A Student's Guide to
Methodology

SAGE has been part of the global academic community since 1965, supporting high quality research and learning that transforms society and our understanding of individuals, groups and cultures. SAGE is the independent, innovative, natural home for authors, editors and societies who share our commitment and passion for the social sciences.

Find out more at: **www.sagepublications.com**

3rd Edition

A Student's Guide to
Methodology
Justifying Enquiry

Peter Clough *and* Cathy Nutbrown

Los Angeles | London | New Delhi
Singapore | Washington DC

The first edition was published 2002 and reprinted in 2003, 2004 (twice), 2005, 2006 (twice).

The 2nd edition was first published 2007, reprinted 2008 (twice), 2010, 2012

SAGE Publications Ltd
1 Oliver's Yard
55 City Road
London EC1Y 1SP

SAGE Publications Inc.
2455 Teller Road
Thousand Oaks, California 91320

SAGE Publications India Pvt Ltd
B 1/I 1 Mohan Cooperative Industrial Area
Mathura Road
New Delhi 110 044

SAGE Publications Asia-Pacific Pte Ltd
3 Church Street
#10-04 Samsung Hub
Singapore 049483

Library of Congress Control Number: 2011935860

British Library Cataloguing in Publication data

A catalogue record for this book is available from the British Library

ISBN 978-1-4462-0861-8
ISBN 978-1-4462-0862-5 (pbk)

Typeset by C&M Digitals (P) Ltd., Chennai, India
Printed by MPG Books Group, Bodmin, Cornwall
Printed on paper from sustainable resources

MIX
Paper from responsible sources
FSC® C018575

Contents

About the authors   vi
Acknowledgements   vii
Preface: how to read this book   viii

PART 1   RESEARCH IS METHODOLOGY   1

1   What is research?   3

2   What is methodology?   24

PART 2   THE PERVASIVE NATURE OF METHODOLOGY   49

3   Looking: seeing beyond the known   51

4   Listening: issues of voice   62

5   Reading: purpose and positionality   105

6   Questioning: the focus of research   139

PART 3   MAKING RESEARCH PUBLIC   173

7   Research design: shaping the study   175

8   Reporting research: telling the story   197

9   Research action: next steps   245

References   251
Appendix 1: research planning audit   260
Author index   264
Subject index   266

About the Authors

Peter Clough is Professorial Research Fellow at the University of Chester. He has been Professor of Inclusive Education at Queen's University Belfast and Liverpool Hope University. Peter has taught in Special and Mainstream schools across the age range as well as on Undergraduate and Postgraduate programmes in Sheffield, Belfast, Liverpool, Hong Kong, Singapore, The United Arab Emirates, India and China. His research interests are in the area of inclusion and exclusion, the exploration of inclusive arts-based methodologies and the use of fictions in research report. Peter is a member of the Editorial Boards of the *Journal of Early Childhood Research and Education, Citizenship and Social Justice* and author of over 40 publications including: *Narratives and Fictions in Educational Research* (2002, OUP) and *Inclusion in the Early Years* (Sage, 2006).

Cathy Nutbrown is Professor of Education and Director for Research at the University of Sheffield, School of Education. She began her career as a teacher of young children and has since worked in a range of settings and roles with children, parents, teachers and other early childhood educators. She teaches on Undergraduate, Masters and Doctoral Programmes and her research interests lie in early childhood education. She is Editor-in-Chief of the Sage *Journal of Early Childhood Research* and author of some 40 publications including *Threads of Thinking* (Sage, 2010).

Acknowledgements

This third edition of *A Student's Guide to Methodology: Justifying Enquiry* has evolved from our many teaching interactions with Masters and Doctoral students in the UK and overseas and we acknowledge, with gratitude, the various roles of our students and colleagues in a number of universities, and in the shaping of some of the ideas contained here.

Thanks to the editors of the *Journal of Early Childhood Research*, the *Journal of Early Childhood Literacy*, the *International Journal of Early Years Education* and *Auto/ Biography* for permission to reproduce the articles in Chapters 4, 5, 6 and 8.

We are particularly grateful to those who have worked with the ideas in the first and second editions of the book and who provided feedback, which we have incorporated into this third edition. Specifically, we should like to thank: Marianne Lagrange and the team at Sage in London, Jools Page, Marlene, Carole, Emily, Adelle, Frances, Philomena, Paul Bunting, John Grant, Ceri Tacey, David Hyatt, Malcolm G., Caron Carter, Karen Hamilton.

Peter Clough and Cathy Nutbrown

We would also like to acknowledge:

Hannon, P. and Nutbrown, C. (1997) 'Teachers' use of a conceptual framework for early literacy education involving parents', *Teacher Development*, (3): 405–420, copyright © Teacher Development reprinted by permission of Taylor & Francis Ltd, http://www.tandfonline.com on behalf of Teacher Development.

Cook, C. (2005) '"It's not what men do": investigating the reasons for the low number of men in the early childhood workforce', in *Perspectives on Early Childhood Education: Contemporary Research* by Katherine M. Hirst and Cathy Nutbrown. Stoke-on-Trent: Trentham Books.

Nutbrown, C. and Clough, P. 'The index for inclusion: personal perspectives from early years educators.' This research paper was first published by The British Association for Early Childhood Education in the Spring 2002 edition of their termly journal *Early Education*.

Preface: How to Read this Book

The following extract was written by Emily, a sociology Doctoral student. It is a raw extract of a note in her research journal where she is thinking through and responding to some of the work she has read on methodology. She is struck by Walker's notion of 'act of faith' and Clough and Nutbrown's position on 'choosing' methods. The following note would be used later to discuss Emily's thinking on some of her research decisions.

Note: Walker (1985: 87) wrote about the choice of methods being an 'act of faith' rather than a 'rational response to a clearly formulated problem'. Now even though that was 1985 I'm not sure that things have changed that much and I'm not sure that this is right. Not then and not now. 'Faith' is about something else, and putting faith in one's decisions, believing they are correct, is not the same as an 'act of faith'. Is it? I'm missing something. Methods and methodology trouble me – I'm interviewing kids with ASBOs (Anti Social Behaviour Orders) and I'm interviewing them because that's the only way I can get anything from them – questionnaires – forget it, focus groups (unfocused groups more like) but sitting in a caff with a fag and endless lattes – (I pay the bill) then we sometimes get somewhere. So – interviewing – not about faith but the only way – the right tool for the job.

Clough and Nutbrown (2002: 27) talk about 'choosing methods'. And say that selecting which methods to use indicates a particular 'take' on the world and how it operates. I can go along with this because though I say that interviewing is the only way; it's not really – I could count the number of kids with ASBOs in Birmingham if I wanted to – but I don't really get excited by that – and that sort of stuff we know. What I want to do is get to what it feels like to have an ASBO – the stories underneath the badge – so I interview.

Where does that get me with discussing my methodology? Well it gets me to the point where I can say (have to say) that I have made certain research decisions here about breadth and depth and about whose voice is important for me.

Walker has a point – you have to believe in what you're doing and be prepared to question (even?) your methods as much as (as he puts it) 'your substantive hypothesis', but in the end there are steps of faith in it all. That said, I think the belief comes at the start, in deciding the research questions and while I can put faith in tried and tested methods that's because others have proved that they work.

OK, so need to grapple with where this gets me in rationalizing research decisions and my conviction that interviewing is THE method.

Emily
Doctoral Student – Sociology

The search for the best way to do things is what, for me, is the key to a good research study. If I think about my own research and those studies carried out by students whom I have supervised, there are two things which cannot really be done without. The first is a good question (or questions) and the second is the means by which that question is investigated. Some work can be flairful and innovative and exciting and different. Other studies are more solemn, meaningful but not head-turning. Whatever the focus, and whether it is my own work or the work of colleagues and students, it is methodology which makes the difference. By that I mean that it is the methodology, the construction and justification of the enquiry which ultimately gives credence to, or calls into question, the findings. And such decisions of how and why can matter long after the study has been completed and reported. I was, a year or so ago, contacted by a colleague who, having read various reports of the REAL project (see Nutbrown et al., 2005), wanted to know precisely how participants for the randomised controlled trial, which was a major part of the work, were originally selected. His question related to a decision taken right at the beginning, before the project began, before many decisions had been made, when just about all that existed were six research questions. But my answer made it possible for him to attribute a different level of 'claim' or confidence to the findings of this quantitative element of the study than might otherwise have been the case. So, early research decisions and the reasons for those decisions matter; and may well have importance long after a study is completed and reported. So, for me, methodology becomes a creative act, in which, before methods are blended and mixed to create new instruments and new avenues, the building blocks of method and justification need to be fully understood. Just as so many of the old masters paid attention to life-like representation long before they moved into abstract and interpretation, and just as musicians must master the basics before they experiment and find their distinctive style or voice, so I think researchers must tread a pathway of learning. We must patiently learn the tools of the trade, which materials are fit for which purpose, and how best to assemble our structures. So, understanding methods and methodology is an essential means by which researchers can develop a confidence to try out, to innovate and to invest some faith and certainty in the rigour of their enquiry. Whatever the research questions, whatever the findings, the methodology must stand a test of time, show itself worthy of the investment of the research act and offer testimony to the credence of research outcomes.

Cathy Nutbrown

Look up 'methodology' in any dictionary and you won't find it particularly useful; and definitions offered in books like this tend – in their attempts to be crystalline – to the obscure if not gnostic. We ourselves offer a number of characterisations, the best of which we still think to be 'a methodology shows how research questions are articulated with questions asked in the field. Its effect is a claim to significance.' But this is still not quite it...

In the few years since we wrote the second edition of this book, a lot has happened for our own thinking about methodology. The reformulation of the book, which is in its third edition, is informed by the uses and critiques of our students and those working in other universities who recommend the book to their students. It is shaped by questions and research designs in published papers, and in theses which we have supervised and examined at universities around the world.

We always wanted this book to be called *Justifying Enquiry: A Student's Guide*, but our publisher reversed this order and effectively relegated that core idea (of justification) to a subtitle – which did not even always appear in the catalogues and the like! It seems that the same is true for this edition! But *Justifying Enquiry* is the real title of this book, and it is this concept of justification of every decision, interpretation, question, that lies at the heart of any research. When the world wants to take apart your study, will the decision you made 'hold water'? Is what you did justified? Can you account for the way you conducted your enquiry? These are the questions we hope this book will help students to ask and respond to.

In an attempt to help readers understand the vapid certainties of phenomenology, Merleau-Ponty advised that 'it is less a question of counting up quotations ... than of *discovering* this phenomenology for ourselves' (1962: ix, original emphasis). And for my part, I think that is precisely the task for the researcher trying to articulate his or her own methodology: what Clough and Nutbrown (or Smith, or Jones, or Brown) offer are no more than maps to a terrain whose reality is discovered and described and justified in the unique circumstances of the study.

As qualitative research designs become ever bolder, the need to discover a 'methodology for ourselves' in each study will become increasingly necessary and increasingly challenging. And, as I have written elsewhere (Clough, 2004), beyond an understanding of mere methods, the persuasive study will demonstrate critical acuity and sensitivity in ethics, in policy and in literary criticism.

Peter Clough

What this book is

This book has grown directly out of research teaching sessions we have led with Masters and Doctoral students over the last twenty years, as well as from our own research studies. The idea for it came from our realisation that students were coming up year after year with the same sorts of questions about quite what methodology *is*, and how it differs from method. It seemed to us that these questions often reflected a tacit assumption that you carried out your study – using 'methods' – and that you finally wrote something called a 'methodology'. This is an understandable assumption, presumably arising from the traditional requirements of the research dissertation or thesis, where methodology tends to be seen as something contained within a single chapter which largely reports 'What I did' (with a little bit of 'Why I did it'). But accounts like this often do little justice to the constant and endless decision-making processes that are a daily part of any research study worth reporting.

What we have developed from these teaching sessions and tutorials is a programme of activities and readings designed to 'turn up the light' on critical decision-making, and many of these now appear in this book. We show how the processes of making methodology are indispensably taking place at all stages of the research – from early, fitful interests or hunches through to the crafting of the final sentence. At all stages decisions are being made, whether it be about the framing of a key research question, the selection of a method, or even the use of a single word. Many of these decisions are of course implicit or otherwise unconscious. The emphasis in the book, then, is on developing a critical approach at all stages, so that it becomes clear in any research report that what the researcher chose to do was not only appropriate, but necessary; we see this as the hallmark of *persuasive* rather than merely adequate methodology.

Our book does not deal with research methods in any detail; there are already many excellent accounts widely available. Rather, the book is concerned with developing a critical research approach more generally; that is, with the more radical and profound processes of enquiry that lie behind the selection or creation of any given method. Through a series of activities and readings, the book is effectively a course in developing *critical research sensibility*. From our own teaching and research supervision we know that students who repeatedly confront their own and others' thinking with awkward questions produce more persuasive and effective research studies. More specifically, students who develop to the point of instinct the critical need to justify their enquiry to themselves at every stage have little difficulty with their final account of methodology: it becomes for them a matter of making concrete for others what has been critically at work throughout the study. To this end, we would urge readers to record responses to some of the activities in a research journal; we should expect that some of this writing would find its way – in some form – into your final dissertation or thesis. We estimate that if you carry out the activities as we suggest throughout this book, you will write around 5,000 words which can be used as part of the articulation of the methodology of your study.

The organisation of the text

We have organised this book in three parts. In Part 1 *'Research is methodology'*, we present our working definitions, which inform the discussions, examples and activities suggested in the remainder of the book. First, we focus on what we see as essential characteristics of social and educational research. Then we set out what we mean when we talk about methodology. These two chapters are important because they set the frame of the book as a whole and introduce key themes which permeate Parts 2 and 3. They also contain a number of activities which, if you work through them, will help you to develop your own responses to our definitions and suggestions about the nature of social and educational research and methodological positions and decisions. However you decide to work through the rest of the book, we suggest that you work through Chapters 1 and 2 first.

In Part 2 *'The pervasive nature of methodology'*, we open up and exemplify the themes introduced in Part 1 and focus (in Chapters 3–6) on: *radical looking, radical listening, radical reading* and *radical questioning*. In this part of the book you may well choose to attend more particularly to one chapter than to others, depending on the structure and thrust of your own study. The order in which you work through these four chapters is not crucial – though there are instances where we refer back to ideas covered in an earlier chapter in so far as they relate to the present discussion. You may prefer to work through these chapters in the sequence in which they are presented, but we have written the chapters in Part 2 in such a way as to make it possible for you to use them out of sequence if your immediate concerns, as they relate to your particular study, suggest that this would better suit your needs.

The concluding part of the book focuses on the processes involved in producing research for a public audience. In Part 3 *'Making research public'*, we focus first on research design (in Chapter 7), showing how the processes of social enquiry discussed in Part 2 can influence the shape and scope of any study. In Chapter 8, we invite you to explore the processes and possibilities of writing the research report, using two examples from our own research to demonstrate how social and educational research might be reported so that it remains persuasive, purposive, positional and political. Finally, in Chapter 9, we suggest how you might use your work in your research journal to plan the next steps in your enquiry. Each chapter ends with an invitation to think about the ethical implications of the ideas discussed in that chapter. Ethical issues are all-pervasive and ethical approval for a study granted by a university is only the beginning; the real work of an ethical research study starts when the study is designed and continues into publication and other dissemination.

Keeping a research journal

An important feature of this book is its interactive nature. Our own work with students studying for higher and research degrees leads us to believe that it is through responding to text as well as reading those texts that their thinking is prompted. So we suggest that as you begin to read this book, you also begin a research journal. Every chapter in the book includes activities designed to help you to reflect on the ideas we are discussing. Many activities ask you to respond, in writing, to a particular statement or article and at some points in the book we suggest that you make an observation or reflect on a particular scenario. These can all be recorded in your research journal.

A research journal can take many forms. Some prefer to keep their journal electronically – keeping their thoughts, puzzles, worries, notes, serendipitous discoveries of references, reflections on conversations and points to raise with their supervisor in electronic form. Others use the opening of a new research journal as an excuse to visit the stationery shop to indulge in the purchase of a new notebook – a sort of ritual to mark the start of the enquiry! The style and form of the research journal is a personal matter because the contents, the structure of those contents, and ultimately the use of those contents will be a personal decision. (No one but you will see your research journal unless you choose to share it with them.) What is important as you begin your research journal is that you choose a format which will make it easy for you to use.

Many of you will be familiar with the idea of keeping a research journal – for some readers this may well be a new idea (or an idea you've heard of but never really adopted). Whenever we suggest the idea of a research journal to our students they always welcome an illustration of what a research journal might look like. So, the example on the next page – taken from one of our student's research journals – provides an indication of the kinds of things you might include in your own. This particular journal was begun as a way of thinking through some initial ideas for a research project based on young people's responses to and images of Anti-Social Behaviour Orders (ASBOs).[1] This extract lists the media cuttings which fuelled the beginning thoughts, and which led to initial drafts of research questions and an emerging notion of the nature and scope of the study. Emily began this journal in order to work out some of those ideas and, as you will see, includes starting points from various sources. The original journal was handwritten and also contained pasted-in newspaper cuttings, scraps from other notebooks and photographs from magazines.

---

[1]The Anti-Social Behaviour Order was introduced by the UK Government in 1999 as a way of dealing with persistent – if criminally minor – infringements of social order: drunkenness, for example, or grafitti or abusive language. A the time of writing, ASBOs are under governmental review.

Emily's Research Journal – example page of collection of summary of newspaper reports on youth and behaviour made in the early days of developing a research question for a Doctoral thesis.

Daily Mirror 3rd November	*The bad boys and girls of Europe: Brit teens worst for drinking and hanging around on streets*	Account of British teenagers being at risk of ASBOs. Flagging up IPPR report to be published next week. (Check this.) Copy on file.
Daily Mirror 3rd November	*Boring excuse*	Brief note on OFSTED report that bad behaviour in schools is partly due to dull lessons. The Sin Bin also recommended as a sanction for disruption instead of exclusion. Copy on file.
Daily Mirror 3rd November	*Perverts in our schools*	Reports that 160+ teachers were suspended in 2005 after allegations of physical and sexual abuse of children. Issues of CRB checks raised. Profiles of 3 – summary of case, photos... Copy on file.
Guardian 4th November	*Stop hugging, school head tells his pupils*	Ban on girls hugging each other during break times because it causes delays in getting to lessons. Interesting comment on radio newspaper review discussions about the relation of this study of positive relationships between pupils and the ASBO reports... Cutting on file.
Guardian 4th November	*Do we need these medals of dishonour?*	Letters responding to report by Youth Justice Board that youths see ABSOs as 'badges of honour'. Cutting on file.
Independent 5th November	*The Sunday Review 'This is our youth'*	At last! Some balance in the reporting of the state of British youth! Profiles, case histories and even a bit of intellectual reflection on changes in adolescence. Really useful informed critique. Copy on file – full of post-it notes.

5th December	*ASBOS for sale*	I found this on Lastminute.com. Along with polar bears and hotel rooms it seems it's possible to buy fake ASBOS as joke gifts! Bad taste I fear...
7th December	*ASBOS in the card shop*	This idea of ASBOS being a joke and a badge of honour proliferates....
8th November	*Research Questions are emerging....* *I'm interested in how young people with/without ASBOS see them.* *How do young people (and their families?) respond to being given an ASBO?* *What impact does an ASBO have on a young person's social behaviour?*	So, focus on the young people and their own responses, beliefs, reactions. Impact on their self image, self esteem, relations with peers etc. ...

Your research journal is your own creation; as you will see from the example above, there are no rules about what goes in a research journal. It is often useful to date entries, especially if they relate to visits to your research setting and meetings with your academic tutor or supervisor. But the point of a research journal is that it helps you to develop your own ideas about research. The example above is taken from the opening of a journal where ideas and stimuli for a research project from all aspects of experience are recorded as they strike the researcher as relevant (however obliquely). Much of this may well be discarded in the final event of designing and reporting a study, but it is always advisable to hold on to ideas that might seem important, even if at the time you do not know why.

Peter Clough and Cathy Nutbrown

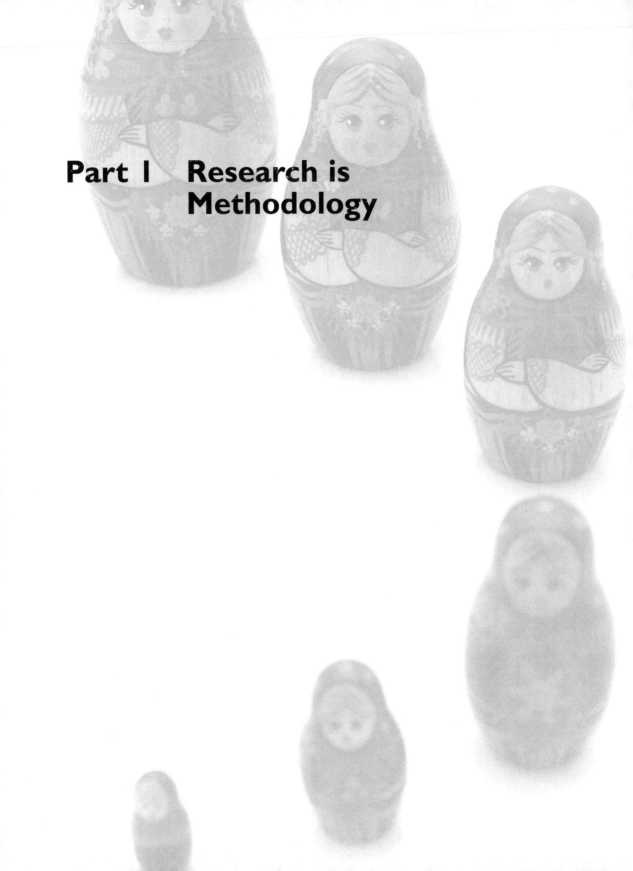

Part 1 Research is Methodology

1 What is Research?

CHAPTER CONTENTS

Introduction   4
Social research is persuasive   5
Social research is purposive   6
Social research is positional   10
Social research is political   14
Traditions of enquiry: false dichotomies   18
Ethics: pause for reflection   22

LEARNING OBJECTIVES

By studying and doing the activities in this chapter you will:

- be able to define 'research'
- be able to respond to the view that social research is persuasive, purposive, positional and political
- be able to articulate the purposive nature of research in the social sciences
- have reflected on the capacity of research in influence change
- be able to express the reasons for doing your own research study
- be able to articulate the potential of your own research to 'make a difference'.

Introduction

> All social research sets out with specific *purposes* from a particular *position*, and aims to *persuade* readers of the significance of its claims. These claims are always broadly *political*.

This definition is our starting point in this book. You may not agree with it, but we hope that by the end of this chapter you will be able to express the extent to which you do, and criticise those aspects that you take issue with.

The chapter is organised around four statements which identify what we see as characteristic of social and educational research. The chapter 'unpacks' these statements, and invites you to make your own responses to them. As we said in the Preface, these responses will contribute directly to the development of your own research methodology.

We think it is important to begin this book by encouraging you to set out what *you* mean by research because it is this which underpins your research study and the decisions you will make within it (just as for us, our own definitions of research directly influence our research design and methodological positions). In this book we are addressing issues for those who are developing research studies for higher and research degrees; thus, this first section will focus on what we mean by research in the context of academic study of academic awards.

The purpose of much research at Masters or Doctoral level is not so much to *prove* things, but more to *investigate* questions, *enquire* into phenomena and *explore* issues. Many researchers either want to understand a situation more clearly or to change things by virtue of their research, and some want to do both. But all research, necessarily, is about asking questions, exploring problems and reflecting on what emerges in order to make meaning from the data and tell the research story. As such, social research is also a moral act within which the researcher holds responsibility for ensuring that resulting change is 'for the better'. In this sense, researchers work for the social 'good'.

Of course, there will always be disagreement about what is 'for the better' and what is 'socially good'. This is why we emphasise the role of *persuasion* in creating a telling account. However, an important function of this *persuasion* is that it makes explicit the ways in which the research specifically avoids doing harm. Across the social sciences, where most, if not all, enquiry treats of human lives and values, the ethical imperative is arguably a primary consideration in research design. Because of this, we have not included a chapter on 'ethics' as such. Rather, we have chosen to include persistent reminders throughout the book that all research activity, from the outset, requires responses to ethical issues.

Social research is persuasive

> Those who carry out social research aim to persuade readers of the significance of their claims.

How does research 'persuade'? To answer this question, we start here by looking at what counts as research for different people: that is, how research is defined in relation to its capacity to bring about change.

Activity 1.1

Take some time to think about the following deceptively simple question; it is asked to help you articulate what *you* mean by 'research'.

What is 'research'?

Make a few notes in your research journal in response to this question.

Over the years, we have been asking our own students to think about their response to the question in Activity 1.1. They have responded in different ways. The following list gives some students' written responses to the same question:

- Research is the investigation of an idea, subject or topic for a purpose. It enables the researcher to extend knowledge or explore theory. It offers the opportunity to investigate an area of interest from a particular perspective.
- The methods you use to obtain information from a variety of sources.
- Investigation and discovery. An opportunity to investigate a theory that requires further interpretation and greater understanding.
- A rigorous enquiry about an area which is of interest for various reasons, e.g. it may be an area about which little is known, or an area which is causing concern.
- Discovery, finding out, study, looking in depth, investigation, reaching new ideas/conclusions.
- The term research is for me a way of describing a systematic investigation of a phenomenon or area of activity. It can sometimes be accurately measured scientifically or data collected can be analysed and compared to identify trends, similarities or differences.

Activity 1.2

We have listed below the terms used in the above definitions of research. Glance through the list and then look back to the definition you wrote in your response to Activity 1.1. Are any of the terms listed here included in your own definition? Are any of them useful to you in revising your definition? Make some notes – in your research journal – on any changes you've made and what you've learned about your own thinking about research.

asking	measure
conclusions	new ideas
critique	opportunity
depth	perspective
discovery	purpose
enquiry	questionning
explore theory	rigorous
extend knowledge	scholarship
evaluate	subject
finding out	systematic
idea	topic
information	trends
interpretation	understanding
investigation	wisdom

Social research is purposive

> What is often forgotten (as too obvious) is that any piece of research in the social sciences emerges from a distinct purpose (whether or not this is apparent to the reader).

As you have seen, our students' descriptions of research convey a strong sense of finding out, of *purposive* enquiry. The task of researchers to 'find out' is highlighted by Goodwin and Goodwin (1996) who emphasise the generation of knowledge, solving of problems and better understanding:

> In a general sense, research means finding out ... the types, or methods [that] have in common the generation of knowledge at varying levels of detail, sophistication, and generalizability. Research results in the creation of knowledge to solve a problem, answer a question, and better describe or understand something. In all these instances, producing new knowledge highlights the research process aimed at finding out. (Goodwin and Goodwin, 1996: 5)

This is not surprising, because, as the following discussion demonstrates, what is important to those who carry out research – whatever its scale – is that it should somehow *make a difference*.

In the following group tutorial various definitions of 'research' are offered and discussed. Focus, as you read, on the ideas which emerge about:

- the *meaning of the term* 'research'
- what research should *accomplish.*

Group tutorial: What do we mean by 'research'?

In preparation for this tutorial the students were asked to write down their response to the question 'What is research?'. They draw on their written notes in the discussion which follows.

SN   OK, well … what I've written here is/it probably sounds, really/I don't know … OK, 'Research is a process of purposeful, in-depth investigation of a particular issue. It follows a defined structured approach to obtain answers which make useful contributions to knowledge or to practice'.

Tutor   So, research is a process – has to be purposeful, and make a contribution to knowledge, OK. But this definition goes on to make us ask a number of questions, such as: What do you mean by 'in-depth'? Does research have to follow a 'defined structured approach'? Does it always have to find 'answers'?

AM   Well I've got a note here about … well … I understand the term to mean looking into an issue that is of interest, or needs analysis, in great detail. By doing this, the issue becomes clearer, is easier to explain and, if it's contentious, becomes more easily resolved. Researching an area helps to tease out the problems and make the picture clearer. This should help focus on the areas that need more work. I was thinking about my problem with focusing in on precise questions there, I think …

MT   Mmm … It's difficult isn't it? When you have to pin it down. I've got a note about, well, I said 'To take a particular issue that is specific and possibly innovative to study in depth' – that's what I think research is … and I said that 'Results can be interpreted by the perspective of others – it stimulates debate and further issues for consideration'.

Tutor   So, research leads to the clarification of issues – and ideas? – and leads to the generation of yet more issues to be considered? Could we say that research often generates more questions than answers?

CT   Possibly, but it does provide a means of finding out about issues of concern or areas of interest. When I was thinking about this I said that it was 'Drawing together a variety of thoughts and opinions in order to move these issues or interests forward and therefore build upon the research findings'. I think research is about encouraging other professionals to challenge or just become interested enough to find out more – so yes – more questions but also some 'responses' to issues … some answers.

MM   It is about generating understanding, greater awareness of an idea, achieving additional knowledge and meaning – isn't it?

Tutor	So, what's emerging here is the importance of research as an *organising structure*, a means by which a body of knowledge is assembled in response to questions and new knowledge generated.
SN	Yes, research is often an investigation which is used to gather information. In my notes I wrote ... 'To gain new knowledge and to confirm, or disprove information already known'.
Tutor	So one of the purposes of research is to check out existing assumptions? What about the role of research in bringing about change?
MM	Yes, for example a lot of research is usually an investigation into a topic which is then evaluated. And there are links between educational research and policy-making – those kinds of studies sometimes lead to change in a Local Authority, for example. My key thing about research was that ... 'Research informs events and allows for critical appraisal of the findings'. That's what I wrote.
CT	Research needs to affect thinking and/or practice.
SN	Research can also reveal the unexpected!

Activity 1.3

Before you move on, take some time to think about the following question. It is designed to help you articulate *your* reasons for doing the particular research study *you* have chosen.

What is the purpose of *your* research study?

We asked 114 of our students attending a study school to write down their reasons for undertaking the study they had chosen. The 97 students who responded gave us answers which we sorted into the following six categories:

- to bring about change
- because it was commissioned by funders
- for interest
- to get a qualification
- for self-development
- for understanding.

Of the 97 students, 82 gave a single reason for undertaking their research and the remaining 15 gave two reasons. The reasons given by the students are ranked in order of importance in Table 1.1.

We do not take the outcomes of this small survey to mean that few of our students are interested in gaining their higher degree or that only 17 of the 97 were

Table 1.1   Responses of students to the question 'Why are you doing this piece of research?'

Category	Number of responses (n=97)
Change	30
Self/personal development	29
Understanding	29
Interest	17
Commissioned	5
Qualification	5

interested in their work! We could say that getting the degree is a 'taken-for-granted' reason! What *is* interesting is that important factors for these students were the opportunity to bring about *change* – to make a difference; their own self-development as professionals and the chance to develop new or deeper understandings.

These are examples of their comments in the categories listed in Table 1.1:

Researching to bring about change

- To find out how I can make a difference to practice in order that children's well-being, their learning and their group identity will be improved.
- To enhance my work with children 'at risk'.

Researching for self-development

- To challenge some of my own ideas.
- To extend my own thinking.
- To improve the way I do my job.
- To increase my professional development and understanding.

Researching for understanding

- To develop a greater understanding of pupils' learning in collaboration with their parents.
- To gather background information on how gender is affected by different social and economic backgrounds through a solid review of what's been done already, and then to gather together new information obtained through questionnaires and informal interviews.
- To gain a more in-depth understanding of the people in my team whom I support. I want to understand more about their backgrounds, attitudes towards students, education and their relationships with other workers in the field.

So, students often carry out research with the expressed purpose of bringing about some kind of change – in the situation they are researching, in themselves and in their own understanding.

This is an important point of reflection, because if you are clear about your research rationale you will be better able to highlight your own particular motivational factors and articulate those in your written report. Clarity about research purpose is also essential in making decisions about methodology.

Activity 1.4

Look back at your own response to the question in Activity 1.3.

Are your reasons for carrying out your own study reflected in the categories we identified in Table 1.1? Do you have a different reason?

Social research is positional

Since research is carried out by people, it is inevitable that the standpoint of the researcher is a fundamental platform on which enquiry is developed. All social science research is saturated (however disguised) with positionality.

Research *becomes* research when its written report is made public (Stenhouse, 1975), thus giving expression to the standpoint of its authors in a given context. It is the context in which research is designed, conducted and (eventually) reported which gives it its real meaning. Social research does not take place in isolation; people drive research, they identify the emerging issues to be studied and they create – in context – the methods by which situations are further understood, and they communicate its outcomes to chosen audiences. The positionality of the researcher affects research designs and processes as well as the ethical practices which are inevitably present throughout any study involving human beings. As Hannon has it, research takes place in the contexts of its community environment, in interaction with the rest of life. He suggests that we '[T]hink of educational research as a living plant in interaction with its environment – constantly renewing itself, sometimes growing, sometimes declining...' (Hannon, 1998: 150). This ecological perspective on research encourages the idea of research *itself* changing as wider social contexts and needs for understanding change. The ways in which we choose to conduct our enquiry, the nature of our questions and the moral intents are expressions of our positionality and will govern the ways in which we craft and change the research act itself.

Teaching in different geographical and political contexts has heightened our awareness of the importance of the particular theatre of enquiry in which research takes place, and how those situations inform and shape research questions, the methodological frames, ethical practices and the nature of the reports.

Koch (2001) studied the factors which influence young women students' choices of post-secondary education and was constructed in the context of its location in the Arabian Gulf. Within that context, the research needed to understand and take account of (and ultimately gain expression in) the balance of local and expatriate population and of the political, religious, cultural and economic realities of life in the Gulf States. Similarly, a report by Parackal (2001) examined the perspectives of teachers of children with special educational needs in Beirut, Lebanon. This study is particularly informed and shaped by its context, and must be interpreted in the context of the social structure of the country, with the civil war of 1974–89 seriously affecting educational developments in the country.

Thus the need to research particular issues grows from the contexts in which the researcher operates, and what is an appropriate research question in one context often lacks relevance in others. For example, Khan (2002) studied the development of strategies for managing the behaviour of young children in kindergartens in Trinidad and Tobago without recourse to corporal punishment. This study took place in the context of a developing country where the death penalty was still in operation and where the beating and physical chastisement of children at home and in schools was not out of the ordinary, but where issues of children's rights were beginning to form part of the educational/social agenda. Khan's rationale for her study was born out of a professional and political context and was 'of the moment' in that context. Her clear moral and political position provided both her motivation for carrying out the study and the organising structure of her final report.

Here is another example from political studies of the importance of understanding positionality. Michael Bérubé's (2010) book *The Left at War* is described by the publishers thus:

> The terrorist attacks of 9/11 and Bush's belligerent response fractured the American left – partly by putting pressure on little-noticed fissures that had appeared a decade earlier.
>
> In a masterful survey of the post-9/11 landscape, renowned scholar Michael Bérubé revisits and reinterprets the major intellectual debates and key players of the last two decades, covering the terrain of left debates in the United States over foreign policy from the Balkans to 9/11 to Iraq, and over domestic policy from the culture wars of the 1990s to the question of what (if anything) is the matter with Kansas. ...
>
> *The Left at War* insists that, in contrast to American countercultural traditions, the geo-political history of cultural studies has much to teach us about internationalism – for 'in order to think globally, we need to think culturally, and in order to understand cultural conflict, we need to think globally.' At a time when America finds itself at a critical crossroads, *The Left at War* is an indispensable guide to the divisions that have created a left at war with itself. (http://nyupress.org/books/book-details.aspx?bookId=1016 Description)

In a review of the book, Yakira (2010) asks 'Whose Left, Which War?' and notes, of Bérubé's book:

> Like him, I don't have much respect for reductionist-paternalist explanations, typically endemic in a leftist kind of thinking about, for instance, the 'ordinary people's' support for Thatcher in England, Reagan or Bush in the US (which are the main topics of the last two chapters of *The Left at War*) and – one could add here perhaps – for the Likkud, or Netanyahu in Israel. I could not avoid thinking, however, while I was reading the non-reductionist attempt to understand the 'ordinary people's' rejection of the Left, that Bérubé was doing himself after all a relatively easy job: not less important and some-times more intellectually challenging than the 'ordinary people' is what the 'non-ordinary' adversary of the Left, the intellectual *on the right* for example, has to say. Bérubé typically ignores this kind of being.

Yakira (2010: 2) goes on to explain his feeling of 'outsideness' from the wars discussed by Bérubé, as a result of 'geographical and institutional distance', and also because the book seemed to him to 'lack the reflexive distance needed in order to be able to fully understand the stakes of the positions defended or attacked in this book'. What we have here is a clear positioning of the reviewer of Bérubé's work and a clear recognition of the ways in which work can be interpreted when viewed from different geopolitical positions and life experiences.

Positionality is an issue across the social sciences. As a final illustration we have turned to a study of the effects of winning the lottery on the lifestyle of winners (Hedenus, 2011). In a narrative study of 14 lottery winners, Hedenus presents the perspectives of the winners who seek to show that they are not 'squanderers of wealth' but 'responsible spenders'. However, there are clues to the position of the author when she writes, in the introduction to the paper, of how this study is different from previous work:

> Concerned to show that the lottery winners in general are no squanderers, research-ers and journalists have conveyed an image of the winners as passive and restrained. They appear almost intimidated by their wealth, safely storing it in a bank and for the most part keen to keep their ways unchanged. With a few exceptions (e.g. Abrahamson, 1980; Casey, 2003; Falk and Mäenpää, 1999; Larsson, forthcoming), previous research has not tackled the question of why this tendency has come to dominate among lot-tery winners.
>
> In this article, narrative analysis of qualitative data from a study on lottery winners is employed to examine the interviewees' accounts of how they have lived their lives after the windfall. The aim is to investigate how the squandering-winner narrative may be used by winners in their self-presentations and post-winning narratives, and to consider how the different narratives relate to social norms concerning identity and consump-tion. In this respect, the lottery winners may be viewed as an instance of all those hav-ing to come to terms with sudden wealth. (Hedenus, 2011: 23)

There are times when the positionality of the research(er) may appear to be circumstantial, though we would argue that, as researchers, our positionality is always also informed and sculpted by our values and morals.

Activity 1.5

We have given some examples of studies that have arisen out of the specific moral and physical contexts in which students have found themselves and others from the literature. Your research report will need to include some picture of these contexts as they relate to your own study. Try writing 200–300 words, which begin to map out these factors.
  Consider:

- What is the political context?
- What is the social context in which it will take place?
- Are there religious and/or political factors which will influence your research questions or your research design?
- Are there personal values and morals which shape and drive your approach to research?
- How might these factors shape your research study?

The following example demonstrates the points highlighted in Activity 1.5.
  For her MA dissertation, British Forces school teacher Ceri Tacey chose to research gender issues appertaining to 4 and 5 year-olds in a small British military community. In her introduction to the study report she writes:

Introduction

This research study is set in a British military community overseas and reflects influences that are unique to this society. I set out to explore the question, 'Why do the boys like to build and the girls like to draw?' This question originated from a series of classroom observations in the foundation setting, where I had become concerned by the apparent gender divide in the children's choice of activities, and the impact this could be having on their overall development. Living in a military community, I was increasingly struck by the imbalance of power I observed. This led me to read feminist theories and consequently to the discovery of discourses circulating in our society relating to 'culturally specific categories through which we give meaning to our lives, practice our lives, invest emotionally in our lives and constitute our social structures' (MacNaughton, 1998 p.158). The feminist viewpoint I had taken in relation to the military community led me to believe that the children's stereotypical behaviour in the classroom was caused by home influences. This theory was later confounded, but it formed the basis of my decision to analyse the gender issues surrounding the children in my class. (Tacey, 2005)

Tacey has here painted for us the social and political contexts of the study along with her own theoretical stance, which also informs the political stance she is taking at the outset of this investigation. Tacey's own feminist position, declared at the outset, was in apparent juxtaposition to the power relations which were apparent due to the military hierarchy. This positioning of the researcher in the research context is made clear at the outset.

Social research is political

> Research which changes nothing – not even the researcher – is not research at all. And since all social research takes place in policy contexts of one form or another, research itself must therefore be seen as inevitably political.

There was a strong sense in the tutorial discussion (on pages 7 and 8) that it is what research *achieves* that gives it its definition. It was Lawrence Stenhouse who defined research as 'Systematic and sustained, enquiry, planned and self-critical, which make public criticism' (1975: 87) and, for us, this is as good a definition as any – having, by and large, stood the test of time. Though of course new views of research also see the process as 'messy', and thus less systematic, research is also becoming accepted – particularly that which adopts more boundary-pushing, qualitative methodological approaches. It is, however, the 'making public' which ultimately brings about change and so the central argument about the capacity of social science enquiry to influence change is present in Stenhouse's (1975) view of research.

But to say 'this research has changed this …' or 'that study made a difference to …' is the important defining feature. So, research worthy of the name must bring about some change: change in the researcher, change in the researched, change in the user of research.

Activity 1.6

Think of a research paper which you have read recently.

What did the authors seek to change?
What impact might it have?
On whom?
On what?

In the following example, Adelle has addressed the questions in Activity 1.6 in her journal response to a paper by Faulks (2006). She notes:

> I dithered over this but it's a good paper. This is a newish journal but I'm finding material that makes me think about what I'm doing for my thesis.
>
> Notes on:
>
> Faulks, K. (2006) Rethinking citizenship education in England: some lessons from contemporary social and political theory *Education, citizenship and social justice* Vol 1, No. 2 July 2006
>
> Discussion of the introduction of compulsory 'citizenship' lessons in England, and the controversy surrounding that policy. Argues for the need to review so that such an aspect of curriculum really is effective in 'democratic renewal'. Challenges the Crick report. Has really made me think! Exposes the policy as sociologically naïve and makes the case for broader and 'bolder' approach to citizenship education.
>
> The main impact of this paper (as I see it) is on *me*. I have a much better grasp now of the underlying assumptions and of quite how political (little p and big P) issues of citizenship education really are. All the issues bound up in the sociology of 'emotion, psychoanalysis and feminism stretch citizenship beyond its traditional focus on formal rights and requires us to consider … relationships … intimate citizenship' (p. 130). Plummer's idea of 'intimate citizenship' – wow! (2003) I think it's true to say that I see it all quite differently – rights alongside relationships … in society as well as in the school and classroom.
>
> Plummer, K. (2003) *Intimate Citizenship: Private Decisions and Public Dialogues.* Washington, DC: University of Washington Press.

Having ascertained that most of our students want their research to bring about some (however modest) kind of change, we asked them to tell us briefly what difference they thought their research could make. All 97 students responded that something would happen as a result of their research. Their responses fell into four broad categories of change:

- policy
- practice
- professional development
- stimulus for further research.

Students' expectations for the impact of their research studies are ranked, in order of expressed importance, in Table 1.2.

Table 1.2   Students' expectations of the impact of their research on policy, practice or professional development ranked in order of expressed importance

Students' expectation that their research would make a difference in the area of...	Number of responses (n=97)
Practice (personal/professional)	51
Professional development	32
Policy (institutional/local/national)	11
Stimulus for further research	3

There is a sense here of a desire for *action,* of students wanting to put the outcomes of their research to some practical operation. They said:

Of making a difference to policy

- Studies on the impact of Ofsted inspection on practice are few, therefore, my research will contribute to knowledge on this area.
- Education Services can be very focused on 'educating the child'. I would like to highlight the issues around perspective, contribution and values of parents as a policy factor.
- May be useful in policy development and the procurement of resources.

Of making a difference to practice

- My research will reflect my own practice, and in the way I train others.
- I hope the research will inform future practice in work with people with learning difficulties.
- I hope it will increase continuity of activities between multidisciplinary agencies working with women in the community.
- I'm planning to use it to develop new guidelines for the induction of new staff into the Unit.

Of making a difference to professional development

- ... it will give me a better understanding of what I do.
- It should influence the attitudes and perceptions of colleagues.
- The greatest difference I can hope it will make will be in terms of personal differences to my understanding and attitudes.
- I hope it will influence/provoke thought in other professionals about issues of gender and exclusion.

Policy, practice and professional development are all politically oriented or motivated arenas and the students' desire to influence developments in these areas of work is, in itself, political.

We can see the attempts to bring about change, or the desire to provide evidence which may be used to argue for change in many studies across the social sciences, as the following two examples illustrate.

In their abstract of a paper reporting a study of the effects of bullying on the labour market, Brown and Taylor (2008) write:

> We explore the effect of bullying at school on the educational attainment of a sample of individuals drawn from the British National Child Development Study (NCDS). Our empirical findings suggest that school bullying has an adverse effect on human capital accumulation both at and beyond school. Moreover, the impact of bullying on educational attainment at age 16 is found to be similar in magnitude to class size effects. Furthermore, in contrast to class size effects, the adverse influence of bullying on educational attainment remains during adulthood. In addition, being bullied at school influences wages received during adulthood as well as indirectly influencing wages via educational attainment. (Brown and Taylor, 2008: 388)

As economists, Brown and Taylor approach the difficulties of bullying in terms of the cost to the economy. In so doing they address the problem of bullying not from a victim–perpetrator viewpoint, but they provide evidence of the cost to society of not addressing and curbing bullying, showing that the effects of bullying can continue long after the bullying acts have ceased. They conclude:

> In order to facilitate research in this area, the collection of more recent individual level data on this crucial aspect of children's experiences at school is imperative. In addition, there is a shortage of statistics on bullying at an aggregate level which has hindered attempts to ascertain the nature of trends in bullying behaviour. In order to alleviate the adverse effects of bullying at school and to effectively deploy Government funding in this area, it is apparent that policy makers need to be better informed about children's experiences of bullying at school. (Brown and Taylor, 2008: 400)

In the field of criminology, Wilson et al. (2010) put forward an approach to managing sex offenders in the community which ran counter to the view that those convicted of such crimes should never be permitted to live back in the community and should remain in custody to prevent the opportunity of reoffending, thus protecting potential victims. In the abstract of their paper they write:

> Sex offenders cause particular concern upon release and are often received with apprehension or hostility by the community. This in turn may increase their feelings of loneliness and poor self-esteem, hindering re-integration and potentially increasing re-offending. Circles of Support and Accountability (CoSAs) were first developed in Canada in 1994 and introduced in the UK in 2000. A 'Circle' consists of a group of four to six volunteers with the offender as the 'Core Member'. Appropriately trained volunteers support and hold to account the core member, who has to volunteer to be part of the scheme, by providing them with social

contact and practical support while at the same time maintaining links to statutory agencies alerting them of any risk issues. Following completion of initial pilots, the scheme is currently being rolled out across the UK. This systematic review will describe the Circles model and its history and summarise the empirical literature, particularly with regards to outcomes. (Wilson et al., 2010: 48)

In reporting on an alternative approach to the release of sex offenders, the authors describe the process (and effectiveness) of a managed system of support, involving volunteers and the offender. They put forward evidence from a systematic review which demonstrates effectiveness, and their position in wishing to bring about change is clear when they conclude:

CoSA represents a community-based response to a community problem which gives a practical alternative to the often unhelpful demonising approach to sexual abuse prevalent in much of the media. (2010: 56)

Traditions of enquiry: false dichotomies

Looking back over your notes and writings made during your reading of this chapter, how do you now respond to our opening statement? We wrote:

All social research sets out with specific purposes from a particular position, and aims to persuade readers of the significance of its claims. These claims are always broadly political.

It has long been argued (for example, Carr, 1995) that distinct paradigms and scientific method are less appropriate for educational research, for this creates a demand for divisions between researchers and teachers. Naturalism (or normative) and interpretive approaches, he argues, should be repudiated and the development of research that is 'both educational and scientific' should be the goal. Could the same be said for other disciplines in the social sciences? For example, does the same apply to sociology? Do distinct paradigms demand divisions between sociologists and social workers, or between architects and builders? How helpful is it to consider the 'distinctive' nature of a discipline in relation to research paradigms? Of course, it all depends on the research question and we shall come to this later in the book.

Just as it may erroneously seem that research methods are simply and readily 'to hand', research is similarly often characterised uncritically in terms of polarisations: it is qualitative or quantitative, or else it is *positivist* or *interpretative*, and so on. The emergence of *critical theory* in educational research offers a third paradigm, linked with the political stance of emancipation of individuals and groups within society. Critical theorists would thus argue that their work is *transformative* in that it seeks to change people and societies. But in terms of the research process – of what actually happens when people *make* research – these paradigms are ultimately no more than *post hoc* descriptions of gross characterisation. In addressing a task we do not immediately go to adopt this or that methodology as such; rather, we again confront specific problems which we come eventually to locate in continually related – rather than opposed – ways of construing the world.

Denscombe (1998: 3) states that 'the social researcher is faced with a variety of options and alternatives and has to make strategic decisions about which to choose'. He suggests six key issues should be taken into account when making decisions about the viability of social science research: relevance, feasibility, coverage, accuracy, objectivity and ethics. A series of questions are posed (under each of these six headings) for researchers to ask at the planning stage of their project. We suggest a seventh factor should be included in this checklist, that of *interest and motivation*, because research projects become part of the life of researchers and it is important that any research 'grabs' the researcher sufficiently to sustain them throughout the study and all its triumphs and disasters!

Some writers continue to support the idea of distinct research paradigms. Cohen, Manion and Morrison (2011) offer the following scheme of what they see as contrasting approaches to research: specifically, normative, interpretive, complexity theoretical, and critical paradigms. Such broad, *post hoc* frameworks can be useful in characterising the means and concerns of any given study, but it must be clear that in practice – in making research as part of a lived world – it is not possible to study 'society and the social system' without at least some interactive notion of and reference to 'the individual', or to 'generalise from the specific' without in some way 'interpreting [that] specific'.

Hence the idea of choice *between* broad approaches characterised in this way is ultimately spurious, and as Merton and Kendall (1986: 549) pointed out, the real choice is that combination of both which makes use of the most valuable features of each. The problem becomes one of determining *at which points* they should 'adopt the one and at which the other approach'.

We can dig deeper into this realm of separate research paradigm and uncover further argument about the relationship between research design and various research methods. The 2011 American Educational Research Association meeting took the theme *Inciting the Social Imagination: Education Research for the Public Good* (AERA, 2011). Reflecting on the programme, the AERA President and Programme Chair said that:

> No single theory, method, or policy can serve as the silver bullet to transform education and to ensure robust learning opportunities for all our nation's students. Our slate of Presidential sessions, and our featured speakers and activities, reflect a range of

approaches, methods, theoretical orientations, and disciplinary foci all organised around a central goal: to leverage educational research and scholarship to advance the field, to contribute to the knowledge base, and to promote the public good. (AERA, 2011: 3)

The thousands of papers spanning all areas of education and the full breadth of the methodological continuum demonstrated many and varied positions and approaches to research in the multivariant field of education and socially responsible educational research.

With the wide range of texts on research methods currently available, there is a wealth of opinion on record. Let us consider one further position at this point. Writing about research design in social research, de Vaus (2001) argues:

> Failing to distinguish between design and method leads to poor evaluation of designs. Equating cross-sectional designs with questionnaires, or case studies with participant observation, means that the designs are often evaluated against the strengths and weaknesses of the method rather than their ability to draw relatively unambiguous conclusions or to select between rival plausible hypotheses.
>
> Similarly, designs are often equated with qualitative and quantitative research methods. Social surveys and experiments are frequently viewed as prime examples of quantitative research and are evaluated against the strengths and weaknesses of statistical, quantitative research methods and analysis. Case studies, on the other hand, are often seen as prime examples of qualitative research – which adopts an interpretive approach to data, studies 'things' within their context and considers the subjective meanings that people bring to their situation.
>
> It is erroneous to equate a particular research design with either quantitative or qualitative methods. (de Vaus, 2001: 9–10)

Making method/ology

Decisions about the location of a particular piece of research (or a researcher) within a research paradigm and the selection of methods for research studies can only be made in the light of specific situations and particular phenomena. To be sure, there already exist traditions and 'blueprints' of practice which suggest – more or (often) less critically – ways of proceeding and which frequently condition our view of how phenomena should be investigated. But these should never be seen as techniques which can be lifted wholesale from other accounts and imported uncritically into an enquiry motivated by specifically different situations and subjects.

Research is, by definition, a search for form quite as much and at the same time as it has any content to report. Methods should be seen as being constructed (for particular purposes) rather than selected (for any general usefulness).

Such a view amplifies the earlier claim that the task of a methodology is to explain the particularity of the methods made for a given study. A characteristic purpose of a methodology is to show not how such and such appeared to be the best method available for the given purposes of the study, but how and why *this way of doing it was unavoidable – was required by – the context and purpose of this particular enquiry*. Thus, we suggest that methodological considerations stem from the obvious; that different researchers can offer different interpretations of the same data. Methodology requires researchers to *justify* their *particular* research decisions, from the outset to the conclusion of their enquiry.

The final difference between a persuasive and a merely sufficient methodology is that the convincing one takes little for granted. It worries endlessly at its own terms and is not content to justify its decisions largely by reference to other research. To be sure, research must be contextualised in terms of what other enquirers have claimed as findings (and it is normally the job of a literature review to do most of this), but it should also be located – and justified – in terms of an argument about the very nature and structure of knowledge and knowing.

Many popular texts on research methods offer information on 'contrasting' approaches (for example, Cohen et al., 2011). Indeed, Denzin and Lincoln continue to denote the 'either/or' response:

> The word qualitative implies an emphasis on the qualities of entities and on processes and meanings that are not experimentally examined or measured (if measured at all) in terms of quantity, amount, intensity, or frequency. Qualitative researchers stress the socially constructed nature of reality, the intimate relationship between the researcher and what is studied, and the situational constraints that shape inquiry. Such researchers emphasise the value-laden nature of inquiry. They seek answers to questions that stress how social experience is created and given meaning. In contrast, quantitative studies emphasise the measurement and analysis of causal relationships between variables, not processes. Proponents of such studies claim that their work is done from within a value-free framework. (Denzin and Lincoln, 2005: 10)

But in reality, many researchers in the social sciences do not select one research paradigm to investigate all their questions, choosing *either* a normative *or* an interpretive approach. In our own work, we have – during the course of our research careers – worked within both positivist and interpretivist paradigms. Would we want to describe ourselves as 'either' qualitative 'or' quantitative researchers? The important point here is that we adopt research stances *as they are appropriate to our work*. There are important questions to unpack in the extract above, and perhaps the issue of greatest concern is that of values. Are studies which employ quantitative approaches *necessarily* value-free? Is such a state possible, or desirable? And is it realistic to approach research design by making the choice between 'either' the 'objectivity' of a normative model 'or' the 'subjectivity' of the interpretative model? Research studies often move between these broad approaches selecting the most appropriate for each part of the study. The issue is not so much a question of which paradigm to work within but how to dissolve that distinction in the interests of developing research design which serves the investigation of the questions posed through that research.

Ethics: pause for reflection

In this chapter we have suggested that all research is persuasive, purposive, positional and political. In your research journal consider these questions:

- What ethical issues should be taken into account in researchers' intent to make their research persuasive?
- What ethical issues underpin the purpose of any research study?
- In what ways does the positionality of a researcher determine ethical responses to their research?
- If all research is, in one sense or another, political, how does this manifest itself in ethical responses to an enquiry?

You will have your own responses to the above questions. However, we suggest that it is crucial that researchers, in their desire to 'persuade', maintain a careful transparency around their work and diligently report all aspects of their studies, analysing data and reporting findings faithfully. Research studies are often ethically or morally driven; some studies arise because the researcher has a clear purpose. In our own work, for example, we are committed to (among other things) promoting social inclusion in education and to the importance of early childhood education in building citizenship. These commitments constitute an ethical underpinning that drives our research, that has at its heart a purpose to persuade readers of our research reports, and that these issues are important and worthy of further attention. In this sense, our 'positionalities' are interwoven with our purpose: we do what we do because we are committed to the purposes of our research – they matter to us. And as such, the ethics of the studies we undertake have to be carefully worked out so that we acknowledge our positionalities from the outset, and design our research to take account of the ethical issues which underpin what we do. From this position, our studies of, for example, citizenship, inclusion and early childhood have a political mission, to make a difference, and in this sense there is an ethical and moral underpinning that pervades our work and that runs through a desire to make a difference 'for the good'.

If you have worked through the activities in this chapter, making notes and composing paragraphs as we have suggested, you will have written around 2,000 words which can be later incorporated into your dissertation or thesis.

CHAPTER SUMMARY

In this chapter we have:

- *Encouraged you to reflect on a range of definitions and to develop your own definition of research*
- *Provided an overview of research as a persuasive, purposive, positional and political activity*
- *Considered the purposive nature of research*
- *Considered the positional nature of research*
- *Discussed the function of research as a process of political change*
- *Discussed the relationship between research paradigms and the nature of social research as persuasive, purposive, positional and political*
- *Reflected on the ethical issues arising from the chapter contents*

FURTHER READING

Cohen, L., Manion, L. and Morrison, K. (2011) 'The nature of enquiry: setting the scene', Chapter 1 in *Research Methods in Education* (7th edn). London: Routledge.

> This chapter sets out a contextual basis for educational research in relation to some of the foundations of inquiry, including scientific and positivistic methodologies; naturalistic and interpretive methodologies; mixed methods; and post-positivism, post-structuralism and postmodernism.

Snape, D. and Spencer, L. (2003) 'The foundations of qualitative research', Chapter 1 in J. Ritchie and J. Lewis, *Qualitative Research Practice: A Guide for Social Science Students and Researchers*. London: Sage.

> In the first section of this chapter the authors seek to define qualitative research, drawing on its history and identifying philosophical and methodological issues in the paradigm.

2 What is Methodology?

CHAPTER CONTENTS

What do we mean by 'methodology'?	25
Distinguishing between 'methods' and 'methodology'	31
What is methodology for?	36
Why are research questions important?	40
Generating and justifying research questions	41
Ethics: pause for reflection	46

LEARNING OBJECTIVES

By studying and doing the activities in this chapter you will:

- be able to articulate what is meant by the term 'methodology'
- be able to eliminate confusion between 'methods' and 'methodology'
- understand why methodological issues are important considerations for your own research study
- be able to discern the ethical issues which pervade methodology
- understand the central role of 'research questions'
- be able to compose and justify your own research questions
- be able to write some 300 or so words which you can later use to discuss your research questions and the methodological justification for the mode of enquiry you have chosen to investigate them.

What do we mean by 'methodology'?

> A methodology shows how research questions are articulated with questions asked in the field. Its effect is a claim about significance.

This chapter addresses an issue which many people coming new to research find confusing, and that is the difference between methods and methodology. We suggest that, at its simplest, this distinction can be seen in terms of *methods* as being some of the ingredients of research, while *methodology* provides the *reasons* for using a particular research 'recipe'.

The chapter explores the relationship of methods and methodology, and the ongoing task of *justification* which a methodology represents. Thus methodology starts quite simply by asking questions such as: '*Why* interview?', '*Why* carry out a questionnaire survey?', '*Why* interview 25 rather than 500 participants?' Decisions such as these are apparently often practical, but they carry very deep, often unarticulated, implications. They are often based on values and assumptions which influence the study, and as such therefore need to be fully interrogated in order to clarify the research decisions which are made. The implications of research decisions are often not fully realised (or perhaps realised too late, when data have already been collected). They are often unexplained, and in many cases poorly justified.

Activity 2.1   What is methodology?

Write a short definition of what you understand by *methodology*. We will return to your definition later in the chapter.

'The arrest of experience'

Research puts common experience into brackets, makes 'objects' of experience so that they can be examined and understood. One of the things that research requires people to do is to question assumptions and perceptions which are taken for granted in the normal run of everyday life. Michael Oakeshott (1933) described this as an 'arrest of experience', when we try to step outside our everyday experience of people, objects and places, and subject them to different sorts of examination. Oakeshott reminds us that 'Nature is the *product* not the *datum* of scientific thought' (1933: 191). The information becomes, then, not the *consequence* of a way of seeing, but the *act* itself (an 'object'), and as such must be intentionally opposed to the thing in itself. In this opposition we discover the *nature of the particular*, for science attempts to conceive the world in defined categories and its datum has the required stability only by virtue of the categorical set of which it is an indifferent member. There can, by this definition, be no such scientific experience as that *of the particular*.

Whatever actual methods are ultimately employed in a study, we suggest that the 'arrest of experience' – present in all research studies – can be characterised by four forms of *radical enquiry*. These are *radical looking, radical listening, radical reading* and *radical questioning*.

Radical looking

> *Radical looking* is the means by which the research process makes the familiar strange, and gaps in knowledge are revealed.

What we mean by *radical looking* is exploration beyond the familiar and the (personally) known, to the roots of a situation: this is *exploration which makes the familiar strange*.

All researchers need to develop the capacity to see their topic with new and different lenses in order to look beyond and transform their own current knowledge. Topics present themselves for research in different ways and for all sorts of different reasons. What distinguishes research from everyday interest or curiosity, however, is the opening up of familiar things to alternative ways of seeing. Thus an *interest* in, say, adolescent drug culture only starts to become *research* proper when that curiosity is *systematically informed by perspectives outside the researcher's normal vision*: What is already known about this topic? What have other researchers found? Are there policy contexts which affect this culture? What do adolescents themselves think about the situation? And, most importantly, what are the gaps and can I add to the public state of knowledge?

Answers to these – and many other such – questions do not simply describe the situation under enquiry, filling in informational blanks, as it were. They actually refine and define the topic: this sort of radical looking at others' knowledge allows researchers to examine and then start to discard information as they begin to focus on a particular problem, a particular *gap in knowledge*. Thus, to stay with the example above, there may be a great deal of relevant work on adolescent drug culture, and it is necessary to be critically aware of this. However, by definition, nobody will have carried out your particular study with *these* subjects *this* year and in *this* town.

In Chapter 3 we present an example of a research study which illustrates what we mean by 'looking' and interpret the theme both in terms of *radical looking* and some methods of *observation* and their interpretation.

Radical listening

> *Radical listening* – as opposed to merely hearing – is the interpretative and critical means through which 'voice' is noticed.

What we mean by *radical listening* is a careful attention to all the *voices* which may be heard within and around any given topic. These include both the (literal) voices of research subjects – in interview, for example – and also the voices which are at work in other research reports. This is really part of the same process as radical looking, but it adds emphasis to our view (outlined in Chapter 1) of social research as characteristically *positional* and *political*.

Radical listening, then, involves working out *positionality*. This means trying to understand something of what lies behind what is said by research subjects and written by other researchers; trying to understand this in terms of the speaker's/ author's intentions; and trying to understand what this means within their particular social frameworks. If you accept our argument in Chapter 1 that all research is political, then it follows that whatever evidence you take from research subjects, or other research writers, embodies a particular political position (however implicit this may be). This is what we mean here by 'voice'.

Activity 2.2

Make some notes about:

- What counts as 'voice'?
- Why do you want to listen?
- What do you want to hear?
- Do you want to listen to what you hear?

The articulation of responses to the above questions will provide you with your rationale for the *methods* of listening which you choose to use in your own studies.

The following example is from a student dissertation.

This study explores the issue of consumer 'voice' in a Day Care Centre for adults with learning difficulties. Whilst the Centre has a Management Committee on which consumers are represented,

a. Many 'important' decisions are taken outside of this body;
b. Consumers' views are frequently 'mediated' by carers;
c. Meetings are often cancelled when the carers believe there are insufficient matters of importance.

This study examines the rhetoric of Consumer Participation (which is a much-vaunted item in the Centre's publicity) and sets this against a reality exposed by one-to-one 'unmediated' interviews with seven consumers. The study concludes that there is a number of 'voices' at work in the Centre, both literal and metaphorical, but that the 'voice' of the consumers is muted, if not powerless.

The methodological issues raised by the decision to collect and analyse data which elicit the many voices of participants are important. They carry crucial ethical issues which have to be addressed to take account of the needs and rights of participants alongside the rights of the Centre and its workers. Whether carrying out ethnographic studies or large surveys which involve listening to others' voices in research studies, the justification for listening to a range of voices in a variety of dimensions must be made clear. We shall see more of this in Chapter 4, which includes an example of a study designed to elicit a number of voices. In this example, the methodological 'frame' is as interesting as the substantive 'findings' (or outcomes) of the research. Radical listening, we suggest, should be central to any form of research whatever its substantive content or paradigm.

Radical reading

> *Radical reading* provides the justification for the critical adoption or rejection of existing knowledge and practices.

In Chapter 1 we showed how social research is *purposive* and *positional*, and we see *radical reading* as a process which exposes the purposes and positions of texts and practices. In this way we are using 'reading' both in a traditional sense – as addressing written texts – and in the metaphorical sense – 'How do *you* read this or that situation?' This process is inseparable from *radical looking* and *radical listening*, but what distinguishes *radical reading* is the notion of *criticality*.

> *Criticality* – 'being critical' – describes the attempt to show *on what terms* 'personal' and 'public' knowledges are jointly articulated – and therefore where their *positional* differences lie.

A critical account of anything seeks to be *rational*, but cannot fail to reflect the values and beliefs of its author. The most *persuasive* critical accounts reveal the full range of values at work in the analysis.

We shall return to this theme in Chapter 5 with a discussion of the centrality to the research process of the literature search and review and of the less formal 'readings' of the research settings which researchers inevitably make.

Radical questioning

> *Radical questioning* reveals not only gaps in knowledge but also why and how particular answers might be morally and politically necessitated.

Radical questioning lies at the heart of a thesis and brings together the earlier notions of *radically attending* to a topic or situation or events.

All researchers ask questions. They sometimes ask innocent and naïve questions about their research focus, as well as searching questions about their data, their processes on analysis, their ethical positions and their moral intent. Research methodology involves, as a minimum, four kinds of questioning activity: personal questions, research questions and field questions, all of which give rise to ethical questions:

> **Personal questions.** Researchers must ask questions of themselves about what drives their research and the location of themselves in their research.
>
> **Research questions.** The careful formulation of 'research questions' – which form the main stage of any research study – is key to the realisation of a successful research study, however large or small.
>
> **Field questions.** These are quite literally questions which are asked 'in the field'. The formulation of these empirical questions follows the development of research questions and planned acts of data collection in the field should always be directly related to the research questions.
>
> **Ethical questions.** These questions pervade all research studies, however straightforward the research might seem. Questions of how and to what extent to inform, consult and protect participants and the researcher lie (even if beneath the surface) in all other questions. The ability to identify the ethical questions that are engendered by research is a skill which all researchers must practise in the pursuit of enquiry.

Of course, many research studies will also involve the questioning of research participants, in which case there are further decisions to be made, in terms of: who to ask what to ask when to ask; going back again (re-asking); being specific; being open. These form the fine detail of field questions.

In the acts of looking, listening, reading and asking it is also important for researchers to 'get the feel' of their research settings and situations. They need to be sensitive to 'hunches' which they might later investigate, or which might alert them to the need for particular responses to situations. In suggesting that researchers 'feel' their settings, we are arguing the need for a holistic response to research design. Chapter 6 further develops these themes.

Activity 2.3

Consider the functions of looking, listening, reading and questioning in relation to your own (proposed) research study. Which of these tasks might presently seem to have more prominence in your own research?

(Continued)

> *(Continued)*
>
> Do you think that the idea of 'feeling' your research setting has any valid function in the context of your particular study? Make a few notes in your research journal before you move on. You may wish to add to your notes on these topics as you work through the book.

Philomena's interest was in the career choices of women returning to work after having children and raising their families. In her response to Activity 2.3 she wrote in the research diary:

> I think this study is mostly about listening. I'm not aware (at the moment) of much that's been done systematically about this topic, but what I've come across is mainly survey based stuff like data from census etc. What I want to do is quite simply listen; let them guide me as it were – I don't have any preconceived ideas about the issues or any set questions... I like that idea of 'feeling the setting' – also of feeling my way around first of all...

This is a good example of the way in which a literal form of listening can lead to the metaphorical idea of 'feeling the setting' – which is to say, 'hearing' the ideas at work in an issue or a location.

'Feeling the setting' of research can sometimes involve the researcher in a lengthy process of learning and building relationships. For example, Kawulich (2011) describes some 15 years of research into the interests of the Muscogee people of Oklahoma. She writes:

> For many years, I had read all of the books I could find on Muscogee (Creek) culture, because the Creek people originally inhabited the state of Georgia where I live and because I'm a 'wannabe' – someone who claims Indian blood but cannot prove that hereditary connection (2011: 59)

She goes on to describe how she developed a relationship which would be important in gaining access to the communities of the Muscogee people and got a feel of the community in which she would undertake her research:

> This relationship building process entails becoming familiar with the setting, determining how to act in ways that are culturally appropriate, and establishing relationships with key informants who can assist with the sample selection process. ... I had begun taking beading classes at the Oglewanagi Indian Center in Atlanta led by several members of an intertribal dance troupe. After several months, they invited me to join them as they traveled to powwows (intertribal social dances) on weekends, and I was able to observe

the customs and cultures of various tribes; at each powwow, I would ask the vendors and dancers whether there were any Creek people there. I later learned that powwows are not a typical part of Creek culture. Learning about various tribal customs was helpful later to my understanding of Creek culture, particularly, the importance of 'family,' respect, and community. (Kawulich, 2011: 59–60)

Not all research requires such an investment in time and learning, but most (if not all) social research involves the researcher in 'feeling' the research setting to some extent.

Distinguishing between 'methods' and 'methodology'

The job of method is only to 'hold apart' the researcher and her objects, so that we can tell the difference between them. Methods do not tell us what the thing is; they do not even describe it. All they tell us is the circumstances under which the researcher met the object; and they normally seek to provide a guarantee that researcher and object are distinct from each other. 'Postmodern' accounts say it is impossible to do this.

First we shall discuss the relationship between research methods and methodology, and argue that one of the tasks for a methodology is to explain and justify the particular methods used in a given study.

Selection of methods may be an act of faith rather than a rational response to a clearly formulated problem. The method may even be an intrinsic part of the problem, rather than extrinsic and disconnected from it. Just as recipes are not simply things that are done to food, but become concepts within which method and substance are compounded, so 'method' in research can become an intrinsic part of the project. The methods we choose are, in this sense, there to be tested, just as much as the substantive hypothesis. (Walker, 1985: 87)

In a sense there is not a deal to say about research methods as such; they are in the end tools, no more, and we may appear to take them from the shelf when we need them.

But methods only – and this is crucial – *only* arise in the service of quite particular needs and purposes. Their usefulness falls away if and as these needs are met and these purposes fulfilled. To be sure, as critical readers of a research report we may wish to know how such and such an insight was arrived at, and hence we may check the researcher's claims to validity and reliability, say, by asking questions of her method. But if the work ultimately has significance for us, it is because its quite particular purpose has been achieved; and to do this, it will have called on the construction of quite particular tools.

In a study of children's views of their early years settings, Nutbrown (forth-coming) argues that the 'known interviewer' is a preferred option to asking children to talk with the researcher as 'stranger'. In the construction of this particular tool, Nutbrown justifies her decisions thus:

> We know (Nutbrown and Hannon, 2003) that interviews with young children have to be brief and meaningful. Though the term 'interview' is used throughout this paper, in reality, the experience for each child took the form of a one-to-one conversation (guided by the same set of prepared questions asked to all children) with a familiar and interested adult. Questions to children were designed to find out how they most like to spend their time and what they thought of the equipment and experiences provided in the setting for them, and the relationships they formed with staff and other children. The children were very keen to talk about the things that they did and what they liked, and gave informative responses. The adults who carried out the interviews worked in their preschools and so were known to the children, respected children's right to refuse to take part, and ensured that the children knew they could choose to stop at any point. Indeed, a small number of interviews were incomplete because interviewers felt children were unsettled so suggested that they stopped the interviews. Interviewers used a pro forma to note what the children said *verbatim*, having explained to the children that because they were interested in what they had to say, and wanted to remember it to pass it on to others who wanted to know what children thought of their preschools. When the interview procedure was explained to him, Marlon said *'So, I'll tell you and you write it…right?'*, showing considerable understanding of what to expect in the process.
>
> Most interviews were in English, it being the first language of the majority of children interviewed, but one setting carried out two interviews in both English and Urdu because a member of staff in the setting spoke Urdu and the children were accustomed to using both languages.
>
> The 'known adult' – as interviewer – makes the research conversation with the child more meaningful (and increases the likelihood that the children's views might have impact at the preschool level, rather than being 'simply' data for a research study). Those who work with the children on a day-to-day basis are in a better position to understand the sometimes idiosyncratic nature of children's responses and also to act on what the children say if possible and appropriate. Billington (2009) has argued that many vulnerable young children have a number of unfamiliar adults asking them questions, and advocates research which gives children the opportunity to participate with people known to them. This fits with a children's rights approach, and so in this study the 'objectiveness' that might (or might not) have been achieved by having an unfamiliar independent interviewer was abandoned in favour of a situation where the quality of the relationship between the child and the adult questioner was already positive and established. (Nutbrown, fourthcoming)

It is for this reason that the idea of method as an indifferent tool is seldom borne out by the experience of researchers. A method turns out not to be a spanner – or even a micrometer – but rather something which has to be painstakingly custom-built from other drafters' cast-offs which, while providing a general guidance, were not made *for this particular job*. It is actually this particularity which it becomes the task of methodology to explain.

'Choosing' methods?

It is true – if a truism – that channels of communication determine what may pass along them. Research methods observe this rule. A statistical survey, for example, generates one particular form of information at the expense of others, and you would not normally expect to learn much about the *experience* of respondents from this sort of enquiry. For example, a survey of students' experiences of their universities will provide quantifiable data about the views of large numbers of graduating students but little detail of the stories behind, say, students' assertion that they 'enjoyed' their courses of study. Similarly, The UK National Census (2011) asked the following question:

How is your health in general?

- Very good
- Good
- Fair
- Bad
- Very bad

This question would provide an indication of how healthy people *think* they are, but there are no definitions of what is meant by 'Very good', 'Good', 'Fair', 'Bad', or 'Very bad' health, and such a question provides no indication as to the experiences of people who report these various 'states' of health.

Another question asked:

How well can you speak English?

- Very well
- Well
- Not well
- Not at all

But again – no definitions of these categories are given and there is no possibility on a survey of this kind to find out how people are learning English, if they feel they want to, why they wish to improve their English, and so on.

Alternatively, an ethnographic study may tell you a great deal about the culture of any given situation and the people involved in it, but you would not easily be able to infer *generalities* about *other* situations from this sort of data. For example, Hurdley (2006: 717) explored the reasons why people displayed objects in their homes. She wrote:

> Although mantelpiece displays were the principal focus, other display areas were considered, and interview respondents were invited to tell stories about the provenance and meaning of objects. Analysing such narratives as social performances demonstrates the extent to which the apparently 'private' experiences of the self are manifested by means of display objects and domestic artefacts.

In this study the emphasis is on individual stories and the personal aspects of lives, rather than the generalisable or large-scale, with four stories being selected from 30 interviews, to illustrate the themes within the study.

Whether using large-scale questionnaire surveys, or smaller-scale and deeper interviews, in delimiting the sorts of information which may be accessed, channels of communication – in this case, particular research methods – represent (though often tacitly) differing views on how the world is constructed and how it operates.

Let us take an example of the genesis and development of a piece of research. Let us say, for argument's sake, that we wish to find out about the political consciousness of 18–21 year-old nursing students. Now there is clearly a number of ways in which we could do this, though it would be hard to avoid using either interview or questionnaire (or both). But the point is that the choice of method will itself depend on much earlier, often tacit, decision-making processes about the *nature* of *knowledge itself*. Are we to assume, for example, that the political beliefs held by our subjects are something which are more or less ready to hand, and which require merely the right question – the appropriate cue – to bring them to expression, and to record? Alternatively, might we assume that a political belief is something which may well be latent, requiring extended and almost certainly interactive interviewing to bring it to light not only to the researcher, but to the subjects themselves? And, in any event, can there be such a thing as context-free and enduring political beliefs, or are they rather tied to specific events? Specific cultures? Specific geographies? Specific times? How important is the nurse education curriculum, the course ethos and their hospital and community nurse experience placements to understanding the students' views?

Or take a different set of questions: how should we select whoever it is we want to interview or issue with a questionnaire? Why him and not her? Why 25 rather than 105? Or, from later moments in the process of carrying out the research, what will 'count' as evidence and what be 'discounted'? When data are 'cleaned' and 'tidied', what is discarded and why? And what about the part researchers play in designing and carrying out any study? Can social researchers be 'neutral', be 'objective'? And should we?

Partial answers to all these and the many more questions will be found as functions of our choice of methods; but the coherence and – above all – power to persuade others of our research will derive ultimately from the *painstaking justification we offer for the decisions we have made.*

Activity 2.4

You want to find out the views of employers on employing young people with a criminal record. How will you approach the task?

Will you interview? How many? Who? Where?
Will you carry out a questionnaire survey by post? How many? Who? Where?

Using the ideas in Figure 2.1 begin to make some of the research decisions identified above. In the process you will make decisions based on the kinds of information you want and the values you identify as important. Do you want the information to be 'slight' or 'deep'? Such a decision will directly impact on your research decisions.

Make some notes on your planned strategy and, importantly, *why* you make particular research decisions.

By way of example, we have plotted two studies on to Figure 2.2. In the first, example Study *a* focused on the perspectives of three long-serving social workers on changes in social work practice over the course of their careers. Study *b* surveyed 489 police officers (of varying career experience and length of service) for their views on community service orders as an alternative to custodial sentences.

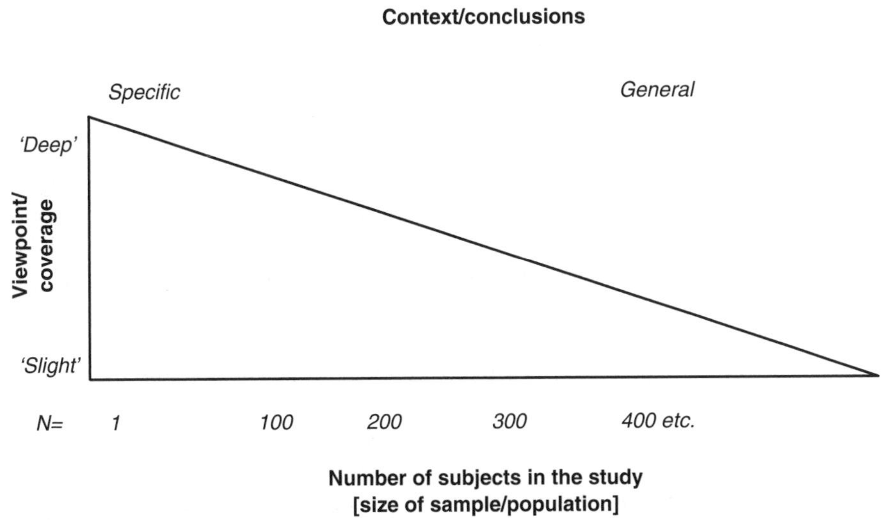

Figure 2.1   Factors to consider in making research decisions

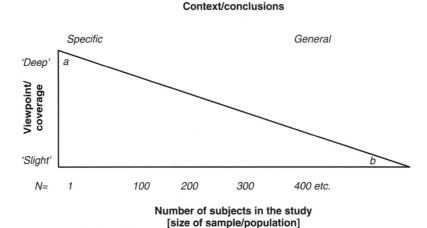

Figure 2.2   Factors to consider in making research decisions: two examples

a **Life history study focusing on three social workers.... N = 3**
b **Survey of attitudes of police officers to community service orders N = 498**

So, we suggest that it is not so much a case of 'choosing' methods as 'making' specifically crafted tools for a specifically generated set of questions which respond to a particular 'problem'. This theme will be addressed through various examples in the book.

What is methodology for?

> A methodology shows how research questions are articulated with questions asked in the field. Its effect is a claim about significance.

Trying to produce a definitive definition of methodology as used in the social sciences, and to serve the purposes of all researchers, is rather like trying to catch water in a net. Different researchers offer slightly differing definitions according to their own training, discipline and purposes. Thus Kaplan sees the aim of methodology to be:

> to describe and analyse ... methods, throwing light on their limitations and resources, clarifying their suppositions and consequences, relating their potentialities to the twilight zone at the frontiers of knowledge. It is to venture generalisations from the success of particular techniques, suggesting new applications, and to unfold the specific bearings of logical and metaphysical principles on concrete problems, suggesting new formulations. (1973: 93)

Miles and Huberman on the other hand, emphasised 'puzzlement' in pointing to the role of methodology:

> In our survey of qualitative researchers, we asked about issues that were unclear and puzzling. One researcher replied: 'Everything is unclear and puzzling. ... Improved methodology, however, raises confidence to a much more significant plane and provides a more certain base (though not an absolute one) for action'. (1994: 3)

And they argued for transparency in research processes:

> It is not just that we must somehow 'please' our critical colleague audiences; the deeper issue is avoiding self-delusion. After that we can turn to the task of being honest with our readers about how we did the study, and what worried us about its quality. Without such methodological frankness, we run the risk of reporting 'knowledge that ain't so'. (Ibid.: 294)

Different again in terms of scope is the requirement of Cohen, Manion and Morrison (2011: 73) that research decisions are made on the basis of the notion of 'fitness for purpose'. And so, from such 'fitness' research decisions are developed.

However, for all their differences, these and other definitions of methodology share a common idea of *justification*. This is why, in our own definition, we do not emphasise a *conceptual* essence for the term, but rather suggest an *operational* description which will be positively useful in justifying any given research design.

Traditionally, for philosophers the twin terms of methodology are *ontology* and *epistemology*, understood as the study of 'being' and of 'knowing' respectively. Basically, an *ontology* is a theory of what exists and how it exists, and an *epistemology* is a related theory of how we can come to know those things. For a philosopher, these are specialist, complex and profound fields of enquiry, but their importance is not restricted to philosophical enquiry, though their relevance at the point of setting out on an empirical research activity may not seem immediate.

Indeed, if every research thesis had to fully elaborate its ontological and epistemological background, then the wheel would truly be endlessly re-invented. However, if we examine any piece of empirical research, it is clear that there are at work a great many assumptions about what the world is, how it works and how we can claim to know these things.

Activity 2.5   What assumptions do you make?

In your research journal respond to these questions about the assumptions which underpin your study. (Clearly, the extent to which you can respond to the following questions will depend on the stage you have reached in your own study.)

(Continued)

(Continued)

- What assumptions about the topic are inevitably present in the way I conceive of the study?
- What specific questions – in the light of my assumptions – am I asking in this particular study, and which events and circumstances prompted them and gave them a particular urgency?
- Why and how did these assumptions, questions and circumstances suggest or require the particular methods I chose?
- What assumptions about 'how the world operates' – and how we can know it – are given with these methods?
- Why, then, are they particularly suitable for investigating the phenomenon in question?
- How did the process of my research change or qualify my assumptions? In what ways am I changed by the research?
- And in what ways is the community's understanding changed by what I have achieved? If, as we are trying to suggest, research actually defines the field, what redefinition (however small) is suggested in my work?
- What might another researcher learn from my experience?

By way of example, we return to Emily's developing study of youths with Anti Social Behaviour Orders. This is what Emily wrote in response to Activity 2.5:

Assumptions I am making about my ASBO study:

I am assuming that some young people with (and without) ASBOs will be prepared to talk to me, that enough people are fired up enough about the whole topic to spare time to talk. Specific questions relate, really, to self-image of the young people with ASBOs and it is the media hype and OTT coverage that has really given me the 'burn' to base my thesis around this.

Methods: hanging out I think, ethnography of a kind, but also talking, interviewing, getting some trust, but various forms of face-to-face talking. Unstructured, and as far as I can, without prejudice... I'm assuming here that people will talk to me and tell me things 'how they are' but there may be a bit of telling me what they think I want to hear or even talking to shock me! I'll need to sort this out, could be quite tangled. I do think this will make some sort of contribution to understanding, it will give an insight into young people's perspectives. I want, above all, to understand the 'currency' of the ASBO, what it means to have one 'on the street' (and not to have one). Ethical minefield in view... tread with care! Wear protective clothing! Be prepared for a new language...

It is the task of methodology to uncover and justify research assumptions as far and as practicably as possible, and in so doing to locate the claims which the research makes within the traditions of enquiry which use it. Equally, it is our task, as researchers, to identify our research tools and our rationale for their selection.

When Emily, rightly, wrote that she saw an 'ethical minefield in view' she was referring to the range of tricky issues likely to confront her as she planned and carried out her study. For interviewing young people with (and without) ASBOs raises issues about: her own safety, confidentiality of the participants, what she might do with information about criminal activity which is shared with her, when and how to withdraw from the field if things get difficult, who to approach and how to get permission for the young people to participate, giving 'currency' or 'kudos' to the idea of getting an ASBO by making it the focus of a research study. These are just some of the ethical issues which Emily had to address in her research and in her *metho-ethical* approach to the design, development and reporting of the study.

We have developed our operational definition from our own work with research students who, in time-constrained studies for Higher degree awards, are not immediately concerned with the fine-print of the epistemological and ontological foundations of their studies! But nevertheless they must articulate the 'being' and 'knowing' aspects of their studies in order to give meaningful report to the research act. However, it is our experience that the really successful – that is, the *persuasive* – studies are those which demonstrate a clear, logical and reflexive relationship between research questions and field questions and, in the process, provide deliberate, careful consideration of ethical questions. Further, this relationship is not one which is articulated only or largely in a so-called 'methodology chapter', but one which is also *evident throughout the work*. The relationship of research questions to literature review is a matter of methodology; the relationship of literature review to fieldwork is a methodological issue; the relationship of the fieldwork to the analysis of data is a methodological concern; the relationship of the framework for analysis to the research report is methodological. The ways in which ethical issues are addressed are a methodological matter and equally integral to the study.

> At the heart of all these interwoven research activities are endless processes of selection; and in constantly justifying this selection, a 'good methodology' is more *a critical design attitude* to be found always at work throughout a study, rather than confined within a brief chapter called 'Methodology'.

But what does this mean in practice? How might you work so that you were at all times *methodologically self-conscious*? We will discuss this further in Chapter 4.

So, what does it mean to adopt a *critical design attitude* in a research study? How does the *methodologically self-conscious researcher* behave? Our central concern is that student researchers are asked not 'Have you done your Methodology chapter?', but 'What are the methodological structures and operations of your study?' And 'How are these presented and justified in your thesis?' In this sense research *is* methodology.

Throughout the book we shall keep our operational definition to the forefront of our discussions. In the following section we explore further our definition of *methodology* by looking in particular at the relationship of *research questions* to those which are asked in empirical situations, and which we identify as *field questions,* and their relationships and implications for *ethical questions*.

Why are research questions important?

> It is important to distinguish between research questions – those that originate, shape and are to some extent answered by the study – from field questions – those that are actually put to people in whatever form.

We asked 13 Doctoral students who had successfully framed and refined their research questions to talk about why they felt the formulation of research questions was an important early stage of their research act. All participants readily agreed that research questions were important and went on to explain why they mattered to their own studies. They wrote:

- My questions matter because they set the parameters for my study.
- These questions matter for me because they define the issues pertinent to my research, will help me to clarify the situation and find ways forward.
- My research questions set out the principles that the study is based on.
- These questions matter because it gives my research a clear focus. It is important that the research I do benefits others and not just me, and it is important that I know why I am doing the study.
- For me, it is important to return to such questions during the research process – to remember what I'm doing and why!
- Research should be enjoyable for the researcher, so the research topic is important to me. My particular research questions help me to clarify, and therefore justify, my own work and to work out the reasonings for doing it.
- These particular research questions are important in the clarification and development of the practical aspects of research.
- My research questions help focus attention on the more important aspects of writing up the study.
- They [the research questions] enable me to clarify thoughts about underlying reasons for the study I've chosen to carry out.
- The research questions are important because they are firstly important to me – they help me to be clear about what's important in what I'm doing.

- They are important in helping me to develop good research practice.
- The formulation of these questions has helped me to be clear in my thoughts and they give my research direction.
- Developing my research questions and then sticking closely to them in designing the small-scale study has kept my study going in the right direction.

Activity 2.6

Whether you have decided on your own research questions or whether you are still deciding on the precise form of words, look over the comments made by research students above and note down the responses which fit, in some way, your own feelings about your research questions.

Note the key words and phrases that occur in several different responses. Ask yourself, whether it is appropriate for you to include such terms in your own discussion of the importance of research questions.

The themes emerging from the responses of our students can be grouped into four categories: defining limits, clarification, empirical issues and ethics.

Research questions require researchers to:

- define the limits of their study
- clarify their research study
- identify empirical and ethical issues
- identify necessary work on empirical questions
- plan responses to ethical issues

Generating and justifying research questions

In our own work we have developed two simple tools that can be employed in the generation of research questions: the 'Russian doll' principle and the 'Goldilocks test'. Applying the Russian doll principle means breaking down the research question from the original statement to something which strips away the complication of layers and obscurities until the very essence – the heart – of the question can be expressed. This may well mean phrasing and rephrasing the question so that each time its focus becomes sharpened and more defined – just as a Russian doll is taken apart to reveal finally a tiny doll at the centre.

The generated questions can then be subjected to the 'Goldilocks test' – a metaphor for thinking through the suitability of the research questions for a particular researcher in a particular setting at a particular time. So, we can ask: Is this question 'too big', such that it cannot be tackled in this particular study at this time? Perhaps it is a study which needs significant research funding or assistance which is not usually available to students doing research for an academic award? We can ask: Is this too small? Perhaps there is not enough substance to the question to warrant investigation. We can ask: Is the question 'too hot'? Perhaps the issue is so sensitive that the timing is not right for investigation or researching it at this point would be not only difficult but damaging in the particular social context. These questions will enable us finally to identify those questions that might be 'just right' for investigation at *this* time, by *this* researcher in *this* setting.

The following example will illustrate the application of the 'Russian doll' principle and the 'Goldilocks test'.

Case Sketch 2.1 Hoywell Hub

Frances, one of our Professional Doctorate students, came to the first of the Research Methods workshops with the following outline of the situation which she wanted to research:

> I work as Senior Youth worker at the Hoywell Hub, a centre for young people open every evening in the middle of Hoywell (a large suburban council estate within the Metropolitan Borough of B.). My research problem is quite a simple one, but I don't suppose the solution is! Basically, the Hub is becoming two communities – one black and one white. This isn't too uncomfortable – although there have been a few nasties – most of the time, but it seems to me to go against what the Hub, and the community itself, are about...

The group discussed her idea for about 10 minutes. Then Frances read a later note from her research journal:

> This is not like 'Can education compensate for society?' and I know the larger problem is much bigger than this research exercise is about, but there should still be something I could do, if only to alert people, perhaps a small project during the summer weeks, something to bring the two groups together... The Assistant Director has said I can have two half-days a week (for 3 months) to do some research. So what's the project I can do – that's what I need to work out...

Frances had made a further note about possible sources of information, which included: Other Youth Workers; Young people themselves (!!!); 3 Headteachers (1 High School, 2 Primaries); 2 GP practices, Health Visitors etc.; 3 social workers; Police/community wardens etc.; Parents?????.

We listed ideas on a flip chart and following another 10 minutes of discussion, Frances concluded: 'I haven't the foggiest idea of what the research question might be! My other possible topic is levels of literacy amongst our users.' We persuaded her to stick with the Hub as a topic for the moment! (Although one of the group pointed out that the two ideas might well link.)

This group of Doctoral students had become used by now to working with the Goldilocks test and Russian doll principle together as a way of isolating a key Research Question, and they set to with enthusiasm, first pooling their various suggestions thus:

Draft research questions for the Hoywell Hub study

1 Why are things going wrong at Hoywell?
2 What do members of the community think about what goes on at the Hub?
3 Is Hoywell Hub meeting the needs of the community?
4 Why are two racially defined subgroups emerging at Hoywell?
5 What is the way forward in development work with young people who use Hoywell?

Frances decided that she would work on these and bring her ideas to the next session.

One way of refining research questions and applying the Goldilocks test and the Russian doll principle is to write the questions in order and, next to each question, decide on its 'Goldilocks' status and draw out any factors which will help you to refine the questions. Table 2.1 shows what our students did with the Hoywell Hub questions and the final column records Frances' thinking and decision-making.

Table 2.1   Hoywell Hub research questions and the Goldilocks test

No.	Draft research questions	Goldilocks test	Russian doll principle
1	Why are things going wrong at Hoywell?	Too big	This statement is too general for a research question. It needs to be shorter, and more focused and perhaps lead to positive strategies rather than reasons why failings are occurring.
2	Why are two racially defined subgroups emerging at Hoywell?	Too big and – not right!	This is too big to help in developing the research design. But it is key to the issues I am facing and so the study needs to address this in some way.
3	Is Hoywell Hub meeting the needs of the community?	Too big	Well, maybe not so much 'too big' as too broad and not sufficiently refined – but there is something in this question which also needs to be included in the study.
4	What do members of the community think about what goes on at the Hub?	Too big	Again, there's too much here to do, but I do need to know what the community thinks… and what happens when the users of the Hub leave and make their way home…
5	What is the way forward in development work with young people who use Hoywell?	Still big… but is this right?	I have stated what I want to study i.e. social/ emotional development, and been more specific about the age range. By focusing on one child the study will be manageable.

In the second Research Methods workshop Frances talked with the group about how she had been thinking through her ideas. Somehow, the right summer research project was eluding her. After further discussion in the group a fellow student suggested that the study might not actually involve a project which actually *did* something with the two racially distinct groups, but rather reflected on how the Hub is used. The study could develop a strategic plan for the use of the centre for the next five years. This would involve all the participants whom Frances had originally thought she might need to include in some way in a project to bring the Hub users together. While the project did not take the form Frances had envisaged – with actually developing practice – it did seem to be the obvious thing to do to address changes in the community, its make-up and the expectations and needs of the young people.

Activity 2.7

Table 2.1 offers a strategy which you might use to support the development of your own research questions. When you are ready to do so, we suggest that you use a version of Table 2.2 to generate and refine your own research questions. There could be any number to begin with, and these will gradually be reduced in number as the questions themselves are gradually refined and clarified.

Table 2.2   Framework for refining research questions

No.	Draft research question	Goldilocks test	Russian doll principle
1			
2			
3			
4			
5			
6			
7			

In a different study, Karen, working on her MA dissertation, used the ideas in Tables 2.1 and 2.2 to work out her research questions for a study of a young child's capacity for social interaction with children and adults. In Table 2.3 we can see Karen's refinement of her research question. Satisfied with a working research question, Karen went on to use the same framework to think about the field questions she wanted to ask. We shall return to this in Chapter 6.

In this chapter we have emphasised the pervasive nature of methodology and the importance of framing questions which inform the creation of research methods. We shall return to these themes later.

Table 2.3   Using Goldilocks and Russian dolls to refine a research question on babies' social interaction

No.	Draft research questions	Goldilocks test	Russian doll principle
1	Have advances in childcare changed the social interaction patterns of babies and young children in recent years, or do they still have a largely egocentric perspective towards the environment, adults, and their peers?	Too big	This statement is too long for a research title. It needs to be short, accurate, informative and interesting.
2	Can babies and young children socially interact with adults and peers in the childcare environment?	Too big	Too vague and generalised. Need to clarify exactly what I hope to see, and specify the age range of the children.
3	Can children socially interact with peers and adults in the childcare environment?	Too big	Too vague and generalised. I have also limited my choices by removing the word 'babies'. What is it that I specifically want to know?
4	Have the social interaction patterns of babies and young children changed in recent years or are they still largely egocentric?	Too big	Although I have been more specific relating to what I want to study, i.e. whether the social interaction patterns of babies and young children have changed in recent years, this topic is still too big. I need to be more specific and scale down the research question to ensure it is more achievable.
5	Can a child under two years old socially interact with other children and adults?	Just right?	I have stated what I want to study i.e. social/ emotional development, and been more specific about the age range. By focusing on one child the study will be manageable.

The methodology of any study is unlikely to be complete until the research is arrested for the purposes of report. A methodology worthy of the name will be continuously and reflexively developed as the study proceeds – in much the same way as the data which emerge from methods reflect back on and qualify the suitability of those methods for the purpose in hand.

Endnote

Narrowly understood, a research methodology is sometimes seen as standing slightly outside the main achievement of a study. It is a sort of guarantee – in the common sense of the term – whose small print may be technically necessary but hardly essential reading for the operation of the product! What we argue here, however, is a broader view of methodology as the very seat of justification of any claims which might follow. Methods mediate between research questions and the answers which data partially provide to them; methodology justifies and guarantees that process of mediation. In the end, the characteristic task for a methodology is to persuade the reader of the *unavoidably* triangular connection between *these* research questions, *these* methods used to operationalise them and *these* data so generated.

Activity 2.8

Before you leave this chapter, think about your own research study. Ask yourself:

Why are you doing this study in this way?
Can you justify the research decisions you have made?

Make some notes about the justification of your research design in your research journal.

Ethics: pause for reflection

How do research ethics influence the design of research questions?
What are the ethical implications of *radical looking*, making the familiar strange, in research?
Adopting *radical listening*, the interpretative and critical means through which 'voice' is noticed, is an ethical position; what are the ethical implications for interpreting the voices of participants?
Consider how *radical reading* and critical reading of research are in themselves ethical practices.

(Continued)

(Continued)

How can *radical questioning* enhance ethical research decision-making?

In what ways can your research questions help you to plan responses to ethical issues which arise in your study?

In this chapter we have discussed examples of studies focusing on young people in receipt of ASBOs and research focusing on a child under 2 years. What ethical issues might arise when researching participants who might be considered 'vulnerable'?

It is important that these questions are responded to in the light of specific studies, addressing the particular issues which each research question raises in the context of ethical decision-making. From the beginning idea of a study, the ethical issues which underpin and extend within that idea are already bubbling. From the point when research questions are formulated, the ethical issues which might arise and will need to be addressed must also be allowed to rise to the surface and be given due consideration. All research that involves human beings and their data is shot through with ethical issues. Some are dealt with in very straightforward ways, and others need more careful, thoughtful and sensitive resolutions.

When engaging in *radical looking*, making the familiar strange, researchers need to remain sensitive to the personal data of lives which can surface. How are such data recorded? How are they stored? What is 'cleaned out' and what is 'tidied' to exclude some of the more tricky issues? If social researchers practise *radical listening,* they must then consider their practices for both representing and acting on the 'voices' they have heard. Researchers must consider how to listen with care and how to record the voices they hear with accuracy and report them faithfully. Likewise, *radical reading* of situations, events and of the literature require an ethic of care and responsibility. When 'reading' situations, researchers must ask how their 'reading' relates to the reality of the lives engaged in their 'readings'. Equally, it is a responsibility of scholarship (and an ethical duty) to undertake a review of the literature which considers all aspects of the field, including those from positions which may not be shared by the researcher. The act of *radical questioning* in research is to be undertaken with great care and requires continued practice and skill. What not to ask, and when not to ask certain questions, is a matter of careful judgement. Equally, it is essential to the integrity of any study that questions are asked of the literature, that studies are scrutinised for their ethical and methodological justifications, for research judgements arise from good questioning.

Finally, when participants are considered to be (in any way) 'vulnerable', the researcher must pay additional attention to their needs. In the case of young people who have been in (or who are on the edge of) trouble with the authorities, and with very young children, their rights and needs as research participants must be paramount, and researchers will need to proceed with clarity and care as well as with well informed judgement.

CHAPTER SUMMARY

In this chapter we have:

- *Provided an overview of what we mean by methodology*
- *Discussed the distinction between 'methods' and 'methodology'*
- *Discussed, with examples, the function of methodological consideration in the context of your research study*
- *Discussed the function and importance of research questions*
- *Provided a structure within which you might generate and justify your research questions*
- *Encouraged you to express, in writing, your own positions on the key elements of the chapter in relation to your research questions and methodology*
- *Reflected on the ethical issues arising from the chapter contents*

FURTHER READING

Agee, J. (2009) 'Developing qualitative research questions: a reflective process', *International Journal of Qualitative Studies in Education*, 22 (4): 431–447.

> Agee states that:
>
> > The reflective and interrogative processes required for developing effective qualitative research questions can give shape and direction to a study in ways that are often underestimated. Good research questions do not necessarily produce good research, but poorly conceived or constructed questions will likely create problems that affect all subsequent stages of a study.
>
> In this paper she discusses the development of research questions and their refinement in order to shape qualitative research.

Kawulich, B.B. (2011) 'Gatekeeping: an ongoing adventure in research', *Field Methods*, 23 (1): 57–76.

> In this paper Kawulich discusses issues relating to permissions to carry out research, selecting participants, researcher presentation, respect and issues of negotiating with gatekeepers.

de Vaus, D. (2001) *Research Design in Social Research*. London: Sage.

> For a succinct summary of the importance of clarifying research questions and their operational and conceptual definitions read 'Tools for Research Design' (Chapter 2). This chapter focuses on the clarification of research questions and concepts from the outset of a study.

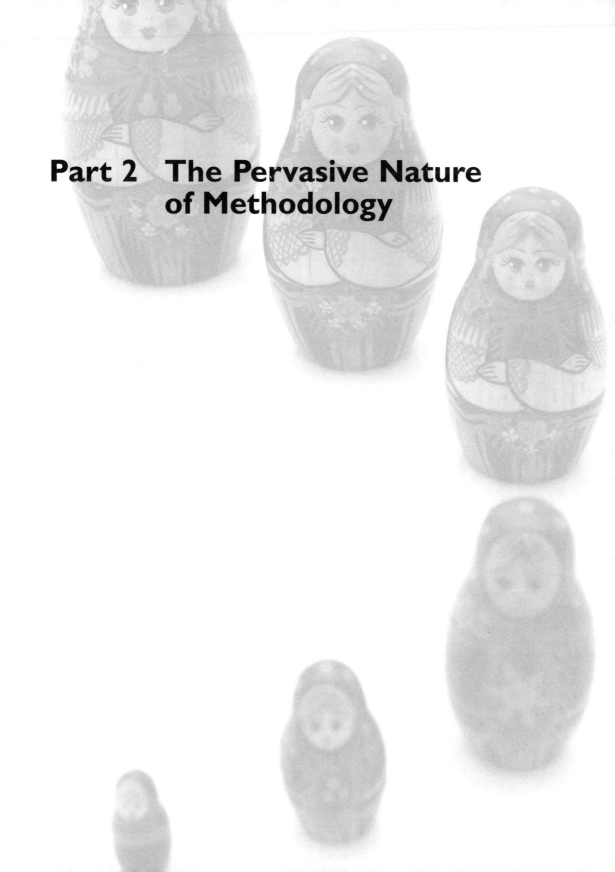

Part 2 The Pervasive Nature of Methodology

3 Looking: Seeing Beyond the Known

CHAPTER CONTENTS

Introduction   52
Making the familiar strange   53
Observation in research   54
What are you looking *for?*   59
Ethics: pause for reflection   60

LEARNING OBJECTIVES

By studying and doing the activities in this chapter you will:

- develop an awareness of the importance of radical looking at all points during the research process
- have an understanding of the strategies which can be used in research involving different ways of seeing
- have studied two examples of research which demonstrate different dimensions of 'radical looking'.

Introduction

> What we mean by radical looking is exploration beyond the familiar and the (personally) known to the roots of a situation. This is exploration which makes the familiar strange.

If we travel to a different country, we see everyday things in a new light and sometimes find ourselves becoming curious about the ordinary: traffic systems, shopping, eating, dress codes and other routines of life can be sources of fascination because, although we *recognise* them, we may not fully understand them nor do we know precisely how we should behave within the nuances of that *particular* society. Travel, in effect, offers us the opportunity to hold our own experiences up to the light and reflect on how we do things in the context of another culture. *Radical looking* can, in effect, involve the researcher in the role of a *traveller* who is curious about the systems, cultures, practices and policies of the life of the setting in which she has decided to work.

To give a quite literal example of this, Nutbrown (2001) reports the experience of looking *outside* the UK provision at early childhood education. This offered an opportunity to reflect again on more familiar contexts. In a report of her experience of visiting some Italian pre-schools she wrote:

> Visiting any early childhood setting is a privilege, such was the case in visiting the Reggio Emilia Pre-schools. Pedagogistas, Atiliaristas, parents and children allowed us to witness their work and to discuss with them the intricacies of their thinking which led to the kinds of practices which were compelling and meaningful. Observations of course are so personal, and interpretation of what is seen depends upon the eyes through which those observations are made. This account is therefore a reflection of my own experience of those encounters; my own construction of Reggio 'as I saw it'.

Mirrors

> There are mirrors everywhere in the Reggio centres. They fill large corners of rooms, they hang from the ceiling, and they dangle in small fragments from mobiles made by the children. They encourage looking, looking at oneself, they make for reflection – and in some cases multi reflections of the same image through mirror after mirror after mirror. The opportunity of so many mirrors invites reflection; reflection on oneself, one's work and one's own observations and assumptions.
>
> Through the mirrors of Reggio Emilia centres I saw much that I recognised, much that makes sense in terms of what I believe is 'right' for children, I saw many of my own values, and many of my principles in practice. I saw too, so much of the excellence of teaching young children that can also be seen in many nurseries and early childhood centres in the UK. (Nutbrown, 2001: 120–2)

This extract illustrates our point that looking at others can help us to reflect on our own experiences. Simultaneously, historical reflection can enable us to look back at the events of the past (McCulloch and Richardson, 2001; Nutbrown et al., 2008). We can also 'dig' into the 'objects' of research settings (much as an archaeologist might do) and thus uncover clues which we then piece together to help us to understand circumstances and policy contexts of the context of study. In these ways all social and educational researchers are historians and archaeologists, aiming to understand origins and contexts of the situations they study.

Further examples of what we call *radical looking* can be found in many sociological studies around the world. For example Wacquant's (2002) ethnographic study, located in the Los Angeles County Jail, contains a vivid description of the prison environment, including:

> A large sign in black block letters stipulates: 'NO TALKING', another blares: 'BE QUIET, KEEP SHOULDERS ON WALL'. Tight lines of inmates hug the corridors decorated with life-sized murals in garish colors, the work of house artists, whose martial themes – 'Tombstone', a scene with a sheriff in a street lifted out of a Western movie, a visual ode to 'Desert Storm', a cluster of strapping cowboys galloping away across the desert at full speed – awkwardly evoke the space that is so lacking and so desired. Blue uniforms for the GP ('General Population'), orange for detainees under medical supervision (which makes them ready targets for violent residents), blue with white sleeves for gang members and convicts from state prisons consigned to the city jail for lack of space in the overpopulated penitentiaries, and green for the 'trustees'. (2002: 375)

In a study of quite a different topic, Srinivas (2010) describes the place of cinema in the South Indian city of Bangalore, and describes part of the location of the study thus:

> With its high-rise, glass-fronted buildings, trendy boutiques, department stores, five-star hotels, and restaurants, the Cantonment is a place to spend time with family and friends and people-watch. Cafés, ice-cream parlors, and small eateries provide spaces for socializing for groups of middle-class high school and college students, young professionals, and families. People stroll on the elevated walkway and sit on the benches; they buy snacks from the street vendors and window-shop. Markers of the city's colonial past are everywhere: a statue of Queen Victoria remains at the Cubbon Park end of M.G. Road, a spot for street vendors to gather and a favorite perch for pigeons. (2010: 193)

Radical looking, then, requires that researchers develop the skills of travellers and historians in so far as they look at events close to them *as if* they were different or distant.

Making the familiar strange

All researchers need to develop the capacity to see their topic with *new and different lenses* in order to look beyond and transform their own current knowledge. Topics present themselves for research in different ways and for all sorts of different reasons. What distinguishes research from everyday interest or curiosity, however, is the *opening up of familiar things to alternative ways of seeing*.

When we try self-consciously to draw on something of ourselves to understand a newly encountered event or phenomenon, we, in some senses, are *making the familiar strange* in the act of seeking to understand – we are remaking new 'versions' of the story. As well as the political motivation of making explicit and visible those aspects of life which often remain invisible, autoethnographic writing is often used to make the familiar strange (Shklovsky, 1965; Clough, 2002; Kaomea, 2003), to bring into focus those taken-for-granted happenings of life.

Two groups of people often studied in social science research are children and the disabled. But it is only relatively recently that children and disabled people have become participants rather than 'objects' of research; it is only recently that their voices have been heard. In Chapter 2 we suggested that an *interest* in a subject only starts to become *research* when a curiosity is systematically informed by perspectives outside the researcher's normal vision. This means asking questions about what is already known, what previous research has been done, what policy contexts affect the situation and what the participants themselves think about their present position. In asking such questions, the researcher engages in *radical looking at others' knowledge*. Responses to such questions refine and define the topic. The process involves the researcher in examining, and either incorporating or rejecting information as s/he begins to focus on a particular problem, a particular gap in knowledge.

Activity 3.1   Making the familiar strange

Try this task.

Imagine you are a cleaner in the institution or organisation where you carry out your research. Describe how the organisation looks, how it works, from a cleaner's viewpoint.

Seeing things from the point of view of someone else, who occupies a different role, gives an indication of what we mean by adopting a research stance which involves radical looking, the *opening up of familiar things to alternative ways of seeing.*

In the next two sections we provide two examples from our own research to demonstrate aspects of radical looking and interpret the theme first in terms of observation and, second, in reflective responses to data and their analyses.

Observation in research

Although observations are often referred to in terms of particular techniques, what we want to attend to here is the nature of looking. Our working definition of observation here is simply 'looking' – looking critically, looking openly, looking sometimes knowing what we are looking for, looking for evidence, looking to be persuaded, looking for information.

In this section we shall point you to some ideas about, and methods of, observation and draw on a research report which used observations.

Activity 3.2

Think about what *you* mean by the term 'observation'.

Reflect on this definition – as you work through this chapter you may well find yourself reworking your definition.

Below is a list of different ways of looking or observing. Different techniques will be useful for different settings and you will need to consider the ethics, practicalities, and justification of each of those you choose to use.

- Checklists
- Structured observations with a schedule
- Time sampling
- Mapping
- Target pupil observations
- Video and photographic records
- Unstructured observations
- One-way mirror observations.

These techniques are discussed in several texts on research methods. The main issue is to be clear about what you want to research and why, and then find the best way of working on your research question.

Observation is a widely used research method and is perhaps all too easily undertaken. Some early questions will help to justify the decision to use this method: what is the purpose of the observation? What is the focus of the observation? What data gathering methods will best serve the purpose? How will the data be used?

Activity 3.3   Making observations

Beginning their section on observation (Chapter 23), Cohen, Manion and Morrison write:

> The distinctive feature of observation as a research process is that it offers an investigator the opportunity to gather 'live' data from naturally occurring social situations. In this way, the researcher can look at what is taking

(Continued)

(Continued)

place *in situ* rather than relying on second-hand accounts. The use of immediate awareness or direct cognition, as a principle mode of research, thus has the potential to yield more valid or authentic data than would otherwise be the case with mediated or inferential methods. And this is observation's unique strength. (Cohen et al., 2011: 456)

In your research journal identify three advantages and three drawbacks of using observation techniques to gather data in your research study.

The following examples of observation illustrate a range of styles, topics, techniques and issues.

Observing Matthew

Matthew's Treasure Basket

Christmas had seen the arrival of Matthew's Treasure Basket. At 6 months old he was just the right age to begin his exploration of the natural materials offered to him. At the time of the observation, Matthew, just turned 9 months old, was used to handling, mouthing, sorting and selecting his favourite items from his basket.

Matthew's mother, Kate, places the Treasure Basket with its abundance of natural materials in the middle of a large cleared space in the room. She then asks Matthew gently if he would like to play with his treasure. He waves his arms and legs frantically as his eyes rest on the basket. Kate places Matthew close enough for him to reach right into the basket. He immediately reaches in with his right hand and selects a long wooden handled spatula. 'oohh, ahh,' he says and looks directly at his mother. She smiles at him in approval. Still holding the spatula he proceeds to kneel up and lean across the basket in order to reach a long brown silk scarf. He pulls at the scarf and squeals in delight as he pulls the fabric through his fingers, 'oohh, ahh' he repeats. He lets go of the spatula and abandons the scarf to his side, his eyes rest on a large blue stone, he picks up the large stone with his right hand and turns it over on his lap using both hands. Still using both hands he picks the stone up and begins to bite it, making a noise as his teeth grind against the hard surface. He smiles; looking at his mother as he repeatedly bites the stone over and over again. He stops, holds the stone up to his face and looks at it intently, then puts it to his mouth once more. He then picks up the wooden spatula again and whilst holding it firmly in one hand, he turns the contents of the basket over with his other hand, squealing loudly with delight as he discovers the matching long handled fork. Matthew looks at his mother and waves both items in the air smiling and rocking on his knees saying 'oohh, ahh'. He turns away from the basket and waves the long handled implements up and down in his hands, first one then the other then both together. He turns back to the basket with a puzzled expression and for a few seconds, stops waving the items. He drops the fork and reaches back into the basket and randomly picks up items one at a time, looks at them and then discards them on the floor beside him. He continues this pattern for several seconds until he comes upon a long handled brush. He picks up the brush, pauses and then waves it in his left hand, all the time continuing to hold the wooden spatula in his right hand. For several seconds he proceeds to bang the long handled items together, smiling as the two wooden items make a sound as they come together. He then spots the wooden fork he had disposed of earlier and letting go of the brush picks up the wooden fork and bangs it together with the spatula. 'baba, baba, da, da, da' he says, then a little more loudly he repeats 'baba, baba, da, da, da'. Just when it seems that he is giving signals that he has finished with the items in the basket he notices another long scarf. Letting go of both the wooden items he reaches into the basket and tugs the scarf, he pulls it over his face and blows raspberries. He smiles at his mother and she smiles at him. The material falls to the floor and Matthew looks up at his mother and waves his arms up and down. Kate, realising that Matthew is signalling that he has finished with his Treasure Basket for today, reaches down and holds her arms out to him. Matthew instantly smiles, holds his arms up to her. As she sweeps him into her arms, Matthew snuggles into his mother's neck and with his thumb in his mouth says 'kai, kai, kai' a pleasurable comfort sound that Matthew vocalises when seemingly enjoying close contact with his family members. (Nutbrown, 2010: 65–8)

Observing 'Alice' 2.5 years

Moya and Alice are painting a duck which they have made over the past days, by covering an inflated balloon with papier maché and attaching wings and a head made from foam rubber. Moya is using the stuffed Mallard duck as a reference point. Moya talks about the duck, its feathers, the colours in the wings and neck.

> Moya 'Can you see that brilliant purple there on his neck?'
> Alice 'Greeny there...'
> Moya 'And a sort of browny...'

They stick some coloured feathers on the duck, chosen by Alice from a bag of feathers dyed in a range of vivid colours. Alice spends some time looking through the bag of feathers as if it is treasure; she seems immersed in the colours and the movement they make as she waves each in the air. She smiles.

Moya quietly ensures that the paint is in plentiful supply, topping up each container before it runs out. Alice applies layer after layer of paint. Moya remains seated with her, occasionally talking about the colours, the direction of the duck's feathers, the shine of the paint, but often providing quite silent, sustained support.

For some 20 minutes Moya and Alice stick feathers to the duck – Alice lingering over her choice of colours, exploring their movement and their texture and placing them on the duck.

Alice's hands are as colourful as the duck; she is immersed in this sustained experience of colour and texture.

Alice moves to work on the neck of the duck and her actions change from slow lingering brush strokes to long, quick, quite vigorous movements of the brush as she adds colour, purple, then orange up the neck of the duck. Wack! Wack-wack!

She smiles to herself – then turns laughing to look at Moya. Moya laughs too! Moya and Alice have been working on her duck for 45 minutes.

'He's wet! He's been swimming!' says Alice and she and Moya go to the hot air hand dryer where Alice tries to dry her duck.

She shows her duck to one of the practitioners 'Ducky!' she shouts proudly – in a sing songy celebratory voice. 'Ducky!' (Nutbrown and Jones, 2006: 30–1)

Observing 'a boy at the airport'

…. working at a special school, a seemingly wonderful opportunity presented itself. A trip to Lapland to meet Father Christmas. I was filled with trepidation for I knew that one of the young children in my group, an autistic boy, would find it extremely difficult to cope with such a change in routine. Encouraged by arrangements to intervene if this proved to be the case, off we set.

Not long after arriving at the airport the child became very upset and lay on the floor in the middle of the departure lounge shouting repeatedly 'this boy doesn't like crowds' surrounded by a curious public backing away. (Mary McVeigh, in Nutbrown and Clough, 2006: 136)

Watching kids 'hanging around'

I went in to get a paper, there was no one else in the shop but me and the young woman behind the counter. She looked slightly unnerved and had sort of frozen to the spot where she stood. … 'Can I just… Er … a Guardian… £1.00? Yes?' I said.

'Oh! Yeah, sorry…' She took my five pound note and without taking her eyes off the teenagers hanging around the shop front, put the money in the till and passed to me four pound coins. 'Thanks.'

'Something up?' I asked.

'They're always hanging round. Sometimes they come in and pretend they want to buy something, if it's raining they come in… They don't really do anything but I get, well, I wish they weren't there…'

I looked, baggy jeans, frayed and torn, hoodies, lolling sort of stances, mumbling, staring, kicking invisible objects on the pavement… Not doing anything really, just… there… present… Watching…

'They trouble you?' I asked.

'Yes, I just don't trust them, they're just "there" ya' know?'

I took my paper, and left the shop, one of them caught my arm as I passed him 'Watchit mate…'

I walked on, deciding not to challenge… I guess that's what most people do, just walk on…

Activity 3.4

Thinking about the examples you have just read, try to identify the ways in which *'the familiar was made strange'* in order to provide the accounts.

What are you looking *for?*

Radical looking means much more than using observations to generate data for a research study.

> *Radical looking* holds within it the important dimension of looking *for* as well as looking *at*, the act of seeking *meanings* as well as *evidence*.

The examples in this chapter have provided illustrations of what we mean by looking *for* and demonstrate how *meanings* are generated in response to the act of *radical looking* through data to see the truths they hold. Whether the focus is a Los Angeles prison, cinemas in Bangalore, a baby playing, a child painting, or young people outside a shop, all are examples of researchers looking *for* something and responding to what they see by creating text which reports the meanings the researchers have made from that they have seen.

Activity 3.5

Try to identify the acts of radical looking present in your own research study. Are you looking *for* as well as *at* and are you the seeking *meanings* as well as *evidence* from which those meanings are derived?

As your study progresses you will, no doubt, add to these notes in your research journal. Such changes in research strategy and construction are important developments and form part of the account of your analysis. (We shall discuss this further in Chapter 7.)

As the book develops it will become clear that *radical looking* is actually inseparable from the other radical practices which we discuss, and how radical looking – both looking *at* and looking *for* – is one of the tools of all social scientists.

> **Ethics: pause for reflection**
>
> What are the ethical implications of *radical looking*? Does the act of looking with *new and different lenses* in order to learn something new carry implications for the seeking of informed consent? Is it always essential to gain permission from those you are looking *at*?
>
> If research is the *opening up of familiar things to alternative ways of seeing*, what are the implications for the researcher who sees something which is immoral, illegal, harmful or unpleasant?
>
> When researchers look *for* as well as *at*, as they seek *meanings* as well as *evidence*. What are the ethical implications for faithful interpretation of those meanings and that evidence?

It is important to be clear, in the act of radical looking, that the worlds of others are being subjected to some form of scrutiny. The extent to which permissions need to be sought needs careful thought. Radical looking often involves the use of photography – often with the participants being asked to take images of things and people in their environment. Photographic data present their own unique ethical difficulties and the decision to 'look' through the lens of a camera must be taken only after full and intense attention to the ownership of the images, the permissions which might be needed and the 'good' or 'harm' the use of images as data might do. Researchers need to remember that they are not journalists, and (for the protection and comfort of all involved) they need permissions to take and use photos as research data. What photographs present in terms of ethical dilemmas are often unknown until the moment of interpretation; the researcher may not know what he or she is looking at until they re-look at the image away from the scene of the research. Checks and balances are needed and each study will need to include consideration of these in order to protect participants from danger or embarrassment.

We suggest that researchers must be in no doubt as to how they will act if there is a need to protect their participants, for whatever reason. There is no compromise on this. The well-being and safety of participants and the research comes first and if the study is jeopardised as a result, then so be it.

Of course, it is not always the case that researchers are open about their studies. There are still examples where covert research is undertaken, and it can gain approval from university Research Ethics Committees. Calvey (2008) discusses the ethics of covert research, drawing on a six-month covert ethnography of 'bouncers' in Manchester. In his paper, Calvey challenges the accepted practices of informed consent and highlights the case for covert research as part of a debate on social science research methodology and ethics.

Radical looking carries with it an expectation that the researcher gives effort and energy to faithful interpretation of what he or she sees, and this necessitates finding ways of taking meaning from what is seen and reporting that evidence in ways which remain true to the research scene. To this end it is an ethical responsibility to explain in any research study how the researcher went about interpreting the data and making transparent instruments and processes of analysis. All too often there is a silence between data and findings – the all important process of analysis – or interpretation – which sits between the data and the findings is often missed or skimped.

CHAPTER SUMMARY

In this chapter we have:

- *Defined and demonstrated our view of radical looking in research and argued the importance of radical looking at all points during the research process*
- *Outlined the function of making the familiar strange*
- *Discussed some practices and issues of using observation as a research tool*
- *Demonstrated, through two examples of research, different dimensions of 'radical looking': looking at; looking for; looking for evidence and looking for meanings*
- *Reflected on the ethical issues arising from the chapter contents*

FURTHER READING

Silverman, D. (2006) *Interpreting Qualitative data: Methods for Analysing Talk, Text and Interaction* (3rd edn). London: Sage.

See particularly Chapter 7 'Visual Images'.

Wacquant, L. (2002) 'The curious eclipse of prison ethnography in the age of mass incarceration', *Ethnography*, 3 (4): 371–97.

Discusses the difficulties of researching in prisons and the importance of portraying the prisons from the unique vantage point of 'inside'.

Calvey, B. (2008) 'The art and politics of covert research: doing "situated ethics" in the field', *Sociology*, 42: 905.

Consider Calvey's arguments for covert research. What is your view?

4 Listening: Issues of Voice

CHAPTER CONTENTS

Introduction   63
'Voice' and research experience   63
Focused conversation as a research method   86
'Voice' and internet-based social enquiry   96
'Interpretation' of research voices   99
Ethics: pause for reflection   102

LEARNING OBJECTIVES

By studying and doing the activities in this chapter you will:

- have an understanding of the importance of 'voice' in social science research
- be aware of the literature on 'voice' in social science research
- have an understanding of the processes of obtaining and reporting data from focused conversation and focus groups
- be able to write a robust justification for generating data through group talk and writing
- be aware of ethical implications
- understand the issues and processes involved in 'interpreting' research voices.

Introduction

> *Radical listening* – as opposed to merely hearing – is the interpretative and critical means through which 'voice' is noticed. *Radical listening* also requires researchers not 'just' to hear, but to consider what action may result from their listening.

In this chapter we focus specifically on the importance of 'voice' in social science research and the justifications for incorporating and interpreting research voices in particular ways. We begin with an overview of what we mean by *radical* listening: a careful attention to all the *voices* to be heard on a given topic of study. Giving prominence to 'voice' in educational and social science research emphasises our view of social research as *positional* and *political* (see Chapter 1). Having established what we mean by voice, we provide one example of developing 'method' in order to serve the research task of giving voice to a group of research participants and incorporating the researcher's voice within that experience; this example is included to illustrate the methodological structure which governs a research study. Next we further discuss issues and implications of 'giving voice' to research participants and the methodological justifications for such research. Finally, we examine some of the issues which arise when researchers attempt to interpret the voices of others.

'Voice' and research experience

In this section we offer an overview of what we mean by 'voice' in educational and social science research, both in terms of the voice of the researcher and the voices of the research participants.

The voices of researchers

> '... The informed researcher's voice no longer provides an authoritarian monologue but contributes a part to dialogue.' (Mitchell, 1993: 55)

In the twenty years since Mitchell's reflection on researcher voice, research in the social sciences has developed apace. The 'messiness' of research and the impossibilities of disentangling the positionality of the researcher from his/her methods and values is now broadly acknowledged. Researchers are part of their research – whether it is the criminologist studying the effects of long-term prison sentences on offenders (Farrall et al., 2011), the economist focusing on the effects of bullying on the economy (Brown and Taylor, 2008), or the landscape architect seeking to improve public play spaces for disabled children (Woolley et al., 2005).

Research is, by definition, a search for form quite as much – and at the same time – as it is a search for 'content' or knowledge to report. As Walker (1985: 46) observed almost forty years ago, methods are intrinsic to research. They are no mere adjunct, but part of the unfolding story – and research in the social sciences in recent years attests to this. But for the purposes of this chapter we want to take ideas of 'method' a little further, so as to get 'on the inside' of doing research. So, when Mitchell writes that '...the informed researcher's voice no longer provides an authoritarian monologue but contributes a part to dialogue' (1993: 55), he is arguing that the researcher's voice is – or should be – as much present as that of the research participants.

But what does Mitchell really mean here? What might it mean for a researcher to 'contribute' to dialogue? And what form should this 'part' take? What would such research look like? Feminist research has advocated the integrity of self and research participants *in* research, and as Ann Oakley reflected on the role of 'self' in research, there remains a lesson here for social science research in general:

> A feminist methodology of social science requires that this rationale of research be described and discussed not only in feminist research but in social science research in general. It requires further, that the mythology of 'hygienic' research with its accompanying mystification of the researcher and the researched as objective instruments of data production be replaced by the recognition that personal involvement is more than dangerous bias – it is the condition under which people come to know each other and to admit others into their lives. (Oakley, 1993: 58)

Activity 4.1

Consider Ann Oakley's words and make some notes on your reflections.

What might she mean by 'the mythology of "hygienic" research'? Can you find an example of reported research which might be claimed to be 'hygienic'? Why might she consider this a 'myth'?

What might be the implications of Oakley's statement that 'personal involvement ... is the condition under which people come to know each other and to admit others into their lives'? What are the implications of this for researchers?

The inseparability of research and researcher is, many would argue, an essential feature of research in the social sciences; and the methodology which drives such research is as much to do with personal values as it is to do with 'rigour' and 'hygiene' in research methodology. In a sense, methodology is as much about the way we live our lives as it is about the way in which we choose to conduct a particular piece of research. Methodology is about making research decisions and understanding (and justifying) *why* we have made those decisions. Our research methodologies are rooted in our own personal values which, in some form, inform our ethical and moral responses to problems and challenges. So what might we make of this in relation to the origins of our research studies? What roots (or re-routes) us to the research theme we work on? Why does an academic in a Department of Politics focus, for example, on the roles and contributions of women in modern European politics? What prompts a professor of Law to focus his research on International Human Rights legislation? Why does a sociologist choose to focus her attention on definitions and responses to child abuse in different societies around the globe? What prompts an academic in a School of Management to develop research into the management of household finances and economies? And what lies beneath the interest of a professor of Education in children's developing literacies in online environments?

Our point here is that researchers are rarely distinct from their research topics (though doubtless some rare examples may be found). One colleague recently remarked: *'I can only commit to doing something I believe in – and when I do that, I give it my all'*. We suggest that there is an intimacy between the researcher and his/her research focus and so the notion of an 'hygenic' and sanitised approach to research is, we suggest, mythical. There is inevitably an element of the personal in any research project, though we would also say that the nature of the project and the methodological approaches taken will also impact on the level of intimacy and the extent to which the researchers and the research is entwined.

You may well have already decided on your research questions, or at least have begun to develop the specific area in which your research will focus. Are you aware of where this interest comes from? What, for example, motivates someone to research adult literacy in community organisations? Or the 'deviant' behaviour of 13-year-old boys? Or human rights abuses in parts of the Middle East? Or the experiences of wheelchair users in accessing public buildings and spaces in a large US city? Or women's experience of higher education in Scotland? Or public reaction to the reporting of expense claims submitted by UK Members of Parliament? Or public views of the economic crises of the early twenty-first century in Europe? What is it, in those who research, which forms that *particular* motivation?

Clough and Corbett (2000), in tracing some routes to inclusive education, interviewed a number of influential figures in the field. Several expressed their hunches about the roots of their own research interests and their 'accidental-or-not' arrival as researchers in the field of inclusive education. Mike Oliver, for example, said:

> I think the whole issue about my own experiences as a disabled person in terms of how that has influenced my thinking as a sociological theorist and a political activist may be one of the reasons I am interested in male country and western singers. They always sing about the road and the train. They are always on a journey to somewhere. I think I've been on a journey as well, in which my own understanding of myself has changed. You know, I started out 25 years ago as a typical academic, saying 'Let's be objective. Let's study the world'. I was advised not to get into disability because it was too personal. Then I moved into recognising that personal experience gives you an added dimension to use to authenticate the work. Then I moved on to feeling that it is not an adequate model in itself either, because you are what you are. You've got to embrace rather than merely use what you are. (Oliver, 2000: 112–13)

Peter Clough picks up the theme of research/professional origins:

> I am struck by the number of people I know whose initial experience of working in special education seemed, as it were, accidental. Yet at the same time I don't really believe in this 'accidental' account; without being fatalist or therapist about it, I think that most people's involvement in 'special' education is – or becomes – knit fairly densely with their 'personal' lives and there's usually some (psycho)logic to it. (Clough, 2000: 65)

Finally, one of our own students, in respect of her own completed study of the experiences of mothers of children with disabilities, wrote:

> Selecting a topic for a dissertation according to many is a challenging task. To me, the subject I selected was an issue I was yearning to research for some time. It was about mothers' experiences of the emotional and social implications of having a child with disabilities. I wanted to tell the mothers' stories.
>
> I've always believed that parenting is a tough job and an even tougher job is parenting a child with special needs. Until I became a mother in a similar situation I had always thought that having a child with a disability always happened to someone else and possibly could never happen to you. ... It was when I found myself to be one of those mothers that I realised the daunting task of bringing up a child with disabilities and the yawning gap between these families' experiences and the rest of the world. ... My objective was to present the personal experience of a small number of families, to tell their stories to a world which, on the whole, remains ignorant and perhaps distant from them, simply because they do not know. (Perera, 2001: 92)

Activity 4.2

We have given three examples of personal perspectives on research/careers origins. Whether or not you relate to these particular examples, we suggest that *somewhere* in your past or more present history might lie the roots of your interest.

Think about your own personal relationship to your research topic and your research questions. Write a brief paragraph or some initial notes about the derivation of your research.

It is not necessarily the case that this will prove to be an immediately revelationary exercise. We suggest that this is a point where you may wish to ponder upon and, perhaps, return to the question:

'Why *are* you doing what you're doing?'

And also to ask yourself:

(Continued)

(Continued)

'Do *you* think it is important to generate a response to such a question?'

Note: It is worth giving some thought to this, because many Doctoral vivas open with the question which goes something like '*Tell us about your research and why you chose to do this study*'. How would you answer this sort of question?

Our central point here is that our *identity* – as man, woman, academic, mother, father – is (to a greater or lesser extent) a driving force in our research foci. *What* we do and *how* we do it is informed by who we are, how we think, our morals, our politics, our sexuality, our faith, our lifestyle, our childhood, our 'race', our values. In other words, we are (as researchers) our own blueprints for our research methodology. We can, in the conduct of our research, form our own specific and unique justifications for our enquiries from the existing values, morals and knowledge bases that we bring to our research. In this sense, then, is it realistic to divorce ourselves from our research? Is it intellectually honest to separate our*selves*, to silence our voices as researchers within our research proc-esses and reports? And if we choose to include our own voices in our research report, how are we to do so without risk (or accusation) of introspection or self-indulgence?

Suzi is 35. She has recently been made redundant from a role in education admin-istration as part of budget cuts in her organisation. She's decided to turn this diffi-cult moment in her life into a positive opportunity and has enrolled to do a part-time PhD at the local university, using some of her redundancy package to pay her fees for four years. Suzi is keen to uncover some of the experiences of lesbian women in the workplace. She plans to carry out life historical interviews with them, seeking to tease out their stories, the impact of the (often subtle, often blatant) prejudice, on their personal and professional lives. She is inspired to do this because of her own experiences (positive and negative) as a lesbian woman, and the impact some decisions and responses of management and colleagues have had on her and her life.

Suzi's focus of research is inextricably linked to her own life and work – the public and the private are interwoven, and cannot easily be disentangled. Her voice will be central in her study, yet this will not be an entirely autobiographical piece, so Suzi will have to work out a way to include herself in her thesis and, at the same time, how her partner will feature, and make it a work which is not wholly introspective and 'gives voice' to her participants.

Psychology student, Nolan, is looking at the experiences of fathers who have limited or no contact with their children. This is close to his heart, he having left the family home in England four years ago after in an acrimonious divorce. Nolan was reunited with his own two children some two years ago; for over two years he had no contact with them at all – despite a legal right to meet them. Nolan wants to carry out interviews with fathers who do not live with their children and have limited contact with them, to tell their stories and uncover the emotional impact separation from their children has on the fathers. He is clear that his study is told from the viewpoint of the fathers, not the children – though of course the effects of such separations will inevitably be part of the fathers' perspectives. He is wondering whether his thesis should begin with his story.

Studying European Law, Monique is focusing her research on the impact of rape on women's self-esteem and sexual identity. She has not been raped herself, but has two close friends in her home town in France who experienced violent rape by known men. Monique has been deeply affected by the experiences of her friends and how they were treated in the justice system – one prepetrator was tried and convicted, the other was never charged. Monique wants to document the stories of European women who have been affected by rape (either their own or that of a family member or friend) and their accounts of the justice systems in their countries. She has permission to include something of her perspective on the post-rape trauma of her friends, but she's not sure that potential participants will be happy to talk to her because she herself has not been through the experiences they have. She is trying to decide how to state her positionality in her thesis and to her participants. Her supervisor is not yet convinced that she has formulated the right research questions.

Whatever the study, many researchers find themselves close to their topic. In the context of voice, it is important to take some decisions about the extent to which the researcher's voice is heard in the study. Perhaps one question to ask is whether the study warrants just enough researcher voice to allow readers to appreciate their positionality, or should there be more, should the researcher tell their story too?

The voices of research participants

There has been a growing interest in the representation of the 'voices' of research participants, especially in relation to the acknowledgement of those participants whose voices are often not heard (the young, the old, the abused, the vulnerable, and so on). One such example is the work of Flewitt (2005), who has examined the different ways 3-year-old children communicate and make meaning at home and in a pre-school playgroup. She writes:

> This ESRC-funded study explores how 3-year-old children use a range of 'voices' during their first year in preschool, investigating how they make and express meaning

'multimodally' through combinations of talk, body movement, facial expression and gaze in the two different settings of home and playgroup. Using longitudinal ethnographic video case studies of four children, two boys and two girls, the study identifies patterns in the children's uses of different communicative strategies that relate to the dynamics of the institutional and immediate contexts in which they are situated. The findings imply that the current focus on talk in the early years may be detracting from the diversity of ways children make and express meaning. (2005: 209)

This is an example of how researchers need to find new ways of listening, and new interpretations of what counts as 'voice'.

Clough (1998c) explored the difficulty of '"giving" voice' in a research report of a group of 'bad lads' in a large school, fairly downtown in a poor, large city. The broad project was to understand the culture of 'special' education in that school (see Clough and Barton, 1995), but – more specifically – Clough's attempt to get a handle on the 'bad lads', draws on 'an amalgam of raw transcribed observation, interview events, notes of conversations, my own research journal and imports of my own knowing and belief' (Clough, 2002: 67) and leads him to reflect on what he calls 'inhibited voices':

Voice does not itself struggle for rights, but is disposed after rights are established; voice is licensed by these rights. It follows from this view that the task for research is largely one of 'turning up the volume' on the depressed or inaudible voice.

Listening to subjects with special educational needs throws into a particular relief all the generically difficult issues of researching 'voice' – issues to do with who is listening to whom, why and – above all, perhaps – in whose interests? For, like most research subjects in the majority of studies, they are identified because they reflect – if not quite represent – a particular population; they represent the experiences of a more or less distinct category (black males, NQTs, Y8 girls, etc.); thus, by definition, subjects with special educational needs are identified because they are categorically different (if not deficient). In such research they are primarily interesting, therefore, because of a perceived difference – however benignly understood, and however politically motivated the study. ...

The research act of listening to voice must always involve the (broadly defined) processes of both mediation and translation; and these functions may be particularly indicated where there are doubts about the capacity of the subject to express an intention; doubts, that is, about his or her powers of articulation. This is, of course, a function of a much larger question of the power relations between the researcher and the researched.

For the most part, life stories are articulated by the conventionally articulate (see Booth and Booth, 1996, for an extended discussion and bibliography). How is such advocacy justified, and at what cost? Sparkes (1994), for example, justifies such acts of writing – by people who hold advantaged positions – in terms of their more effective challenge to their privileged peers *by virtue of those positions*; he argues that studies by marginalised individuals/groups may reflect false consciousness, or may be 'coated with self-protective ideology'; and, more pragmatically, he questions whether – almost by definition – the marginalised individual possesses the resources (of various cultural capital) for effectively telling his or her own story.

For some writers, the project is thus an attempt to forge dialogical empathies between the alienated, between each of our 'othernesses' (e.g., Rorty, 1989). Thus Geertz seeks to enlarge

> the possibility of intelligible discourse between people quite different from one another in interest, outlook, wealth and power, and yet contained in a world where, tumbled as they are into endless connection, it is increasingly difficult to get out of each other's way (1988, p.147).

But this essentially humanist (Barone, 1997) project of solidarity and empathy is not enough for some story writers (and readers), who act politically through 'storied' voice specifically to emancipate; who ultimately seek, that is, a redistribution of power. Thus the search is for the articulation of a persuasive voice which will challenge readers' interests, privileges and prejudices. As bell hooks has it, such writers can provide searing, harrowing 'chronicles of pain' – though she reminds us that these may well serve merely to 'keep in place existing structures of domination' (1991, p.59) if they do not bring about a deep unease in the reader. (Clough, 2002: 68–9)

Activity 4.3

Reflecting on Clough's position on 'voice' in social research, think about the relationship between voice, power, politics and persuasion.

Is there a place in your own research for 'the articulation of a persuasive voice' which will challenge existing 'structures of domination'? Do you agree with Sparkes' stance on the writing of marginalised groups?

What are the implications of this discussion for your own work?

The following paper reports a study which foregrounds young children's voice in research and action. We suggest that you read it with the question in Activity 4.3 in mind.

Citizenship and inclusion in the early years: understanding and responding to children's perspectives on 'belonging'

Cathy Nutbrown[a]* and Peter Clough[b]

Nutbrown, C. and Clough, P. (2009) 'Citizenship and inclusion in the early years: understanding and responding to children's perspectives on "belonging"', *International Journal of Early Years Education*, 17 (3): 191–206.

[a]*School of Education, University of Sheffield, Sheffield, UK;* [b]*Deanery of Education, Liverpool Hope University, Liverpool, UK*

This paper argues for, and demonstrates the effectiveness of, including young children in commenting on and improving their learning environments. It reports the experiences gathered from of 16 setting-based, small-scale, practitioner-led projects. Taking a view of citizenship as 'participation' the paper shows how practitioner-research can support the evolution of inclusive environments for all children. Following a critical review of the literature on citizenship, young children, and 'inclusion' the paper considers the usefulness of the participant methodology of practitioner action research and the concept of 'voice' in educational research and report. Examples of practitioner-research projects involving children aged three to six years identify and illustrate key themes from the data. Thus, they demonstrate: (1) the range of factors which excited or worried the children; and (2) the ways in which children's concerns and ideas were listened to and action for change was developed. The children's ideas and extracts from their comments are included alongside the practitioners' responses in the cases which are discussed. Four main points are considered in conclusion: (1) children's views can contribute to the development of inclusive practices; (2) children's voices are central to studies of their perspectives and the methodological challenges of listening to children's voices in research must be addressed; (3) identity and self esteem are key to the successful promotion of young children's positive sense of inclusivity and belonging in their early years settings; and (4) supported practitioner-research can enhance inclusive early years practices. The paper argues that including children in the identification and exploration of issues important to them promotes a positive sense of inclusivity and that such approaches to developing pedagogies of citizenship and belonging constitute a practical enacting of 'voice'.

Keywords: inclusion; citizenship; voice; practitioner-research; participation

Introduction

Floyd and Emile are playing at guns:

Floyd: I'll blaze you
Emile: I'll blaze you, bad boy
Floyd: O I'll waste you
Emile: [long pause] nobody says I'll waste you
Floyd: I'll waste you nigger
Emile: That's a bad word/that's a bad word/o nigger you/I'll spit you
Floyd: I'll poo on you…!!
[Both boys overcome with giggles]. (Extract from observation)

*Corresponding author. Email: c.e.nutbrown@sheffield.ac.uk

C. Nutbrown and P. Clough

Respectful educators will include all children:

> Not just children who are easy to work with, obliging, endearing, clean, pretty, articulate, capable, but every child – respecting them for who they are, respecting their language, their culture, their history, their family, their abilities, their needs, their name, their ways and their very essence. (Nutbrown 1996, 54)

Because inclusive *policies* only really find meaning in inclusive *practices*, this paper argues for, and demonstrates the effectiveness of, including young children in commenting on and improving their learning environments. Drawing on data from 16 small-scale setting-based projects which have developed and evaluated inclusive practices we demonstrate the effectiveness of practitioner-research in changing learning environments to enhance their inclusiveness for all children.

First, we critically examine the literature on citizenship and young children, and on ideas of 'inclusion'. Second, the participant methodology of practitioner action research and the concept of 'voice' in educational research and report is described and justified. Key themes are identified and illustrated from data which directly report the children's words and the practitioners' responses. We conclude with four main points: first, that it is possible to learn children's views of inclusion and belonging; second, that children's voices are central to any study of their perspectives and studies must find ways to 'listen' to their voices; third, that identity and self esteem are two important issues to be addressed through curriculum and early years pedagogy if children are to experience a positive sense of inclusivity and belonging in their early years settings, and finally, that supported practitioner-research is an effective tool both for professional development and for enhancing inclusive practices.

Citizenship and inclusion in the early years: some lessons from the literature

Issues of citizenship

Recent changes in curriculum guidance and statutory requirements for provision for children under five have led to an incorporation of curriculum content which might be described as addressing issues of citizenship. For example, the Early Years Foundation Stage (Department for Children, Schools and Families [DCSF] 2007, para. 2.1) which became statutory in September 2008 states, under what is called 'Positive relationships: Respecting each other', that: 'When each person is valued for who they are and differences are appreciated, everyone feels included and understood, whatever their personality, abilities, ethnic background or culture'. And in the section identified as: 'Enabling environments: The learning environment' it is suggested that: 'When children feel confident in the environment they are willing to try things out, knowing that effort is valued' (DCSF 2007, para. 3.3). These two statements can be read as a clear assertion that inclusion, citizenship and belonging are key to current early years policy in England. But what does 'valuing each child for who they are' look like? And what factors help children to 'feel confident in the environment'?

Though several studies have reported on practitioners (and other adults') views of inclusion (Cornoldi et al. 1998; Croll and Moses 2000; Purdue, Ballard, and MacArthuer 2001; Clough and Nutbrown 2004; Nutbrown and Clough 2004), few studies have considered young children's views of what it is to be included, or to 'belong' to a group, a school, a setting, or a community. Discussing childhood and citizenship in the Israeli context, Ben-Arieh and Boyer (2005, 33) suggest that:

International Journal of Early Years Education

> Citizenship is not merely a formal status… Citizenship is the prerequisite for belonging to a group and as such bears a significant impact on identity formation. Therefore, citizenship is crucial for the well-being of human beings in general and for children in particular. Children's civil status (and their citizenship) determines their rights (including their social, political and civil rights).

'Citizenship' has been a modern policy issue for schools in England for more than a decade (Qualifications and Curriculum Authority [QCA] 1998), described for pupils aged 11 years and above as 'Playing a part in society' for the following purpose:

> Citizenship gets pupils working together on issues of concern. It gives them the confidence and skills they need to act with others to tackle real problems in society. They do this by researching and debating complex political, moral and social challenges facing society now and in the future. (QCA 2008 para. 1)

Ben-Arieh and Boyer (2005) agree, however, that much less attention has been given to children's citizenship and to the implications such citizenship has for their lives and well-being. Discussing work on citizenship and young people's participation in a civic context, Wyness (2006, 209) claims that:

> International and national political agendas have prioritized children's issues in the past decade or so. However the nature of the commitment to children themselves participating in arrangements that affect them and their communities are highly ambiguous. Whilst children's voices have become progressively louder, the extent to which these voices are articulated within spaces for participation over which children can genuinely claim ownership are often compromised by political structures determined by adults.

It is this combination of *voice* with *action* that, we suggest can lead to genuine *participation, inclusion* and *belonging*, for, as Lundy (2007) has it, 'voice is not enough'. Adams' (2005) consideration of the teaching of citizenship in primary schools demonstrates that practical involvement is key to learning to be a citizen and taking a view on issues affecting people. In exploring how citizenship might be taught, Anderson (2005) promotes teacher enquiry through the use of fictional texts with children in order to promote thinking around issues of citizenship and responsibility. Whitburn (2003) describes practice in Japanese schools which help young children to be independent and take responsibility, as self reliant members of a group. She concludes: 'In a densely populated country, I am conscious that 'learning to live together' is one of the most important and difficult tasks ahead' (175).

In order to establish quite what we mean when we speak of such 'belongingness' we need first to clarify and define what *we* mean when we use the term 'inclusion'.

Inclusion is a social and political struggle where individual identity and difference has prominence. In the early years achieving inclusive settings means change for the entire setting and *all* practitioners who work there. Practices of including or excluding disabled children have been found to vary considerably in Europe (Nutbrown and Clough 2004; Clough and Nutbrown 2004), and in New Zealand (Purdue, Ballard, and MacArthuer 2001). But it is important to recognise that issues of *inclusion* are part of the core of current UK governmental agenda applying to *all* children, not 'only' to children identified as having particular and identified learning needs.

Over the last 20 years or so, inclusion has come to mean increasing participation *and* removing exclusionary pressures, social inclusion in UK policy terms *problematises* the social exclusion of disenfranchised groups and their disengagement from

C. Nutbrown and P. Clough

society (Sparkes 1999). Social exclusion theories and policies seek to avoid deficit approaches and explanations (Leney 1999), but their existence can contribute to the creation of excluded groups or individuals.

Within current policy discourses individual children may be constructed by practitioners in terms of the need to *raise achievement* on the one hand and *promote inclusion* on the other. Though things are rarely polarised in these ways such can happen, as (Levitas 1998, 7) noted, 'in a society whose structural inequalities remain largely uninterrogated'. A practitioner might, therefore, be viewed as either (within the *raising achievement* discourse) implementing planned steps in order to bring about learning in children or (in the context of *inclusion*) as working to the practices of the setting – following rules, procedures and routines for example which may be *more* or *less* inclusive. High quality practices will, of course, seek to include all children and support them in reaching their potential.

This paper reports the outcomes of practitioner-research projects where practitioners designed small-scale studies to develop *cultures of inclusion* . By listening to young children's voices and valuing their suggestions, they changed their settings and practices – often in quite modest ways – to promote more enabling environments which were more inclusive of *all* the young children who used them.

A working definition of inclusion

Finding a definition of inclusion which works in policy and practice, for settings and individual children is a challenge. In this paper we use the term to mean *maximising participation* in, and *minimising exclusion* from, early years settings, schools and society. Inclusion is a much-used term, often assumed to be universally understood. But inclusion means different things to different people and can often reflect stages of development of inclusive practices. Indeed, 'inclusion' can only really mean anything in practice, and there are as many *versions* of inclusion as there are settings, practitioners, children and families who together make up particular living and learning cultures.

Sparkes (1999) identifies school exclusion as a contributing factor in lower educational attainment. Some parents of young children may well have experienced exclusion from school and as a result may have low levels of literacy and educational attainment, and experience poor housing, unemployment, poverty, ill-health, lack of access to services. Levitas (1998) sees social exclusion as defined in terms of poverty, moral and behavioural delinquency of the excluded and paid work, or the lack of it. However, academics, practitioners or politicians choose to construct or theorise such states of living; for many families, social exclusion means living within this range of difficulties, as day-in-day-out they face the realities of poor housing, unemployment, poverty, ill-health, lack of access to services and low levels of educational achievement. Young children, many young children, are excluded in one way or another for a variety of reasons. Because the nature of their exclusion is multicomplex we do not, in this paper, adopt a simplistic, homogenous definition of inclusion/exclusion – rather we take a more complex view of inclusive issues which is broadly comprehensive. We are similarly concerned that the identification of potential groups 'at risk' of exclusion or the identification of particular foci of inclusion and exclusion, could also serve to 'narrow down' our meaning of the term and the issues at heart here. So examination of examples of inclusion (which highlight, for example, gender) together with analyses across types of settings serve to highlight practices where both

International Journal of Early Years Education

simple, and new or radical, approaches to inclusion can be developed through listening to young children.

In mapping out various territories of inclusion Nutbrown and Clough (2006) show (Box 1) that 'potential arenas of inclusion and exclusion are extensive and far reaching, affecting the lives of many children and their families'. The list in Box 1, while not necessarily comprehensive, serves as an indicator of the multifaceted nature of exclusion and highlights reasons why many young children and their families might face exclusion.

Box 1. Some arenas of inclusion/exclusion (Nutbrown and Clough 2006, 5).

Age	Language
Achievement	Location
Challenging behaviour	Mental health
Disability	Obesity
Disaffection	Physical impairment
Educational qualifications	Poverty
Emotional and behavioural difficulty	'Race'/ethnicity
Employment	Religion
Gender	Sexual orientation
Housing	Social class
Illness	Special educational need

So, given that the policy context in England urges that 'differences are appreciated, everyone feels included' (DCSF 2007, para. 2.1), we need to understand how young children think about *difference*; a fundamental element of developing inclusive practices and policies. From a very young age, children can form political and cultural preferences (Connolly and Kelly 2002), some of which may lead to tendencies to exclusionary values and behaviours. Gender issues in play (Gussin Paley 1984; Davies 1989; Tarullo 1994; MacNaughton 1999) and gender identity are a strong feature in young children's lives (Connolly 2005). Tarullo (1994) suggested that girls and boys form different experiences of the world and some show different preferences in their play (Maccoby and Jacklin 1974; Gussin Paley 1984; D'Arcy 1990. Studies over several decades have identified differences and curiosities around gender and play; Derman-Sparkes and Taus (1989, 43) suggested that:

> Between the ages of two and five years old, children are forming self-identifies and building social interactions skills. At the same time, they are becoming aware of and curious about gender, race, ethnicity and disabilities. Gradually young children begin to figure out how they are alike and how they are different from other people, and how they feel about those differences.

As such studies indicate, children are often keenly interested in difference, and so making difference *positive* rather than *negative* is an important aim for early childhood professionals. In a large-scale survey of children aged three to six in Northern Ireland, Connolly and Kelly (2002) identified the detail of cultural and political awareness of young children. Their conclusion that close working practice with parents and the local community is key, an important maxim for all settings wherever they are located.

C. Nutbrown and P. Clough

Inclusion and citizenship in childhood

Alderson, Hawthorne and Killen (2005, 31) articulate the difficulties which arise in defining the relationship between 'citizenship' and 'childhood'. They note: 'Citizenship from birth entitles the child to a legal identity, and the right to expect certain services, protections and amenities from the state. Babies can easily be included in these concepts of rights'. The notion that childhood is socially constructed from the beliefs, expectations and values of adults is widely reported (James and Prout 1997; Mayall 2002; Alanen 2001). Cunningham's (2006) social history of 'childhood' in England since the Middle Ages illustrates these different 'constructions' over time – influenced by economics, politics, philanthropy and necessity. However, as Morss (2002) demonstrates, such constructions of childhood are complex and theories of social construction can themselves be deconstructed and reconstructed to satisfy the position of researchers and theorists.

Children are highly capable learners, not only cognitively, but also socially and emotionally (Dunn 1987; Gardner 1993; Hutchby and Moran Ellis 1998; Alderson 2000; Nutbrown 2006). Mayall (2002) identifies children's abilities to challenge, negotiate, and participate in social interactions with children and with adults, and increasingly, the traditional notions of a helpless child are being challenged, certainly in terms of learning competence and the study of education in the early years (Vakil, Freeman, and Swim 2003; Coles 1997). In this sense then, we can argue that children can be seen as citizens, from their earliest years, because they are able to express ideas and wants and to contribute to decision-making that affects them.

To be meaningful and effective, inclusion must mean much more than the shared location of children, and much more than the sharing of locations with children with a range of learning needs, abilities and difficulties. The study reported in this paper defines inclusion as ensuring that all the children in a setting 'belong' and that every child has an opportunity to 'speak and be heard'.

'Voice', action research and participation: methodological issues

The study adopted a participant methodology whereby practitioners developed their own action research projects in their own early childhood settings. Practitioners in 16 early childhood settings of different types: state-funded, independent and voluntary, developed setting-specific, small-scale action research projects. The themes they addressed were diverse, as were the methods used to develop and implement the projects. What united them all was the common concern of all the practitioners to develop their understanding of children's views of their environments and what it was to feel a sense of 'belonging'.

We were concerned from the outset to develop and adopt inclusive methodologies across all the setting-based projects. Thus, in a similar vein to other recently conducted, inclusive-development projects (Booth and Ainscow 2004; Cook 2004) we asked practitioners to develop their projects in ways which followed the principles of action research. Practitioners attended a five-day programme during which they developed a good grounding in the principles and practices of action research approaches to project development, implementation and evaluation, they also received ongoing professional development support while they carried out their projects.

Action research was chosen in order to ensure that the practitioners were able to develop their studies within a framework of research support and as such this follows the established traditions of action/practitioner-research whereby educational practice

International Journal of Early Years Education

becomes more *reflective* (Stenhouse 1975), brings about *change* (Zuber-Skerritt 1996) and is *collaborative* (Kemmis and McTaggart 1992). It is this collaboration between practitioners and children, in the projects on which this paper is based, that brings to the work a sense of inclusivity and heightens the children's sense of 'belonging' in their early years environments.

While this paper cannot, in the space available, provide detailed reports on the projects themselves, a sense of the range of the projects in which practitioners and children were involved is important to the context and to an understanding of the breadth of definition of inclusion and belonging. The action research projects in the 16 settings focused on the following topics, many of which were prompted by suggestions from the children:

- Involving parents in the setting.
- Making the outdoor play space a place where all children felt comfortable and secure.
- Reviewing the arrangements for transition from preschool to the Foundation Stage unit.
- Changing the toilet area so that the children who were frightened were able to feel more at ease.
- Helping children to settle their disputes.
- Finding ways to allow boys have access to the home corner play space.
- Including children's views on their own progress and achievement in their assessment profiles.
- Making lunchtimes more peaceful and positive social times.
- Offering healthier mid morning snacks.
- Developing new and workable practices on violent weapon play.
- Developing Key Person approaches with babies and toddlers so that their care is more attuned to their needs.
- Introducing baby signing to give them more autonomy and enable them better to communicate their needs and wants.
- Consulting children on new all-weather clothing to be purchased.
- Introducing Persona Dolls to help children learn more about other children's lives.
- Including more fathers on outings.
- Reviewing the pace and opportunities provided for children in day care from 08:00 to 18:00.

'Voice'

Jan recorded the following as a small group of six-year-old children played at the outdoor sandpit:

Andrew: We don't play with them we don't
Alice: I wouldn't play with them
Andrew: My Dad says I/my Dad says
Alice: You see you mustn't/cos you're trouble/in trouble
Andrew: Daddy says they're bad and they don't [inaudible] and at the shop
[Miss Fisher interrupts]
Miss F: Who's that Andrew? Who don't you play with?
Andrew: Nobody Miss Fisher/Alice put that back

C. Nutbrown and P. Clough

Miss F: No Andrew/I mean who don't you want to play with?
Alice: It's a bad word, Miss
Miss F: What's the bad word Alice? What's the bad word? Mm? Alice?
Alice: Andrew you took it from me/you took that
Miss F: Go on Alice tell me/tell me the bad word
[Alice leaves the sandpit; Andrew starts playing with Danielle…]

It was only after the session when Jan (the researcher) talked this exchange through with Miss Fisher that it was recalled that, some four weeks earlier, there had been a visit from two people from the Traveller Support Unit during which some of the older children had talked about some popular terminology and hence 'bad words'.

Sometimes the things young children say raise concerns of racism, segregation and so on, thus, silencing young children's voices can often be a first instinct if they use language or express opinions which adults find unacceptable – whatever the reason (Lane 2008). Silencing may well have been the instinct of the adults who overheard Floyd and Emile whose conversation opened this paper. But if we listen rather than oppress children's voices we can learn from them (Lancaster 2003). For example, some studies suggest that positive benefits can derive from practices which tolerate (rather than suppress) gun and weapon play (Holland 1999). Listening to young children and understanding something of how they are thinking about others who are different from them can help practitioners to develop strategies which challenge prejudices. One such example is the Media Initiative in Northern Ireland which has successfully supported children and practitioners to challenge segregative and exclusionary practices (Connolly et al. 2006). In the study reported here all 16 practitioners had aspects of their work that they wished to change, but they wanted to learn and take account of children's views before they made plans to change anything.

Allen and L'Anson (2004) discuss the challenges of eliciting children's views on complex issues. Yet despite the difficulties, recent studies have argued that it is both possible, and even essential, to seek children's views on the issues and situations which affect them. In the primary years there has been a slowly developing interest in seeking pupil's views, for example in a study of pupils knowledge of 'place', Pike and Clough (2005, 116) state that: 'What is notable from the research literature concerned with primary children's knowledge of distant places is the lack of the child's voice'.

Similarly, Nutbrown and Hannon (2003) have argued for the voices of children to be heard in studies of family literacy and Carter (2006) has consulted children on issues of friendship. Indeed, in the last decade, children's perspectives have increasingly been seen as an important focus of educational and social research (Aubrey et al. 2000; Christensen and James 2000; Greig and Taylor 1999; Holmes 1998; Lewis and Lindsay 1999). Exploring children's perspectives can be illuminating, but presents methodological challenges (Burnett and Myers 2002; Carter 2006; Critchley 2002; Marsh and Thompson 2001). Arguably, the involvement of children as research *participants* rather than research *subjects* should be afforded them as a matter of right (Nutbrown 1996) in order that their voices are heard and their viewpoints are taken into account in the development of policy and the evolution of practices which are designed to involve them. Some of the methodological considerations in this research can, therefore, be situated within the study of 'voice' in social science research in general, which has emerged in recent years as a politically and morally positioned research response to issues faced by oppressed and silenced minorities: black women, people with AIDS, students with disabilities and learning difficulties, disaffected youths and parents of disabled children (Fine 1994; Tierney 1993; Clough 1998;

International Journal of Early Years Education

Pereera 2001; Goodley 2007). Tierney (1993, 111) writes that differences of (for example) race, class, gender and sexual orientation: '...ought to be honoured and brought into the centre of our discourses about education and its purpose'.

Nutbrown and Hannon (2003) have argued that 'age' can be added to Tierney's list of differences, as educational research gradually moves to a position where children – especially *young* children – *are* seen *and* heard. Relatively little attention has been given to *listening* to children and soliciting their views on matters of daily life and learning. However, this is changing as a range of approaches and techniques have been developed (Lancaster 2003; Clark and Moss 2001, 2008; Clark, Kjorholt, and Moss 2005) and children's views on 'ordinary, everyday aspects' of their own lives have been sought (Dyer 2002; Filippini and Vecchi 2000; Nutbrown and Hannon 2003).

Ethical considerations

The ethical issues in this study centred largely on issues of informed consent – both from parents and children – and of ensuring that children were at no time uncomfortable or unhappy. The issue of taking up children's time for research purposes was also considered, and practitioners felt that this was morally justified because they were developing new approaches to pedagogy in which children were included as participants, and their involvement was in matters which affected them and their early years environments. The following adaptation of the practices and protocols developed by Nutbrown and Hannon (2003) were put in place in the study described here:

- parental permission to seek the children's views and take photographs was obtained
- protocols were developed that included a clear explanation to the children about the study, and ensured that they understood that they did not have to participate. The children were also told that they could stop whenever they wished
- no data were collected until children's explicit agreement was given
- children were always in familiar surroundings
- data remained anonymous – names of the children and practitioners have been changed – (photographs have not been used in dissemination for reasons of child protection agreements)
- practitioners remained sensitive to children's needs at all times and the comfort and well being of the children was prioritised above data collection
- concerns about taking up or 'wasting' children's time were addressed

In the examples of projects which will follow in this paper, the underpinning beliefs which practitioners held about the children for whom they are responsible are apparent. This enabled practitioners to tackle some sometimes quite difficult, subtle and complex issues in order to create inclusive early years communities. In the remainder of this paper, we report the children's views on 'belonging' and practitioners' interpretations of how such views can be drawn upon to create more inclusive early years environments.

Learning from what young children say

Space does not allow us to discuss all the projects, but the following examples show that children were able express their opinions about various issues which mattered to

C. Nutbrown and P. Clough

them in their settings. Each example gives some of the children's words and a synopsis of changes made by practitioners after listening to and taking account of the children's views when developing their action research projects.

Making the outdoor play space a place where all children felt comfortable and secure

Using disposable cameras, the children took photographs of things they liked (and things they didn't) and then talked about them in small groups. Table 1 lists examples the content of images they took, together with the children's comments.

Action taken included

Pactitioners were particularly aware that many of the children's expressed likes and dislikes were stereotypically gendered. The task, they felt was to create 'zones' within the outdoor space which was more tailored for the different preferences of all the children. They also identified the large task of developing an intervention project which encouraged less stereotypical play.

Changing the toilet area so that the children who were frightened were able to feel more at ease

The children said

> The toilets smell of wee and poo.
> It's scary on the toilet and the light makes a buzzing noise like bees.
> There's a witch in there.
> The toilet with the shower thingy... it's like a snake and it might get you when you're weeing.

Table 1. Examples of the content of images taken by children, together with the children's comments.

I like	I don't like
The big tree: 'we hide under there' (BG)	The spiked wire on the high fencing: 'looks scary, like prison' (B)
My friend: 'Zac is my friend' (B)	The drains: 'they smell' (G)
Mrs T: 'She's right nice, and she smiles and has red fingernails!' (G)	The bike shed: 'It's got spiders'(G)
The big climbing frame in the sunshine: 'I get up the top and I shout "HELLO" reet loud!' (B)	The big climbing frame: 'it's too high for me, I feel scared' (G)
'Digging! You can dig up worms and things' (B)	'When it's cold and my fingers hurt' (G)
The red bike: 'It's the best 'un. The wheels are big and you can go zummm right downhill' (B)	'The boys when they make you get off the bikes, but I like the pink bike – it's got a nice little bell' (G)
'Running round!' (B)	'When the big children come out and their footballs come over [the fence] and hit us, or they shout too loud' (G)

Notes: B, boy(s); G, girl(s); BG, boy(s) and girl(s).

International Journal of Early Years Education

It's a long way to the toilet when you're outside and you can't undo your trousers.
They're not like my toilet at home.
The toilet paper is horrid and makes my bum hurt.
I think a monster will come up the toilet and eat my bottom.

Action taken

More discussion took place with the children around how to make the toilets better. This included, changing the décor, and involving the children in choosing colours. Installing a radio (many of the children said they had music playing in their toilets at home when they went to the loo). The budget was adjusted to include a better quality of toilet paper and air freshener blocks were placed in safe places. The florescent tube which flickered and buzzed was, it seemed, an annoyance to staff as well as a cause of anxiety for some of the children – this was replaced.

Helping children to settle their disputes

The children said

> I get mad when I get hit and then my dad says ''it 'im back'. So I do and then Mrs F does me for it. You get dun if people tell or Mrs F sees you.

> I get Mrs F to sort it out and she says 'I'll have a little word' and she does and sometimes they stop.

> We have to have a talk and then we say sorry and then I go a bit hot cos I feel a bit bad cos I pinched or bit somebody and they don't like it.

> I get Mrs F and she says 'Let's have a little word' and we do and we shake hands.

> I get Mrs F and she sorts it out. I can't sort it out on my own I'm too little.

Action taken included:

Staff realised that the children relied heavily on adult involvement and intervention to settle disputes. Because staff (Mrs F particularly!) stepped in so promptly to settle disputes, the children lacked strategies to resolve their own conflicts with each other. It was decided that staff needed some professional development support to learn skills of encouraging children to be more self reliant when they were in conflict situations and then to incorporate these into their practice.

Finding ways to allow boys have access to the home corner play space

The children said

> I like 'baby born' best; I like the black dolly. Wish we could have Barbies at nursery, we like Barbies but nursery 'an't got 'ny and the bits get lost if you bring your own so I don't.

> The boy doll is horrid, it's got a willy wot wees/when he wees it's horrid, yuck! yuck!

> The boys can't come in here 'cos they make a noise and they mess it up, and they act like dogs and angry husbands

C. Nutbrown and P. Clough

> Sometimes I put the ironing board across the doorway so the boys can't get in... 'cos there's no door and you need one.

Action included

As well as maintaining the usual home play space, staff included other role-play areas which they chose in consultation with the children. Over time they established a garage, a tropical fish shop, a hairdressing salon, a chip shop and an office (familiar practice in many settings, but new to this one). Several of these new opportunities gave rise to fewer instances of gender-dominated play and created spaces for boys to engage in more positive role-play activities which were not dominated and controlled by the girls. To date, practitioners in this setting continue to help boys negotiate their way 'past the ironing board' in to the home corner which remains (often) a mainly female domain.

The previous examples show how children's views became translated into practical solutions and gave rise to changes, most of which improved their experiences in their settings and made for more enabling environments.

Discussion and conclusion

This paper has challenged notions that young children lack competency and has evidenced how young children can make meaningful contributions to inclusive practice.

Our analysis leads us to identify four main points of conclusion:

(1) It is possible to learn children's views of inclusion and belonging.
(2) Children's voices are central to any study of their perspectives and studies must find ways to 'listen' to those voices.
(3) Identity and self esteem are the two most important issues to be addressed through curriculum and early years pedagogy if children are to successfully experiences a sense of inclusivity and belonging in their early years settings.
(4) Supported practitioner-research can be an effective tool both for professional development and for enhancing inclusive practices.

Young children have their own particular views of inclusion and belonging which are often different from those held by adults. The experiences reported here show that, given the opportunity to express those views (though they may sometimes be fluid), children can contribute their own unique viewpoints on situations in their early years settings. The examples demonstrate how including children in the identification and exploration of issues important to them promotes a positive sense of inclusivity.

Any study which seeks to include young children's perspectives must take issues of 'voice' as central to the methodology and find ways to 'listen' to those young voices and act on what they say. Though it will not always be possible to accommodate fully all the views and suggestions made by children, it is the case that many of the views that young children offer can often be incorporated into changes in practices and settings which make the place more inclusive and enabling for all who attend. The work reported here moves from the important pedagogic position of listening to and consultation with children (Clark and Moss 2001, 2008; Clark, Kjorholt, and Moss 2005) to provide an expression of children's active participation – or active

International Journal of Early Years Education

citizenship. Such approaches to developing citizenship and belonging constitute a practical enacting of 'voice'.

If current objectives in early years policy in relation to inclusion and citizenship in England are to be realised; identity and self esteem are the two most important issues to be addressed. If children are successfully to experience a sense of inclusivity and belonging in their early years curriculum and pedagogy must attend to aspects of practice that make all children feel valued by enabling them to contribute their ideas and know that their contributions matter. This paper has shown that, for young children, a sense of inclusivity and belonging in their early years settings stems from practitioners ensuring that young children feel good about themselves, feel positive about the differences they see in other children and are secure in their own sense of place in their early years community.

Finally, what was achieved in the project reported in this paper was the result of a team effort which involved universities, practitioners, settings, children and their families. It involved investment in supported practitioner-research that proved to be a practical and effective strategy for change: developing and implementing new, more inclusive, policies and pedagogies. There can be no doubt that bespoke research-based professional development and support was key to bringing about more inclusive practices.

Acknowledgements

We should like to thank the practitioners who allowed us to draw on aspects of their action research in the writing of this paper. We have respected their requests for anonymity. The children would have preferred us to include their real names – indeed all their names and several photographs – but for the moment, adult views of confidentiality and anonymity prevail – we thank them none the less. Earlier versions of this paper were presented at the *American Educational Research Association* April 2007 and *Collaborative Action Research Conference* January 2008; we are grateful to discussants and participants for their comments.

References

Adams, P. 2005. Citizenship: How is it different to PSHE and how can it be done? *Education 3–13* 33, no. 3: 57–62.

Alanen, L. 2001. Explorations in generational analysis. In *Conceptualizing child–adult relations,* ed. L. Alanen and B. Mayall, 27–38. London: Routledge Falmer.

Alderson, P. 2000. *Young children's rights.* London: Jessica Kingsley.

Alderson, P., J. Hawthorne, and M. Killen. 2005. The participation rights of premature babies. *The International Journal of Children's Rights* 13: 31–50.

Allen, J. and J. L'Anson. 2004. Children's rights in school: Power, assemblies and assemblages. *The International Journal of Children's Rights* 12: 123–38.

Anderson, B. 2005. Can a community of enquiry approach with fiction texts support the development of young pupils' understanding? *Education 3–13* 33, no. 3: 9–14.

Aubrey, C., T. David, G. Godfrey and L. Thompson. 2004. *Researching early childhood education: Debates and issues in methodology and ethics.* London: Routledge.

Ben-Arieh, A., and Y. Boyer. 2005. Citizenship and childhood: The state of affairs in Israel *Childhood* 12, no. 1: 33–53.

Booth, T., and M. Ainscow. 2004. *Index for inclusion: Developing learning, participation and play in early years and child care.* Bristol, UK: Centre for Studies in Inclusive Education.

Burnett, C., and J. Myers. 2002. Beyond the frame: Exploring children's literacy practices. *Reading: Literacy and Language* 36, no. 2: 56–62.

Carter, C. 2006. The playground buddies project. In *Inclusion in the early years: Critical analyses and enabling narratives,* ed. C. Nutbrown, and P. Clough, 88–93. London: Sage.

C. Nutbrown and P. Clough

Christensen, P., and A. James. 2008. *Research with children: Perspectives and practices.* 2nd ed. London: Routledge.

Clark, A, A.T. Kjorholt, and P. Moss, eds. 2005. *Beyond listening: Children's perspectives on early childhood services.* London: NCB.

Clark, A., and P. Moss. 2001. *Listening to young children: The Mosaic approach.* London: National Children's Bureau and Joseph Rowntree Trust.

Clark, A., and P. Moss. 2008. *Beyond spaces to play: More listening to young children using the mosaic approach.* London: NCB.

Clough, P., ed. 1998. *Articulating with difficulty: Research voices in inclusive education.* London: Sage.

Clough, P., and C. Nutbrown. 2004. Special educational needs and inclusive early education: Multiple perspectives from UK educators. *Journal of Early Childhood Research* 2, no. 2: 191–211.

Coles, R. 1997. *The moral intelligence of children.* London: Bloomsbury.

Connolly, P. 2005. *Boys and schooling in the early years.* London: Routledge Falmer.

Connolly, P., S. Fitzpatrick, T. Gallagher, and P. Harris. 2006. Addressing diversity and inclusion in the early years in conflict-affected societies: A case study of the Media Initiative for Children – Northern Ireland. *International Journal of Early Years Education* 14, no. 3: 263–78.

Connolly, P., and B. Kelly. 2002. *Too young to notice? The cultural and political awareness of 3–6 year olds in Northern Ireland.* Belfast: Northern Ireland Community Relations Council.

Cornoldi, C., A. Terreni, T. Scruggs, and M. Mastropieri. 1998. Teacher attitudes in Italy after twenty years of inclusion. *Remedial and Special Education* 19, no. 6: 350–56.

Cook, T. 2004. Starting where we can: Using action research to develop inclusive practice. *International Journal of Early Years Education* 12, no. 1: 3–16.

Critchley, D. 2002. Children's assessment of their own learning. In *Research studies in early childhood education,* ed. C. Nutbrown, 53–66. Stoke-on-Trent, UK: Trentham.

Croll, P., and D. Moses. 2000. Ideologies and utopias: Education professionals' views of inclusion. *European Journal of Special Needs Education* 15, no. 1: 1–12.

Cunningham, H. 2006. *The invention of childhood.* London: BBC.

D'Arcy, S. 1990. Towards a non-sexist primary classroom. In *Dolls and dungarees: Gender issues in the primary school curriculum,* ed. E. Tutchell, 79–88. Milton Keynes, UK: Open University Press.

Davies, B. 1989. *Frogs, snails and feminist tales.* Sydney: George Allen and Unwin.

DCSF. 2007. *Early years foundation stage.* London: HMSO/DCSF.

Derman-Sparkes, L., and K. Taus. 1989. We're different… And we're friends! *Scholastic Children Today* 4, no. 3: 43–6.

Dunn, J. 1987. The beginnings of moral understanding. In *The emergence of morality in young children,* ed. J. Kagan and S. Lamb, 109–17. Chicago, IL: University of Chicago Press Falmer.

Dyer, P. 2002. 'A box full of feelings': Emotional literacy in a nursery class. In *Research studies in early childhood education,* ed. C. Nutbrown, 53–66. Stoke-on-Trent: Trentham

Filillini, T., and V. Vecchi, eds. 2000. *The hundred languages of childhood: Exhibition catalogue.* Reggio Emilia: Reggio Children.

Fine, M. 1994. 'Dis-stance' and other stances: Negotiations of power inside feminist research. In *Power and method: Political activism and educational research,* ed. A. Giltlin, 42–62 London: Routledge.

Gardner, H. 1993. *The unschooled mind: How children think and how schools should teach.* London: Fontana.

Goodley, D. 2007. Becoming rhizomatic parents: Deleuze, Guattari and disabled babies. *Disability & Society* 22, no. 2: 145–60.

Greig, A., and J. Taylor. 1999. *Doing research with children.* London: Sage.

Gussin Paley, V. 1984. *Boys and girls: Superheroes in the doll corner.* Chicago, IL: The University of Chicago Press.

Holland, P. 1999. Is 'zero-tolerance' intolerance? An under-fives centre takes a fresh look at their policy on war/weapon superhero practice. *Early Childhood Practice* 1, no. 1: 24–45.

Holmes, R.M. 1998. *Fieldwork with children.* London: Sage.

International Journal of Early Years Education

Hutchby, I., and J. Moran Ellis, eds. 1998. *Children and social competence.* London: Falmer.

James, A., and A. Prout. 1997. *Constructing and reconstructing childhood.* 2nd ed. London: Routledge.

Kemmis, S., and R. McTaggart. 1992. *The action research planner.* 3rd ed. Geelong, Victoria: Deakin University Press.

Lancaster, P. 2003. *Listening to young children: Promoting listening to young children: The reader.* Maidenhead, UK: Open University Press.

Lane, J. 2008. *Young children and racial justice.* London: National Children's Bureau.

Leney, T. 1999. *European approaches to social exclusion.* In *Tackling disaffection and social exclusion,* ed. A. Hayton and A. Hodgson, 33–45. London: Routledge.

Levitas, R. 1998. *The inclusive society? Social exclusion and New Labour.* Basingstoke, UK: Macmillan.

Lewis, A., and G. Lindsay. 1999. *Researching children's perspectives.* Buckingham: Open University Press.

Lundy, L. 2007. 'Voice is not enough': Conceptualising Article 12 of the United Nations Convention on the Rights of the Child. *British Education Research Journal* 33, no. 6: 927–42.

Maccoby, E.E., and C.N. Jacklin. 1974. *The psychology of sex differences.* Vol. 1. Stanford, CA: Stanford University Press.

MacNaughton, G. 1999. Even pink tents have glass ceilings: Crossing the gender boundaries in pretend play. In *Child's play: Revisiting play in early childhood settings,* ed. E. Dau, and E. Jones, 76–89. Sydney: MacLennan and Petty Pty Ltd.

Marsh, J., and P. Thompson. 2001. Parental involvement in literacy development: Using media texts. *Journal of Research in Reading* 24, no. 3: 266–78.

Mayall, B. 2002. *Towards a sociology for childhood.* London: Routledge Falmer.

Morss, J. 2002. The several social constructions of James, Jenks, and Prout: A contribution to the sociological theorization of childhood. *The International Journal of Children's Rights* 10: 39–54.

Nutbrown, C. 1996. *Respectful educators: Capable learners – Children's rights in the early years.* London: Paul Chapman Publishing.

Nutbrown, C. 2006. *Threads of thinking: Young children learning and the role of early education.* 3rd ed. London: SAGE.

Nutbrown, C., and P. Clough. 2004. Inclusion in the early years: Conversations with European educators. *European Journal of Special Needs Education* 19, no. 3: 311–39.

Nutbrown, C., and P. Clough. 2006. *Inclusion in the early years: Critical analyses and enabling narratives.* London: Sage.

Nutbrown, C., and P. Hannon. 2003. Children's perspectives on family literacy: Methodological issues, findings and implications for practice. *Journal of Early Childhood Literacy* 3, no. 2: 115–45.

Pereera, S. 2001. Living with 'special educational needs': Mothers' perspectives. In *Voices of Arabia: Essays in educational research,* ed. P. Clough and C. Nutbrown, 62–9. Sheffield: University of Sheffield Papers in Education.

Pike, S., and P. Clough. 2005. Children's voices on learning about countries in geography. *International Research in Geographical and Environmental Education* 14, no. 4: 114–21.

Purdue, K., K. Ballard, J. MacArthuer. 2001. Exclusion and inclusion in New Zealand early childhood education: Disability, discourses and contexts. *International Journal of Early Years Education* 9, no. 1: 37–49.

QCA. 1998. *Education for citizenship and the teaching of democracy in schools.* London: DfEE/QCA.

QCA. 2008. Citizenship: Information, resources and support for teachers. QCA. http://www.qcda.gov.uk/4791.aspx (accessed 28 November 2008).

Sparkes, J. 1999. *Schools, education and social exclusion.* LSE STICERD Research Paper No. CASE029. http://ssrn.com/abstract=1158920.

Stenhouse, L. 1975. *An introduction to curriculum research and development.* London: Heinemann.

Tarullo, L.B. 1994. Windows on social worlds: Gender differences in children's play narratives in children's play narratives. In *Children at play: Clinical and developmental approaches to meaning and representation,* ed. A. Slade and P.D. Wolf, 16–25. New York: Oxford University Press.

Tierney, W.G. 1993. Self and identity in a post modern world: A life story. In *Naming silenced lives,* ed. D. McLaughlin and W.G. Tierney, 87–100. New York: Routledge.

Vakil, S., R. Freeman, and T.J. Swim. 2003. The Reggio Emilia approach and inclusive early childhood programmes. *Early Childhood Education Journal* 30, no. 3: 187–92.

Whitburn, J. 2003. Learning to live together: The Japanese model of early years education. *International Journal of Early Years Education* 11, no. 2: 155–75.

Wyness, M. 2006. Children, young people and civic participation: Regulation and local diversity. *Educational Review* 58, no. 2: 209–18.

Zuber-Skerritt, O. 1996. *New directions in action research.* London: Falmer.

Participants' voices are now often accessed through methodologies other than the spoken word. These include the creation, collection and curation of artifacts (Pahl and Rowsell, 2010), the making of images through collage or photography (Harper, 2005), the American tradition of telling of stories through quilts (Capozzola, 2002), drama (Clough, 2009) and dance (Blumenfeld-Jones, 1995). In the next section we shall look at one example of developing 'method' which incorporates the voices of researcher and research participants. This example demonstrates how a methodological 'frame' can underpin a research study.

Focused conversation as a research method

The following example is drawn from Nutbrown (1999). Here she discusses the origins, motivations, processes and outcomes of eliciting the 'voices' of a small group of women. As you read, bear in mind our argument that social research is *persuasive, purposive, positional* and *political,* and try to identify those features in the account.

Focused Conversation: the context

The idea of setting up a 'Focused Conversation' between a group of people grew out of my interest in understanding, eventually to write about, the practices of a particular group of under-fives professionals. I wanted to know about their approach to working with parents of young children, their ideas about particular aspects of literacy, and their experiences of being black and bilingual and working in inner-city areas of a large city in the north of England. I wanted to know how they worked, what informed their thinking, what they brought to their role. This account does not describe that experience *per se* but draws on that process to focus on the methods and methodology involved.

Writing as 'process'

The five women who were to make up the group were known to me. We had worked together on issues of practice and early education pedagogy over several years. They were the obvious group to consult when, as part of a research project focusing on ways of involving parents of young children in early literacy development, I needed advice on working bilingually with parents and their young children. It was agreed that we would work together to write about the topic.

Creating the writing process

My best exchanges with the women were our lengthy, detailed, animated conversations, so we decided to begin our work by talking. I invited them to work with me, one afternoon a week for about 10 weeks, and explained that my aim was to 'tap their expertise', learn from what they did, acknowledge the special nature of their role, write something – with them – to ensure that their part was acknowledged at every turn.

We began tentatively, despite our existing relationships, which in some cases spanned more than 10 years. Here we were doing something new. We were treading new territory and we needed to proceed with care. As our first meeting began I was nervous, and very conscious of my position of power. I issued the invitation, I began the meeting, I knew what I wanted to accomplish, I had convened the group, I was seen as the academic, the authority, the writer, and I was expected to 'know'. I was conscious too of my whiteness and of my monolingualism in a group of black women, all of whom were bi- (if not multi-)lingual. We had a number of things in common: we were all women, all interested in young children, and held mutual respect for our different roles in education. Those commonalities, especially the fact that we were all women, became an important dynamic in the particular working group we were to create. I am not implying that Focused Conversation research should be a 'woman only' affair – simply that it was a particularly important characteristic of this group, in this case.

There were new experiences for me, as I broke though the barriers that I perceived from my whiteness and my inability to speak any of the six other languages they spoke (Arabic, Urdu, Punjabi, Bengali, Creole, Chinese). We would work in English – our common language – but we would be talking about other languages. I anticipated that members of the group would use their other languages at times, as we worked through some details of commonalities and differences in language structure, character, heritage and etiquette. So, as we began our writing process, here was I with my one language asking people to work with me, and to do so they spoke in their second (or third) language – to help me understand more of their bilingual work.

We created a way of proceeding with our writing which, as time went on, we remoulded a little but the basic practices and processes remained the same. We worked as follows:

1 We discussed topics which had been agreed well before the writing sessions began, and added to that preliminary agenda as our work progressed and other pertinent issues emerged.
2 We negotiated how we – together – would write about the topics we discussed. One of the women said: 'It's better if we talk, Cathy, and you can write it down'.

She was right of course – the richness of their experiences would only come through within fluid conversational interactions – but if I took the role as scribe for our two-hour sessions I would forfeit my role as participant and be unable to make a faithful record of the conversation which was so important. I could not be a scribe in our two-hour sessions and the other alternative (to include another person to act as scribe) would alter the dynamics of the group, which although newly convened for this purpose was familiar in other professional contexts. We agreed – after some reticence and inhibition – that we would tape record our sessions. We would make sure the tape 'heard' all that we said.

3   We also agreed that my role would be to take the words off the tape and apply an initial structure. The group would look at this first transcript draft and we would shape and reshape the writing from there until we were sufficiently satisfied to make our writing public.

This account draws on the experience of sessions when the group talked about being bilingual. This topic was not one which I had in mind when we began, but it emerged as a fundamental issue which we needed to explore before we could focus in any meaningful way on the topics I thought were important. So the group talked about their experiences of being young and bilingual before we moved on to our previously agreed (pre-experience) agenda.

It was at this point in creating this particular writing process that I learned I was not simply engaged in a process of gathering information in the most effective and convenient way and by a means comfortable for the 'participants' – it was here that I learned that these women were the 'data', they created new knowledge through connective discourse, as they listened and spoke together. For example, on one occasion we were talking about the different home languages the women spoke:

L said, 'Arabic is a language of song and poetry. It is the most beautiful of languages'.

P interjected with a gentle challenge, 'You can't just say that! You can't say your language is the most beautiful – that's because it's yours! We all think our own language is beautiful – it's because it's your own mother tongue!'

The group pursued this theme, eventually reaching agreement that it was how we felt about our own languages which was at the root of L's initial comment. Feeling about their own language was so much part of their multilingual identities.

This was the richness of this group process. One comment – one spoken thought – stimulated another and as the conversation went on a verbal sculpture was created, ideas were crafted, expressed and re-expressed as each one drew on memories of her childhood, and revisited her early life in the light of what she had just learned of another's. These were the moments when I began to think that I was engaged, not simply in a writing exercise, but as a participant in a way of understanding experience which had a unique dynamism.

Our sessions had all the features of a long, animated, passionate conversation. Short pauses, long silences, discomforts, agreements, disclaimers, retractions, clarifications, humour, interruptions, repetition, emphasis, misunderstandings, excitements, conflicts, and discoveries. We created and recognised new points of convergence as we each uncovered something of our own lives and our own thinking.

Some might worry about the 'muddying' of data, of participants influencing the ideas of others, but Focused Conversation work, as I conceive it, aims to do just that – to allow for the convergence of lives and experiences. Stanley and Wise (1993, p. 161), like Oakley (1993), argue for the replacement of 'hygienic' research with the legitimisation of personal involvement:

> Our experiences suggest that 'hygienic research' is a reconstructed logic, a mythology which presents an oversimplified account of research. It is also extremely misleading, in that it emphasises the 'objective' presence of the researcher, and suggests that she can be 'there' without having any greater involvement than simple presence. In contrast, we emphasise that all research involves, as its basis, an interaction, a relationship between researcher and researched. … Because the basis of all research is a relationship, this necessarily involves the presence of the researcher *as a person*. Personhood cannot be left behind, cannot be left out of the research process.

In the case under discussion here, members of the group revisited their own comments and their own assumptions in the light of what they heard from others, for example:

> G made a comment about her experience in the first few weeks of infant school in England. Then she stopped and laughed and said, 'I'll have to think about what I've just said – I'm not sure I mean it!'

That kind of reflection, which allowed individuals to change what they said, reflect on each other's comments, and ask each other if they meant what they had said, was a rich and vital part of the writing process, one which would likely have been missed if we had chosen a different approach to this writing task.

I played a quiet role for the most part – though I did join in some debates; to put another point of view, ask for clarification, push an idea a little further. But I also noted the comments which tailed off unfinished, the thoughts that were interrupted, the threads which seemed to get lost. I noted these so that – when one theme seemed to be finished or exhausted – I could return to that thought. I would say things like: 'C – you were talking about your first teacher' or 'G – a moment ago you mentioned a time in Jamaica when …'. I did this to try to capture every gem of experience that they were sharing.

I also noted those who did not speak for some time, but was careful not to try to draw them into the conversation too soon because they might well have been participating while silent, engaged in listening and reflecting on what they heard. As Lewis (2002) notes with regard to group interviewing, people can take thinking time. The dynamics of this group were such that on occasions people sank back in their chairs, perhaps reflecting on what they heard, trying out some idea in their head. People concentrated to different degrees and levels of intensity at different times throughout our two-hour sessions; boiled the kettle again, left the room for five minutes, without pressure and in the knowledge that silent thought and times of apparent non-contribution were legitimised, even recognised as necessary factors in what was at times a quite intense process.

The writing as 'product'

We were conscious that we were writing to produce a product which would eventually be made public. The writing went through nine drafts and each time new words were added, new thoughts created, old thoughts discarded – or withdrawn from the public eye. What was created was a short piece of writing which told much about the women's experiences and which humbled me as the privileged 'participant' who was allowed to listen to and help compose their stories. In a sense, the product of the process – the finished, public writing – is not so important. What is more important is the process by which data can be created, moulded and reported as a seamless process. What is different about this writing, which emerges from Focused Conversation work, is that the group participants do not simply provide the quotes, they co-author the whole piece.

Seeking the method that 'feels' right

> Selection of methods may be an act of faith rather than a rational response to a clearly formulated problem. The method may even be an intrinsic part of the problem, rather than extrinsic and disconnected from it. Just as recipes are not simply things that are done to food, but become concepts within which method and substance are compounded, so 'method' in research can become an intrinsic part of the project. *The methods we choose are, in this sense, there to be tested, just as much as the substantive hypothesis.*
>
> (Walker, 1985, p. 46, our italics)

There were other alternatives to the process of Focused Conversation which I have described. Instead of opting for a process of collaborative writing, I could have chosen to obtain information from the five individuals concerned, weave this information together in the way I saw fit, consult them on a draft and eventually publish with an appropriate acknowledgement to them for their contribution. The most obvious alternative to this collaborative writing process was first to use individual interviews with each person.

Considering interviews

I could have set about interviewing each of the five women – having some idea beforehand of what we might talk about. This would either have necessitated considerable time and several one-to-one interviews with each person first to establish the agenda and then to explore it with each individual or, as Seidman puts it, to share and understand something of 'other people's stories' (Seidman, 1991, p.1).

Telling stories is essentially a meaning-making process. When people tell stories, they select details from their stream of consciousness. ... It is this process of selecting constitutive details of experience, reflecting on them, giving them order, and thereby making sense of them that makes telling stories a meaning-making experience.

(Seidman, 1991, p. 1)

What I was interested in was not simply their stories and experiences of work with young children, but also the way in which their collective experiences fitted together.

Individual 'long interviews', as discussed by McCracken (1988), might well have provided rich data which could then be analysed according to the categories which I identified as meaningful when I came to analyse the transcripts. Such an approach would have yielded five separate sets of interview scripts – of varying depth – for me to analyse as I saw fit, and it would have been my responsibility to mould their five unique and individual experiences and ideas into a structure that I created. The main disadvantage of this method – for me – lay in the 'separateness' of the five responses, when part of the objective was to understand something of the 'collective' experiences of the group. The aim of this process was not, as McCracken puts it, to 'survey the terrain' but to 'mine it' (p. 17). The method for this piece of exploration needed to suit a process which was 'much more intensive than extensive in its objectives' (McCracken, 1988, p. 17).

The right 'feeling' is seldom discussed as a rationale for deciding on methods of data collection and analysis in educational research but here, for me, it figured highly, and I suggest that 'feeling' (or perhaps we might say 'hunch') is an important methodological consideration. Neither interviews, questionnaires nor individual writing 'felt' right for the task. Somehow – for this particular group of women and this particular task – the accepted research methods of obtaining information did not fit. At the time my aim was to obtain information in order to write some material about a specific topic – I was not (I thought) engaged so much in research as in a process of writing a practical booklet for early childhood educators. I needed a means of gathering the information which would eventually lead to a publishable written outcome. I was seeking some way of combining the richness of detail and experience which could be obtained from long interviews with shared consensus and collective meaning-making which involved all participants. Lewis (2002) discussed the usefulness of group interviews with children, suggesting that this was a useful tool for achieving consensus and evolving views where there could be some element of 'connecting with' or, as Lewis terms it, 'on' (p. 416) to the ideas of other interview participants.

Some thoughts on procedures and processes in Focused Conversations

So how might this experience of a writing process help to shape a research method? Key elements in this particular writing project can be extracted and developed as some kind of guideline on procedures and processes for the use of 'Focused Conversations' in educational research. In doing this I do not want to add methodological complication or construct some pretence of 'rigour' – often processes of writing (and research methods) can be constrained under the guise of rigour or 'quality control'. There are perhaps some characteristics of the specific writing process described above which contributed to its success and which might be used to develop a frame within which other Focused Conversation research can be conducted. The following characteristics are not intended as a blueprint – merely as a 'recipe' (to use Walker's metaphor) to be tried and tasted. It may well be that for some new ingredients must be added and others removed – it depends on the research questions, the circumstances and the participants. It depends on what kind of meal you want to cook, and who will eat of it!

What might make Focused Conversations a useful research tool?

- Familiarity of members of the group
- A group large enough to be a group but small enough for everyone to have a voice (say 4–7)
- An agreed topic of shared experience, knowledge and interest
- Willingness to explore statements and ideas in terms of individuals' own experiences and personal histories
- Willingness and desire to – eventually – make this exploration or the outcomes of it public
- The expectations of the 'researcher' – responsibilities, ethical considerations
- The role of the 'researcher' as group convenor and 'caretaker' of proceedings
- Mutual respect for opinions, culture, experience – everyone has something to offer
- Established confidentiality.

There are established methods in educational and social science research which might be viewed as similar to the Focused Conversation. It is important to locate work using focused conversations within the context of other established methods – if only to avoid some accusation of mis-use of other methods!

Focus Group Interviews

I would not want what I am suggesting here to be misconstrued as a misinterpretation (or poor use!) of the Focus Group Interview. My understanding is that this is a somewhat different process.

Though some definitions suggest similarities between Focus Group Interviews and Focused Conversations, processes are different.

First, some definitions of focus group interviews:

> an informal discussion among selected individuals about specific topics relevant to the situation at hand

> (Beck, Trombetta and Share, 1986, p. 73)

organised group discussions which are focused around a single theme

(Byers and Wilcox, 1988, p. 1)

The goal of focus group interviews is to create a candid, normal conversation that addresses, in depth, the selected topic.

(Vaughn, Schumm and Sunagub, 1996, p. 4)

In describing the processes of Focus Group Interviews, Hess (1968) notes the advantages of this technique over individual interviews to include:

1 **synergism** (when a wider bank of data emerges through the group interaction)
2 **snowballing** (when the statements of one respondent initiate a chain reaction of additional comments)
3 **stimulation** (when the group discussion generates excitement about a topic)
4 **security** (when the group provides a comfort and encourages candid responses)
5 **spontaneity** (when participants are not required to answer every question, their responses are more spontaneous and genuine).

(Hess, 1968)

Vaughn, Schumm and Sunagub (1996) set out five reasons for using Focus Group Interviews:

1 Focus Group Interviews offer variety and versatility to both qualitative and quantitative research methods
2 Focus Group Interviews are compatible with the qualitative research paradigm
3 Focus Group Interviews offer opportunities for direct contact with subjects
4 The Group Format offers distinctive advantages for data collection (encourages interaction; encourages openness; allows and encourages formation of opinions through interaction with others)
5 Focus Group Interviews offer utility.

So far, so good, but these authors then go on to set out an eight-step plan describing how the FGI should be conducted: with rigid rules for a 'moderator' and stringent guidelines on data analysis. A key difference between Focus Group Interviews and Focused Conversation research is that, with the former, the role of participants often ends with the completion of data collection. For me, Focused Conversations can continue to involve participants in the development of data to analysing and reporting.

Others have defended Focus Group Interviews against critics:

Focus Group research has been the subject of much controversy and criticism. Such criticism is generally associated with the view that focus groups interviews do not yield 'hard' data, and the concern that group members may not be representative of a larger population (because of both the small numbers and the idiosyncratic nature of the group discussion). Such criticism, however, is unfair. Although focus groups do have important limitations of which the researcher should be aware, limitations are not unique to focus group research; all research tools in the social sciences have significant limitations.

(Stewart and Shamdasani, 1990, p. 12)

It is interesting that the strengths are not identified as lying in their idiosyncratic nature. The group is not necessarily a representative 'sample' nor is what they say immediately generalisable, they simply provide a collective viewpoint of those present (at that time) in that composition. It is a story, a single account (that is what it is and it need not claim to be anything else). If generalisable findings or representative samples are needed then, arguably, different methods should be used. Stewart and Shamdasani (1990) identify many potential problems and issues in terms of the group being composed/assembled, particularly for the purpose of the research. In the work I have described here the group already existed. Issues of importance that emerged within this group lead to the development of the method of working which I am calling Focused Conversation, in order to stimulate the writing process. Issues of data analysis, also discussed in depth by Stewart and Shamdasani (1990), are rendered less important when the group are the data, the analysts and the authors.

The Focus Group Interview in social science research, originating in consumer and market research, is a very different method from the focus group work described by Madriz (1998) who, researching the lives of women describes her use of focus groups thus:

The singularity of the focus group as a form of collective testimony is that it allows women to exchange, verify, and confirm their experiences with other women of similar socioeconomic and ethnic backgrounds. The interaction in focus groups emphasises empathy and commonality of experiences and fosters self-disclosure and self-validation. Communication among women can be an awakening experience and an important element of a consciousness-raising process because it asserts women's rights to substantiate their own experiences.

(Madriz, 1998, p. 116)

Madriz (1998) describes her use of focus groups to elicit life stories and experiences; her description of the groups, located in a feminist research perspective is different from those focus groups convened and written about by some male researchers who set out with some precision details of the Focus Group method itself. Perhaps this attention to detail of procedure is in part to prevent the 'method' itself being distorted (Morgan, 1998). In contrast, feminist paradigms continue to seek new research ways which, more honestly, include the researcher. (This is not to say that such tools are only used by women researchers – but it does appear that feminist paradigms push at the boundaries of method.) Fine (1994) writes of her need to place herself in her research:

The interviews with the Baltimore women forced us to come clean; I had to reinsert consciously my interpretive self into my writings, with, but not through, the rendition of their voices. Researchers cannot write about/with/through adults' (or adolescents') voices as if the researchers had 'said it all'.

(Fine, 1994, p. 22)

The Focused Conversation which I am exploring as a method is more closely aligned, one could say 'rooted', in the Individual Focused Interview as used in Oral/Life History research than in those methodologically controlled Focus Group Interviews. But Focused Conversation work goes further than Focus Group Interviews which stop at the generation of data. Focused Conversation work, in my interpretation, is not complete until participants have agreed their written version of the events. For Madriz, as with most researchers, most of the time, the power of authorship rested with her:

I see my role as being part of the broader group of researchers who translate women's experiences ... to the reader with the intent of advancing social justice and social change and writing against 'othering'. I am aware, however, that my particular translation of these women's voices is possible because of my middle-class background and particularly because of my education, which gives power to my translation, making it 'scholarly' work.

(Madriz, 1998, p. 117)

The creation of new knowledge – Focused Conversations in Educational and Social Science Research

So, what, if anything, does this 'method' offer to the function of research? How does research using Focused Conversations help to create new knowledge? What place might the Focused Conversation have in Research in Educational and Social Science Research? Through 'talking-for-writing' new ideas can be born, new knowledge can be created, views can be shaped and reshaped. The richness of the process lies in the openness of those who participate and their willingness to allow their ideas to be shaped by those of others, and to examine their own experiences in the light of what they hear others say. It is a process of thinking, where the thoughts – every spoken thought – is captured on tape for future reflection.

Later examination of the first draft of the transcribed tape can lead to a new composition. People may say things like:'I didn't say that ... well maybe I said it but I don't mean it like that – I mean ... ' And that thought, that idea is reshaped again.

The processes I have described here form, for me, one of those new paths in the relationship between 'researcher' and 'research participants'.

For me the value of Focused Conversations in educational and social science research lies in the process of holding on to the talk, reshaping talk and creating a dynamic where one person allows another's words to illuminate and sometimes rephrase their own. Inestimable is the process by which the sources of the data become analysts of

those data and eventually become the authors of what is written from those processes, and the blurring of boundaries between researcher and researched. The words
we speak are not always the ones we want but our own words, reflected back a week
later off the page, can trigger new ideas as well as clarify existing ones (and again, and
again) until our written words say what we are content to say to others whom we
may never know.

This process may well transfer to situations where it is people's thoughts, feelings and
experiences which we want to capture (indeed our own when we become part of the
process). It is a method of gathering data out of our heads, a research method which,
like other forms of data gathered, eventually leads to writing. Focused Conversations
are about voices, experiences, stories and their place in research; about finding new
words, new expressions and new learning about ourselves in a shared dynamic of communication. What is different in this process is that those who are the data are those
who gather the data, remould and reshape the data, analyse those data, draft and redraft
the words which result until the paper is written (and has – in the process – become
research).

(*Source*: Nutbrown, 1999: 4–22)

Activity 4.4

Before you move on, reflect on the example above. Make some notes on the usefulness of generating, interpreting and reporting data through Focused Conversations
in the context of your own research study.

Would a method like this be useful in your own study? Is its methodological frame
one which would support the structures which drive your own research?

'Voice' and internet-based social enquiry

Thursday 2 June 2011

Two years ago I started a classroom blog after having been introduced to this techno-
logical tool during a one-day teacher seminar. Since then, I haven't stopped experimenting
and testing ideas to maximise its use as an effective and innovative classroom resource.
As a teacher of young learners, I can freely say that the benefits of using a classroom
blog are numerous. Apart from proving to be an effective means of communication
with parents on a day-to-day basis, most importantly it has helped create a sense of
belonging to the classroom as a community of learners where the process of learning
is strengthened and intensified through the sharing of classroom experiences as well as
increased exposure to content knowledge through links to online resources (video clips,
PowerPoint presentations, music, research sites and educational websites to name a few)
that facilitate learning and that could be easily accessed from within the classroom as

well as from the home. In this way, learning is also extended outside the classroom walls as the pupils and their families are provided with the opportunity to revisit links, share ideas, comments and make suggestions, thus participating actively in the learning process. Moreover, I also use the classroom blog as a space to initiate classroom research by providing links to direct pupil searches around topics of interest and to seek answers to their own questions.

I must say that, although keeping a classroom blog certainly requires additional time and effort on the part of the teacher, the amount of positive feedback that I have received over the past two years from both parents, colleagues and pupils together with the heightened sense of interest and motivation demonstrated by the learners in my classes have made it a worthwhile endeavour which I intend to pursue further. Blogging is undoubtedly a valuable means of incorporating new technologies in the classroom and of utilising and extending young learners' media literacies.

Rosienne,
Teacher, Malta

One area in which research has developed at a fast pace is in the use of the internet. *Web 2.0* is now becoming of interest to teachers and so, as school use develops, so too does research into pupils' use of such innovations (Davies and Merchant, 2010). Electronic resources add to sources of available literature and also offer new ways of collecting data and communicating with research participants. Forums for internet communication proliferate and chatrooms, msn messenger, web spaces, blogs, wikis, as well as email, are developing and offer convenient sources of data collection. However, these newer technologies also raise new perspectives on ethical and moral issues.

Rudd et al. (2006: 32) note the potential benefits and the pitfalls in working within online communities and online spaces:

> The term 'social software' covers a range of different software currently used online, including internet discussion forums, messaging, social networking and social bookmarking tools, weblogs (or blogs) and wikis. All of these are growing in popularity and are often referred to in relation to a series of developments referred to as 'Web 2.0'. The social nature of learning is reflected in the way the software has developed and the protocols surrounding its use, which focus upon collaboration and social interaction. Another underlying principle is the belief that through responsible, individual contributions, the wider user community will benefit. Social software can be an extremely powerful means of communicating, sharing views and facilitating action. It is essential, however, that safety and security issues are considered and discussed prior to any online activity taking place.

Just as the invention of the printing press gave rise to more widely accessible information, so the internet has provided a global explosion of communication. What is different is the speed of communication, which is not hindered by geographical location, and the way in which information can 'go viral' within seconds of it appearing on sites such as *Facebook* and *YouTube*. This presents huge opportunities for researchers:

> Every generation believes it is singular in its experience of rapid and monumental social and technological changes. Ours is no exception. Early in the 21st century, 'The Internet' marks our epochal particularity. The internet – with all its capacities, inter-faces, uses, and underlying technologies – both epitomizes and enables a seemingly constant barrage of reality-altering, globe-shifting changes. (Markham and Baym, 2009: vii)

This 'explosion' presents challenges too, and researchers using new technologies need to address the challenges and ethical and moral issues alongside the merits and benefits.

In a pilot interview which aimed to understand teenage girls' use of internet chatrooms, the following response was received to the question: Are you willing to tell me the kinds of things you chat about on the www? One 14-year-old girl who replied wrote:

@ yes. we talk about our problems, or if were stuck with NEthing. we cheer each ova up if theyre feeling sad or down. we make each ova laff and have a good tym. we talk about homework and help each other with that. most of the time its just ran-dom conversations about random stuff. share pictures, songs and say things like chek my myspace please and sign it so we keep in touch there as well as msn. we talk about useful websites and music that weve found on there. if people find a site or get a virus email, they will sometimes send a warning to every1 on their contacts and they send it on to their contacts but me and my friends conversations usu-ally involve feelings, problems, laffin, jokin, cheering each ova up, homework and just plain random.

The genre of her response was as important as the substantive content of what she wrote.

Activity 4.5 Keeping 'voice' in the data

Bearing in mind the form in which the participant above chose to respond to the interview questions, using a form of msn speak, what would you do with such data? How would you represent such data in a final written report? How do you begin to ensure that the distinctive voice of this 14 year-old is respected and faith-fully portrayed?

Hine (2009) asks how internet researchers decide on and define the boundaries of their research. She suggests that, as an internet ethnographer, she can adopt unconventional approaches to defining her 'field' of enquiry and the 'sites' of her research. She argues against the notion of the internet as 'place' but rather as another site in social life: 'Social phenomena are not uniquely confined to online of offline sites, and it would be a mistake to allow these notions automatically to provide boundaries for our studies' (Hine, 2009: 18).

Yet confusion can arise, and the ethics of the internet need particular attention – the potential for 'covert' research is huge and it remains in the integrity of the researcher to develop appropriate online practices which respect the privacy and identities of those who provide data.

From a US perspective, Markham (2005) sets out some epistemological and methodological issues related to using the internet to do research and researching the internet. Of online research, she notes:

> Deceptive in its apparent simplicity, qualitative inquiry in this environment requires careful attention to the traditional means by which social life is interpreted and the adjustments that must be made to give value to the online experience and internal consistency to one's methods. (Markham, 2005: 799)

The internet provides a different space for research and researchers and the maps are still being drawn for these evolving territories. What is clear is that while online methods of collecting data are assisting many researchers, there are new ethical and moral issues to negotiate and much of the practices which develop will be a matter of individual researcher integrity.

'Interpretation' of research voices

There is always an ethical problem surrounding issues of 'interpretation'. Just how does a researcher make sense of data derived from the voices of others? Numerous texts on research methods set out 'the method' and include details of 'how to' analyse data. However, it is still a matter (always) of interpretation. Researchers adopt a variety of practices in order to make meaning from the information given to them and garnered in different ways. Hannon and Nutbrown (2001) reported a large longitudinal randomised control design experimental study. It involved much statistical data but also included the voices of over 500 participants: parents, children and teachers. The research report 'gives voice' to the research participants before it presents the outcomes of quantitative data. The interpretation of research voices is not an issue to be confined to purely qualitative or ethnographic research. The important point here is 'faithful' interpretation of what is heard, arising from *radical listening* which has the characteristics of honesty and integrity.

It is generally the case in research studies that interpretation is the job of the researcher. But is there a case in particular studies – on particular topics – for placing interpretation in the hands of the participants? Perhaps this is what Fine might call 'playing with power' (Fine, 1994: 23). 'Playing' it may be, but is this a means by which we can trust that the story told is the story as the participants want to tell it? This means more than returning to the 'participants' or 'interviewees' with a transcript; it means more than asking them to 'approve' a final draft. It means involving them in writing the story – drafting and redrafting, worrying over words and interpretations, thinking about 'the reader' until they (until we) are happy to make our writing public. The power and responsibility of authorship is held in collective.

Tierney (1998) and others who work through narrative and life history research (Clough, 1996; Kiesinger, 1998) consider the place of the researched self and 'others' in the process of research and in the text created. Tierney concludes: 'To seek new epistemological and methodological avenues demands that we chart new paths rather than constantly return to well-worn roads and point out that they will not take us where we want to go' (Tierney, 1998: 68).

Reflecting on his own work, Clough considers the work which results from his own project to explore aspects of 'self' in his research:

> In 1996 I published a story called *Again, Fathers and Sons* [Clough, 1996], a story 'about' Klaus, a 9-year-old boy with moderate learning difficulties, and emotional and behavioural difficulties which had already seen him excluded from two schools. I met him when I worked in the residential unit where he had been placed. Of the 'facts', I should record that this boy and his father 'existed' as they do in the story; my visit to the house and the father's visit to the school 'happened' in precisely the way that my memory reconstructs them in the story. In this sense, there is no *material* import to the story. But its data have no formal record, and its particular structure is achieved through a working out of a very personal agenda and it is verified only in collision with the experience of the reader.
>
> Any discussion of the story of 'Klaus' insists upon particular consideration of research and self. The role of the researcher's self in the construction of research accounts is a ground being cleared in the increasing occupation of educational research with the insertion of the researcher her/himself in the process of research. Reflections on research collected, for example, by Walford (1991), Vulliamy and Webb (1992), and Clough and Barton (1995) emphasise the growing critical, but also reflexive self-awareness of educational enquiry, and in the introductions to each of these collections is seen the impulse to such revelation located and justified in a particular tradition of human science study.
>
> Klaus and I are central to the story – but it is my own identity which lies at the heart of the meaning constructed through this story – a kind of 'testament' (Hutton-Jarvis 1999). My own identity as I constructed it in relation to my own father is central too – stripped as I was of power and confidence in the presence of this other father. (Clough, 2002: 107)

Confidentiality or secrecy?

All research must be interrogated for the means by which it 'protects' the interests of the participants. Researchers make their own decisions about how their subjects' 'confidences' are protected in the reporting of research. Clough admitted some of his struggles with his own father as he searched his 'fossils' in order to understand himself *in* his research. But aside from the standard (and essential) ethical undertakings of confidentiality there may be issues of secrecy to think about. Mitchell, in his book *Secrecy and Fieldwork* (1993), points out that the researcher's relationships with those he/she studies are of the heart and of the mind: they are, he says, 'inseparably and simultaneously both cognitive and affective ...' (Mitchell, 1993: 12). He goes on:

> Looking inward, researchers face the greatest dangers, the dangers of self-doubt and questioned identity. Secrecy, always present, is also always double-edged ...
>
> At risk is the potential of researchers to equivocate in this challenge and rest their ethical cases on methodological routines, while as social selves they remain outsiders, objective analysts with their own over-reaching agendas. Researchers may fail fundamentally to meet the most crucial of fiduciary responsibilities, the responsibility for informed reporting of members' perspectives ...
>
> In insisting on expressive distance, in conducting work from positions of convenience, in relative power of control, researchers may achieve only incomplete understandings ...
>
> In order to understand, researchers must be more than technically competent. They must enter into cathected intimacies, open themselves to their subjects' feeling worlds, whether those worlds are congenial to them or repulsive. They must confront the duality of represented and experienced selves simultaneously, both conflicted, both real ...
>
> Finally and fundamentally, the fieldworkers understand. They can keep no secrets from themselves. In action of consequence, there is no frontier between appearing and being. (Mitchell, 1993: 54–5)

All researchers are on the 'inside' of their research. Some open themselves up to the secrets which insider perspectives reveal and some admit the secrets.

Activity 4.6

Issues of self, voice and secrecy have a direct relation to that of interpretation of research voices in any research study, whatever the scale.

> Think of the people who may participate – in different ways – in your research. Whose voices might you want to listen to?
>
> What are the implications of *radical listening* and 'giving voice' to research participants for: your research design; research questions; data collection; interpretation; and report?

Issues of 'voice', 'self' and 'interpretation' are themes which are also addressed in later chapters. In Part 3 we shall see how radical listening – as opposed to merely hearing – is central to the development of a good research design and writing a compelling report.

Ethics: pause for reflection

Radical listening requires researchers not 'just' to hear but also to consider what action may result from their listening. What are the ethical processes at work here?

What particular ethical issues arise when researching using the internet?

How can researchers make 'faithful' interpretation of what is heard and report their findings with honesty and integrity?

What should be confidential and what should be secret in research? To what extent is it ethical to keep research secrets? Are confidentiality and anonymity always necessary? Might there be occasions when it would not be ethical to withhold identities of research participants?

Radical listening requires researchers not 'just' to hear but also to consider what action may result from their listening. What are the ethical processes at work here?

When, as researchers, we engage in active listening to the accounts our participants volunteer to us, we have a duty to hold what we hear with good care. We must ensure that our notes and recordings are kept safely, of course, but ethical responses to listening go further than this minimal requirement. We must work hard to ensure that what we have heard is treated with respect. By that, it is important that the data our participants give to us when we listen is reported honestly and also in ways which do not embarrass or draw undue attention to those participants. This extends to *radical listening* in relation to internet inquiry too, where the potential for distortion or misunderstanding is greater.

Making 'faithful' interpretation of the data we hear and reporting what we are told and what we hear by other means with honesty and integrity is a key challenge for any qualitative researcher. In some cases anonymity and the use of pseudonyms may suffice, in others researchers may need to consider the use of fictional devices to weave together a single story from fragments of many interviews or other 'listening' data. In this way the 'truths' are told but the identities of participants are concealed and their specific interests are protected.

How do researchers decide what parts of their data should be confidential and what should be secret in research? To some extent the participants themselves can help with these decisions – but, given that one of the first priorities of the researcher is to do no harm (to participants or themselves), it is important to run several checks over the report and to do one's utmost to protect all involved. It is probably the case that all researchers keep some secrets. They may withhold part of the data in order to protect a participant, they may choose not to report some details in order to guard against the identity or full circumstances of some participants being disclosed. It is for the researcher to decide the difference between secrecy and confidentiality, and to decide when confidentiality and anonymity are unnecessary – and indeed, not ethical? There can be occasions when it would not be ethical to withhold the identities of research participants, especially when they request acknowledgement and recognition for their part in the research and where making their identities public would better serve their interests? Every study and every participant is different and needs particular and specific consideration when it comes to such issues.

CHAPTER SUMMARY

In this chapter we have:

- *Discussed issues of 'voice' and research experience*
- *Provided an example of raising, interpreting and reporting voices through focused conversation, and discussed the use of focused conversation as a research method*
- *Explored the methodological issues which arise in the attempt to 'give voice' to research participants*
- *Considered 'voice' and internet-based social enquiry*
- *Discussed the 'interpretation' of research 'voices'*
- *Reflected on the ethical issues arising from the chapter contents*

FURTHER READING

Hine, C. (2009) 'How can qualitative internet researchers define the boundaries of their projects?', in A.N. Markham and N.K. Baym (eds), *Internet Inquiry: Conversations about Method*. London: Sage.

> This chapter unpicks the questions of boundaries and space in the field of internet inquiry and offers useful questions and additional reading. It is followed by a response from two researchers who each provide different perspectives from a US context.

Markham, A.N. (2005) 'The methods, politics, and ethics of representation in online ethnography', in N.K. Denzin and Y.S. Lincoln (eds), *The Sage Handbook of Qualitative Inquiry*. London: Sage.

> This chapter discusses practice, purpose and ethics in online ethnographic research and sets out the field in the every changing online 'moment'.

Clough, P. (2009) 'Finding God in Wellworth High School: more legitimations of story-making as research', *Ethnography and Education*, 4 (3): 347–56.

Abstract

A curious piece of ironic, partially-dramatised auto/ethnography, this paper reflects an ongoing attempt to explore the vapid certainties of my own faith, some of the brittle discomforts of contemporary schooling, and the possibilities of a social science research methodology which can artfully assemble on the same stage belief, empirics and critique. Though actually too didactic to be art – and at the same time too casual to be social science – the paper supposes a set of incidents, based remotely on 'actual' events, which bring into collision some crises of faith, of schooling and of research methodology. I imagine that there is also some rather terrible humour to the piece which might be a radio play.

5 Reading: Purpose and Positionality

CHAPTER CONTENTS

Introduction   106
Criticality   106
The critical literature review   108
Critical interpretations of events   117
Being critical in your own research   121
Ethics: pause for reflection   136

LEARNING OBJECTIVES

By studying and doing the activities in this chapter you will:

- have an understanding of *radical reading*
- develop an awareness of the place of criticality in radical reading of both texts and practices
- have explored examples of critical responses to literature
- have responded to examples of critical readings of events
- have developed your own definition and synopsis of the place of criticality in your own research.

Introduction

> *Radical reading* provides the justification for the critical adoption or rejection of existing knowledge and practices.

In this chapter we discuss the centrality of the literature search and review and the 'readings' of the research settings in which researchers work.

Building on our argument that social research is *purposive* and *positional*, we argued in Chapter 2 that *radical reading* is a process which exposes the *purposes* and *positions* of both texts and practices. By using the word 'reading' here we are concerned both with the understanding of written and semiotic texts and the more metaphorical 'reading' of situations. What do certain signs, conventions and symbols mean? How do *you* read this or that action or event? How, that is, do you interpret the events in the theatre of enquiry?

> **Activity 5.1**
>
> Take a moment to reflect on our definition of *radical reading*. How does this concept help you in your research study? Make some brief notes in your research journal. Remember that is it important not necessarily to agree with our position, but rather to engage with it.

Criticality

> *Criticality* – 'being critical' – describes the attempt to show *on what terms* 'personal' and 'public' knowledges are jointly articulated, and therefore where their *positional* differences lie.

Academic critique does not necessarily mean 'taking issue' with a text but rather 'asking questions' of it. Any critical account seeks to be *rational*, but will also reflect the values and beliefs of its author. It is the presence of the *persuasive* in a critical account which reveals the full range of values at work.

In Chapter 1 we asked, *What is research?* and outlined the specific characteristics of social research as *persuasive, purposive, positional* and *political*. Alongside these important *characteristics* of social research it is necessary to establish an operational understanding of the phases involved in any research study. Such an understanding of the *constructural features* of social research becomes central at this point in our discussion. In a simple operational definition we could say that social research consists of six steps.

We want to demonstrate here how *radical reading* is inseparable from the other three radical processes discussed elsewhere in this book, and show how it is essential in realising the six steps presented in Figure 5.1.

Operationally, research consists of:

1. *framing* a research question,

2. *finding out* what existing answers there are to that question,

3. *establishing* what is 'missing' from those answers, then

4. *getting information* which will answer the question; and

5. *making meanings* from the information which helps to answer your research question; and

6. *presenting a report* which highlights the significance of your study.

Figure 5.1   Six steps in critical social science enquiry

In the following scheme (Figure 5.2) we connect these six steps with the various *radical processes* in the conduct of *critical enquiry*.

	Operational step	Radical processes
1	*Framing* a research question	This cannot be successfully achieved without some *radical reading* of the research literature and/or the 'theatre' of research
2	*Finding out* what existing answers there are to that question	Essential here is engagement with the research literature – *critical reading*
3	*Establishing* what is 'missing' from those answers	Some *radical looking* is necessary here – seeing beyond the known – to find the precise focus of the study which makes your study unique. Criticality in the *radical reading* of literature and 'theatre'
4	*Getting information* which will answer the question	More reading of the literature and *radical listening* and *looking* in the ethical generation of data
5	*Making meanings* from the information which helps to answer your research question	*Radical looking* and *radical reading* of the meanings within the evidence at the stage of analytical and ethical interpretation of data; *critical reflection*
6	*Presenting a report* which highlights the significance of the research report in your study	Telling the research story. Accounting for the findings through *persuasive* ways which make explicit the findings, the *purpose* of the study, the *position* of the researcher and the *political* nature of the research act. The research report brings together these *radical processes* of *looking*, *listening*, *questioning* and *reading* and ultimately *justifies* the responsible and ethical enquiry

Figure 5.2   Six operational steps and their radical processes of critical social science enquiry

---

Activity 5.2

Think about the simple six-step operational structure above. How can you apply this to your own study? In which ways can the various radical acts of critical social science enquiry be identified as present in your own study?

The critical literature review

In this section we shall examine what *radical reading* means in relation to the literature. First, we shall describe practical strategies for *radical reading* of research reports. Second, we suggest how research questions will inform the literature search decisions. Finally, we shall look at some examples of demonstrating a critical response to such reading in the writing of research reports.

Practically, *radical reading* means asking the following questions of what you read:

- *What is the author trying to say?*

    What is the real point here? What is the central argument?

- *To whom is the author speaking?*

    Is this account written for academics? Policy-makers? Practitioners? Is the author really speaking to me?

- *Why has this account of this research been written?*

    Does s/he have a political point to make? How does this relate to current policy?

- *What does the author ultimately want to achieve?*

    Does s/he want to bring about some change? Does s/he want to make a difference? To what?

- *What authority does s/he appeal to?*

    Disciplinarity? Policy evidence? Political mission?

- *What evidence does the author offer to substantiate the claims?*

    Participants' statements? Observations/documentary analysis? Is there any 'missing' evidence?

- *Do I accept this evidence?*

    Is it sufficient to support the claims made in the report? What else could I ask to see?

- *Does this account accord with what I know of the world?*

    Is there a match between my experience and my reading and what I am reading? Does it matter if the report is disconnected from my own world? Can I learn something from that disconnection?

- *What is my view?*

    Based on what principles/ideology/pedagogy/life experiences ... and supported by which authors ...?

- *What evidence do I have for this view?*

    How can I substantiate my own view? Do I draw on what I am reading here? What other sources and experiences have formed my view?

- *Do I find this account credible within the compass of my experience and knowledge?*

    Taking my responses to the above questions, does my reading of this research report lead me to decide that it should 'count' in my own study? Should it be included as part of the bank of information and evidence which shapes my own study?

It is perhaps helpful to think of radical reading as posing two sets of questions: questions to the author and questions put, as it were, 'to myself'. The questions in Figure 5.3 can be used when reading any piece of research literature and offer a distinct and straightforward strategy for making a critical response to what you are reading.

Questions to 'ask' the author ...	Questions to ask myself ...
Why did you write this?	Why am I reading this?
Who did you write this for?	Was it written for 'me'? [Is it helpful to my own study?]
What was your purpose?	What am I looking for?
What questions were you asking?	What questions am I asking? [Of this text; in my own study]
What answers did you find?	Do I find those answers credible?
What is your evidence?	Do I accept that evidence? [Does the evidence support the findings/conclusions?]
What is your conclusion?	Do I agree with those conclusions? [Is there sufficient data and justification for me to make a judgement about the strength of the conclusions?] But above all ...
	What have *I* learned?
	and
	How can *I* use it?

Figure 5.3 Critical reading: some questions

> **Activity 5.3**
>
> With the questions in Figure 5.3 in mind, try reflecting on something you have read recently – a magazine or newspaper article perhaps.
>
> To what extent do you use the strategies for critical reading suggested above to decide on the usefulness of the piece *for your purposes*?

Electronic and digital sources of literature

There has never been such an abundance of resources available to those undertaking academic writing and research. In addition to the well-established academic libraries' 'hard copy' resources there is now a proliferation of web-based literature, with e-books and e-journals being the tip of the literature iceberg. Many archives are digitised and accessible online, and the number of free and open access journals is increasing. It is important to take advantage of such resources and benefit from the variety of Web directories, gateways and other resources.

The development of online academic communities, or academic e-communities, virtual worlds such as Second Life,[1] online see and talk facilities such as Skype,[2] and social networking sites such as *Facebook*[3] or *Twitter*,[4] make it possible for students and researchers to communicate and collaborate with each other across distance and time zones, and to network with the academic community worldwide, thus internationalising research activity in a way which, hitherto, has not been possible for anyone other than those able to afford the time and expense of overseas travel. And the multitude of sites which now provides information about everything comprises an infinite resource. However, it is important not to assume that access is global or universal and, as Markham and Baym (2009: 140) notes, researchers must 'have global sensitivities' when it comes to internet research and issues of access across time, space and cultures. Reading materials, though widely available through electronic sources, are sometimes less accessible to some due to geopolitical and socio-economic reasons. There remain individuals, communities and cultures without internet access, and this may well be a limiting factor in obtaining the wealth of resources not available through the internet.

As with any other source of literature and information, it is important to remain critical about the reliability of sources and to use discussion lists and newsgroups with care, though these too are attracting research interest in their own right. The availability of search engines dedicated to particular topics and the benefits of fast-searched and downloadable documents makes literature searches both easier

---

[1]http://secondlife.com/
[2]http://www.skype.com/
[3]http://www.facebook.com/
[4]http://twitter.com/

and more complex. Literature reviews must now be more thorough, more comprehensive and more international in scope because the availability of resources to university students is now, practically, infinite. Strategies for critical reading need be no different if sources are electronic – it is still important, perhaps more so, to scrutinise the integrity of the source of information, whether it is hard copy or electronic in origin.

Now, we turn to the importance of research questions in the planning of a literature search and writing of a critical literature review.

Using research questions to identify sources for a literature review

The 'Crowsfoot' school questions

In Chapter 2 we showed how our students arrived at Frances' research questions using the Goldilocks test, which helped her to decide on the focus of her research. Similarly, in the case of another student whose focus was inclusion in a secondary school, the research questions were:

1 To what extent do the attitudes of staff affect the inclusion of children with learning difficulties in Crowsfoot School?
2 What steps might be taken to develop more inclusive attitudes and practices at Crowsfoot?

These questions are pivotal in planning a suitably focused *literature search* and in writing a critical *literature review*. One technique for planning a literature search from research questions is to map the key themes on to a Venn diagram. It can help to try to identify three key themes from the research questions in order to develop sufficient focus for the search. The most likely key themes for the Crowsfoot study literature search are: teacher attitudes, inclusive education and learning difficulties. If these are mapped on to the Venn diagram, as in Figure 5.4, the precise focus of the literature search becomes clear. This is the literature which lies in the intersection of the three key themes (marked with the arrow in Figure 5.4).

To plan and write a good literature review necessitates focusing in, from the research questions, to the key themes in the literature and finding what lies at the heart of the study. Focusing in from the *research questions* to identify a small number of *key themes* is a simple but effective strategy for planning the literature search and for making decisions about what to include and what to leave outside the scope of the literature review.

Frances decided that her literature review for her *Hoywell* study had to focus on four main themes: community cohesion, 'race', young people and 'disaffection', education 14–19. Her literature search was not quite so neatly determined as that

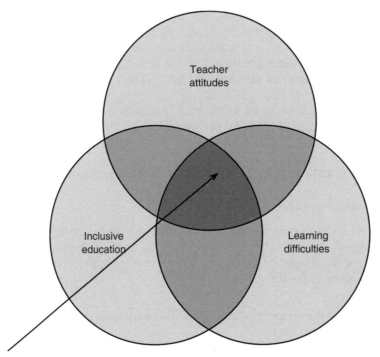

The main focus of the literature search for the Crowsfoot study lies at the intersection of these three key themes

Figure 5.4   Identifying the focus of the Crowsfoot literature search

for the Crowsfoot study but her planning derived from her research questions showed her starting points (Figure 5.5).

Literature and positionality

Finally, in this section, we want to consider the role of the literature in demonstrating positionality. Typically, all research reports (especially those written for award-bearing courses) include some form of literature review. One function of the *critical literature review* is to locate the *positionality* of the research being reported within its field and to identify how that research is *unique*.

One way of positioning oneself in a study is to identify with a particular theory – or a set of theoretical constructs. Silverman's (2001: 78) observation that 'Without a theory, there is nothing to research' is worth attention. There is a word of warning here: it can be tempting to rush headlong into data collection and the excitement of what we might call 'the field', but without a clear appreciation of the theoretical underpinnings of a particular study, little of value will emerge from those data – if they can even be called that, for data are only ever made sensible by the theory which is used to explains them.

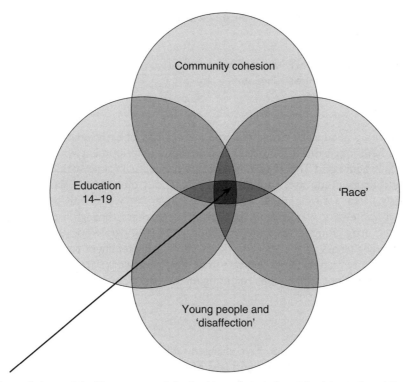

The main focus of the literature search for the Hoywell study lies at the intersection of these four key themes

Figure 5.5   Identifying the focus of the literature search for the Hoywell study

'There is nothing so practical as a good theory' (Lewin, 1951: 169)

Activity 5.4

Using a similar approach to the Crowsfoot and Hoywell studies, use your research questions to try to identify the key themes for your own literature search.

The following extract shows how Hannon and Nutbrown (1997) summarised the literature in their field of study and identified what was *unique* in their own research report. We have included the 'Abstract' so as to give an overview of the whole article and then the 'Introduction' which uses the literature to position the research and its researchers and, in the final sentence, to state the uniqueness of the study being reported.

Teachers' Use of a Conceptual Framework for Early Literacy Education Involving Parents

PETER HANNON & CATHY NUTBROWN
University of Sheffield, United Kingdom

ABSTRACT

Changes in literacy education regarding the importance of early years and the role of parents have implications for teacher professional development which have not yet been fully addressed. This article describes a conceptual framework intended to give early childhood educators a way of thinking about the role of parents in children's early literacy development and how teachers can work with parents. The conceptual framework was offered to a group of teachers through a professional development programme of six seminars. Four sources of data were used to evaluate the meaningfulness of the framework, its perceived usefulness to teachers, and its impact on practice. Findings indicate that the framework largely achieved its intended purposes but some issues requiring further development and investigation are identified.

Introduction

Two aspects of literacy education have changed radically in recent years: first, recognition of the importance of the early stages of children's literacy development, particularly in the pre-school years; and second, acknowledgement of the value of parental involvement, again in particular in the early years. Both have implications for the professional development of early years teachers. In this article we argue that the need is to offer teachers concepts for understanding early literacy development, the parents' role in that development and the teacher's role in relation to the parents. We propose a particular conceptual framework to aid understanding of these issues and report an evaluation of it which involved investigating teachers' views of the framework and studying how it enabled them to develop new practice in early literacy education.

Recognition of the importance of the early stages of children's literacy development has come about as a result of several lines of research. Simple measures of literacy development at school entry (e.g. ability to recognise or form letters, book handling skills) have been shown to be powerful predicators of later attainment – better, arguably, than other measures of ability or oral language development (Wells, 1987; Tizard et al., 1988). Other predictors from as early as 3 years of age include knowledge of nursery rhymes (Maclean et al., 1987) and having favourite books (Weinberger, 1996). The teaching implications of these findings are not straightforward (for it does not follow that concentrating directly on any of these things will, in itself, improve later literacy attainment) but it is at least clear that early literacy experiences of some kind are important. Research has also given us a fuller appreciation of the nature of literacy development in the pre-school period – what Yetta Goodman has termed the 'roots of literacy' which, she argues, often go unnoticed (Goodman, 1980, 1986). Particularly interesting is what children learn from environmental print – a major feature of the print-rich cultures of the Western world – which for some children may be more influential than books. Children's early writing development can also be traced back into the pre-school period, especially if one looks at children's understanding of the function of writing as well as its form (Teale and Sulzby, 1986; Hall, 1987). Other aspects of early literacy development to have been highlighted by researchers include phonological awareness (Goswami and Bryant, 1990), understanding of narrative and story (Meek, 1982; Wells, 1987), and decontextualised talk (Snow, 1991).

Acknowledgement of the value of parental involvement in the teaching of literacy at all ages has also been the result of a large number of research studies (Dickinson, 1994; Hannon, 1995; Wolfendale and Topping, 1996). In the early years, children do not acquire their knowledge of written language unaided – parents and other family members have a central role. A survey by Hannon and James (1990) found parents of pre-school children, across a wide range of families, to be very active in promoting children's literacy. Most would have appreciated support from nursery teachers but did not get it. Some parents go so far as deliberately to teach their children some aspects of literacy (Farquhar et al., 1985; Hall at al., 1989; Hannon and James, 1990). However, although virtually all parents attempt to assist pre-school literacy in some way, they do not all do it in the same way, to the same extent, with the same concept of literacy, or with the same resources (Heath, 1983; Taylor, 1983; Wells, 1987; Taylor and Dorsey-Gaines, 1988; Hannon et al., 1991). Much of the variation in children's early literacy achievement must be due to what parents do, or do not do, at home in the pre-school years.

There is ample encouragement therefore to involve parents in early literacy education, but how that can best be achieved and the implications for teachers' professional development have not been adequately explored (Nutbrown et al., 1991). Part of the problem is that teachers are trained for their role in promoting children's classroom literacy learning. Children's home literacy learning may well be more important but, by its nature, it is usually invisible to schoolteachers, who are not necessarily well equipped conceptually to appreciate its nature or power.

Teachers' concepts of literacy learning have been the subject of several research studies. For example, in adult literacy education there has been research into how teachers' implicit theories structure their classroom practice (Dirkx and Spurgin, 1992). In the school years, studies have also concentrated on teachers' conceptions of classroom instruction and learning (De Ford, 1985; Levande, 1989; Wham, 1993; Guimares and Youngman, 1995). Some authors have noted the significance of children's out-of-school or pre-school learning and explored the implications for how teachers conceptualise what they offer in classrooms (Duffy and Anderson, 1984; Weir, 1989; Cambourne, 1995; Anderson, 1995; Barclay et al., 1995), but there appears to have been little concern for how teachers might influence that

Strands of Early Literacy Development

		Environmental Print	Books	Early Writing	Oral Language
Parents	Opportunities				
Can	Recognition				
Provide	Interaction				
	Model				

Figure 5.6   The ORIM framework (Hannon et al., 2006)

literacy learning through work with parents. In this article we want to consider how a particular conceptual framework might provide the means for teachers to do just that.

(Source: Hannon and Nutbrown, 1997: 405–20).

Note how, having reviewed the literature and positioned their own study within that literature, the authors state in the last two sentences what it is precisely that makes this study unique – what contribution to knowledge this *particular* research study in this *particular* research report is making. The article goes on to explain aspects of early literacy development and the four roles which the authors suggest parents can play in their children's early literacy development: providing *opportunities, recognition, interaction* and a *model* of a literacy user (Hannon and Nutbrown, 1997: 407). They suggest that the various strands of literacy (as identified through the literature review) and the four parents' roles can be combined in a heuristic device which they call the ORIM Framework (Figure 5.6).

Having used the literature to establish a theoretical basis for their ORIM framework (in Figure 5.6) Hannon and Nutbrown (1997) go on to locate the literature they have reviewed in terms of their framework. They map on to the framework the studies they have reviewed (Figure 5.7), thus using the framework to critically review the literature they cite in terms of the home-focused early literacy education. This action provides *evidence* – as a result of *critical reading* and a form of *radical looking* – that most work in the field in which Hannon and Nutbrown were working was more narrowly focused than their own and that some cells in the framework had been largely neglected by researchers. Thus the territory in which Hannon and Nutbrown located their own research was established without ambiguity.

Using another tabular device for critical reflection, Nutbrown (1997) reviewed a number of measures of literacy in terms of her stated desirable characteristics. Having provided an extensive overview of existing measures, she summarised

Strands of Early Literacy Development

		Environmental Print	Books	Early Writing	Oral Language
Families	Opportunities	J	BCDEG HIJKLMN	EFJ	AN?
Can	Recognition	J	EGHIJM N?	EJ	N?
Provide	Interaction	J	BEGH I? JM N	EFJ	A N?
	Model	J	E? HJ	E? HJ	A

Key:
A = Wade (1984); B = Swinson (1985); C = McCormick and Mason (1986); D = Griffiths and Edmonds (1986); E = Lujan et al. (1986); F = Green (1987); G = Edwards (1989); H = Goldsmith and Handel (1990); I = Winter and Rouse (1990); J = Hannon et al. (1991); K = Segel and Freidberg (1991); L = Wade and Moore (1993); M = Arnold and Whitehurst (1994); N = Toomey and Sloane (1994).

Figure 5.7   The ORIM framework: analysis of previous research studies (Hannon and Nutbrown, 1997: 409)

them in tabular form (Figure 5.8) to identify the contribution those particular studies make to the field and – importantly – to demonstrate what was unique about Nutbrown's (1997) own study of the topic.

Critical interpretations of events

So far we have discussed the role of *radical reading* in terms of developing a critical response to literature. Otherwise, and in the actual field, many aspects of research involve 'reading' the research setting as well as reading the literature in the substantive and related fields of enquiry. But what does it mean to take a 'reading' of a research situation? At its simplest level, it involves the researcher in reading – literally – from noticeboards, institution policy documentation, corridors of public buildings and other signs and signals, as well as more subtle data such as body language in interviews or meetings or other interactive settings. The interpretation of silences as well as spoken responses also form part of taking a 'reading' of the setting. Such (in-part) 'intuitive' data is often disregarded but can play a powerful role in forming the researchers' response to work with/in the research setting. Experiences that require an interpretational 'reading' in order to understand the actions and interactions within the situation must also be considered in the forming of research questions and the making of research decisions.

Test	Sets tasks in meaningful context	Covers environmental print	Covers books	Covers writing	Can be repeated	Has scoring system
Jones & Hendrickson 1970	–	♦	–	–	?	–
Clay 1972	–	–	♦	♦	♦	♦
Thackray & Thackray 1974	–	–	*	–	?	–
Downing & Thackray 1976	–	–	*	–	?	–
Ylisto 1977	♦	♦	–	–	?	♦
Brimer & Raban 1979	–	–	*	–	?	♦
Goodman & Altwerger 1981	–	*	*	*	♦	–
Downing et al. 1983	–	*	*	*	♦	♦
Clymer & Barratt 1983	♦	–	*	–	?	♦
Heibert 1983	♦	–	♦	–	?	–
Goodhall 1984	♦	♦	–	–	♦	–
Manchester LEA 1988	♦	–	♦	♦	♦	–
Barrs et al. 1989	♦	–	♦	–	♦	–
Waterland 1989	♦	–	♦	–	♦	–
Sulzby 1990	♦	–	–	♦	♦	♦
Kent LEA 1992	–	–	*	–	♦	♦
LARR 1993	–	*	*	–	♦	♦
Wandsworth 1994	♦	–	*	*	♦	♦
Desforges & Lyndsay 1995	♦	–	*	*	♦	♦
SCAA 1996	♦	–	*	*	♦	♦
Vincent et al.1983	–	–	*	*	♦	♦
Nutbrown 1997	♦	♦	♦	♦	♦	♦

Key:
–   no
*   Minimal coverage
♦   adequate coverage

Figure 5.8   Review of measures of literacy in terms of Nutbrown's desirable characteristics (adapted from Nutbrown, 1997: 68 and 109)

Hurdley (2010) literally 'read' the contents and use by academics of corridors and communal spaces. Her ethnographic study focused on everyday culture in corridors, including the meanings which people re-created in the informality of the corridor space and how her study impacted on their uses of such spaces.

What follows are two examples of writing which emanate from the researcher's 'intuitive' reading of research settings. They are based on data gathered through *radical reading* of each research setting: graffiti, local newspaper reports, postures of staff in meetings, of pupils as they moved around a school, of shop windows, boarded-up buildings, school and community noticeboards, school inspection reports, parents' meetings, the look of the streets, the makes and condition of cars parked locally, the state of the telephone box, the stray dogs roaming the streets. 'Readings' such as these enable a researcher to 'take a reading' of the setting and to compose a written response to that reading.

Activity 5.5   'Taking 'readings' in the field of enquiry

Read the following two examples of research accounts which derive from 'radical readings' of research settings. After your reading try to note down the various things which the researcher 'read' in order to assemble the account.

Example 1

NICK, PAUL AND ME

In one of the Midlands schools we studied, we spent something like 300 days over two years mainly talking to staff within the scope and schedule of the project. Now this school was of great interest: a big (about 2000 students) place fairly downtown in a big city tired with industrial collapse; fitfully tense – in this retrenchment – with a substantial Pakistani community brought so many years ago thousands of miles indifferently as so many operatives; and made slightly famous by local politicians who polarized each other into caricatures of left and right (one Labour councillor described the Tory leader – in his presence – as ''itler wi' knobs on'; this without a smile).

Of a staff of over 140, some eight were employed full time as special educators, mainly supporting children in mainstream classrooms; a further eight worked as language support teachers with the many students whose first tongue was not English. This is by any standard a high proportion of teachers in support-for-access roles.

I shall tell the whole story elsewhere, but in brief there were many mutterings about these support departments, and in particular about the special needs organization; it was falling apart and was becoming friable as its head of department. ...

Few structures held the department together beyond those which organized his own spirit. To be sure, there were timetables, a policy of sorts, schedules for staff to refer children for help. But I insist that these were contingent, mere stuff that routes Nick's energy.

(*Source*: Clough, 1995: 132).

Example 2

I've met my father and his sons in so many Special Schools.

A man I was really frightened of was a miner from Bresswell; he had served in the post-war Army, mainly in Germany, and named his son Klaus in honour and memory, I presume, of a greater life, culture and identity than he enjoyed in this bleak mining village. He had a bayonet over the fireplace. His wife – the mother – had left years before and he had brought Klaus up largely alone with some help from his nearby mother. He was in all respects what would be called, I think, 'a man's man'.

He was five feet eight or so, but broad, and naturally fatty, but strong, too. His face was clearly made to be young – you could see him easily at 20, a sort of Irish look – but had been badly spoiled with hard work, drink and tobacco. ...

My job was to liaise between home and the special school which Klaus attended in respect of his maladjustment. I made my first visit to the house during the half-term holiday in February. Bresswell is low, somehow; there is a severe grid of council estate painted on top of the slight wold of the east Midland. The miners and their families live over the shop: quite beneath the estate is their work, so these are single story bungalows laid out as Coniston Drive, Langdale Close, Bowness Avenue and so on.

I had written – twice – that I was coming, but there was no sign of life when I arrived at 11. The curtains were drawn at all the windows and this was the only bungalow where there was no smoke from the chimney though this was a February morning. I knocked and banged and I would have gone just as the door opened ...

(*Source*: Clough, 1996: 75).

Activity 5.6   Taking 'readings' in the field of enquiry

Try 'reading' your own institution, or your morning bus queue or the supermarket. As you reflect on your 'reading' of the situation think about the following:

What did you 'read'?
What skills and strategies did you use?
What assumptions and responses did you make about what you saw?
How did you make decisions about the meaning of your reading?

The following is an example of such a 'reading':

Tesco Check-outs, Sheffield: 10.15am Saturday 18 March

This is baskets only/max 10 items, but a woman at the front of the queue has 'cheated' by having two baskets! The queue is aware – raised eyebrows, silent tutting – but nobody yet takes this on and there is a brewing anger. She is mid-twenties and very very thin, bleached hair with dark roots showing. One of her baskets has six reduced price chocolate footballs and three (!) green felt hats (St Pat's Day was yesterday.) A Colonel Blimpy-type is seething and looks at me inviting communication or acknowledgement of his seethe but I look away.

My 'reading'/what's going on here?

Rule-making/breaking. Is it gendered? Or something to do with class? Does she know she has broken the rule? If not, etc. ... Interested in my own response to this; probably prejudiced – note I describe her as something of a class stereotype (but would rather take her side than Blimpy's/Express-reader etc!).

Being critical in your own research

This chapter has focused on critical responses to the literature and to the interpretation of research settings. Before we leave the theme of radical reading we want to suggest a final form of critical response to texts and situations in respect of your radical reading of your own research report. While writing your dissertation or thesis, bear in mind the skills of radical reading which you brought to bear on the writing of others and employ these to read your own writing within a critical frame.

Activity 5.7

Try this:

Read the following report of a study of the reasons for the low percentage of men in the early childhood workforce (Cook, 2005). Then consider the critical reflection which one student wrote in response to it.

'It's Not What Men Do': Investigating the Reasons for the Low Number of Men in the Early Childhood Workforce

CLAIRE COOK

Overview

In the summer of 2002, I was working as an Audit and Information Officer for North East Lincolnshire Council's Children's Information Service (CIS). The CIS in North East Lincolnshire is part of the Early Years and Childcare Department and we were given a number of the Early Years Development and Childcare Partnership (EYDCP) targets, set by the Government. A number of these targets centred around implementing the Government's National Childcare Recruitment Campaign at a local level. The CIS then became responsible for promoting careers in early years education, childcare and play-work to potential new recruits.

However, along with all the other EYDCPs throughout the country, we were not simply asked to increase the Early Years and Childcare workforce but also to increase the percentage of under-represented groups in the sector. These under-represented groups included people aged over 40, people from ethnic minority groups, people with disabilities and men. We took the recruitment campaign on board wholeheartedly and organised numerous marketing activities to encourage these under-represented groups to join the workforce. This included organising recruitment fairs, placing advertisements in the local press and on local radio, producing leaflets and information packs and pub-lishing articles in specific magazines and newspapers targeted at these groups.

Although these marketing activities did increase interest from the targeted groups, this interest was short-lived. This was particularly the case with men. At the time of the study, in North East Lincolnshire 2.08% of the staff within the Foundation Stage in the LEA maintained sector and 1.69% of the staff in the Foundation Stage in the private, voluntary and independent sector were men. The proportion of men in the pre-school childcare sector was even lower: 1.4% in group-based settings and 1% with childminders. These low percentages of men were not just a reflection of North East Lincolnshire but were a national concern, with national figures standing at approximately 2.8% of nursery teachers, 2% of day nursery staff, 1% of pre-school playgroup staff and 1% of childminders (DfES 2002). Despite the efforts of North East Lincolnshire CIS to increase the number of men in the early years and childcare workforce, the numbers have not significantly increased since the targets were first set.

Clearly, advertising campaigns targeted at men have little impact on increasing their representation within the Foundation Stage and pre-school childcare workforce. There have to be more deep-rooted reasons for the low numbers of men in the sector, rather than that men have never considered it as a career option. I believed that having more men within the sector was a worthwhile aim to strive for, rather than just another Government target that we must work for. Having more men working with under fives would surely have a massive positive impact on children, parents, the dynamics of the workforce and society at large. So why weren't more men coming forward? Until we knew the true reasons for this we would never make any impact on the statistics. More importantly, children, parents, the workforce, men and society would as a whole continue to be impoverished.

I started to undertake a review of the literature into men working with young children and found evidence to support my belief that having a more balanced workforce would be beneficial for children, the workforce, parents and for society as a whole. The benefits for children included providing a balance of male and female perspectives (Lee 1993), encouraging boys to believe that it is natural for men to care for children (Nilsen and Manum 1998), improving the academic achievements of boys (Gold and Reis 1982) and providing a male role model of long-term presence, reliability and trust (Williams 1998). The benefits to the workforce included promoting a healthy balance in the staff team, providing a challenge for female workers, providing an opportunity for colleagues to learn from different experiences (Men and Childcare Scotland 2000) and providing opportunities for open debate and discussion (Jensen 1996). The benefits for parents included encouraging fathers to come into the nursery and become involved in the education of their child (Jensen 1996, Ghedini et al. 1995). The benefits for society included promoting equality in the labour market (Jensen 1996) and creating a more realistic representation of society for children in the nursery (Cameron, Moss and Owen 1999).

Past research had uncovered four reasons for men not choosing to work with young children. These included career issues (such as pay, status and employment conditions), gender-biased attitudes (including the belief that working with young children is an extension of mothering and is not masculine), fear of discrimination from family, colleges, employers, work colleagues and parents and of false allegations of child abuse. I wanted to find out whether any one of these reasons was stronger than the others resulting in the low number of men in the early childhood workforce. I also wanted to know how each of these reasons related to and affected each other so that a strategy could be found for challenging the causes of the low number of men in the early childhood workforce and for increasing the number of men in the sector. This would enable us to achieve all those benefits for children, the workforce, parents and society and also meet Government targets!

I found that the majority of the previous research into the issue of men working with young children had focused on the views of parents and early childhood workers. I decided to approach my study from a completely different angle and to investigate the views of tomorrow's workforce: our current secondary school pupils in Year 10. I assumed that young people aged fourteen and fifteen would have fairly well developed ideas about what they would like to do once they left school and that if they had negative feelings about working with young children at this age, it would be unlikely that they would choose to undertake childcare or foundation stage teacher training. I also wanted to find out whether young males had gender-biased attitudes towards careers, in particular careers involving young children, whether young males would like to work with young children and their reasons for either wanting to or not wanting to do so. Above all, however, I wanted to know how young people, both male and female, felt about men working with young children and whether there was one reason in particular to account for the low numbers of men in the early childhood workforce.

Methods and methodology

I decided that a questionnaire would be the most appropriate way of obtaining a large amount of quantitative data from a large sample of school pupils relatively quickly and easily. I also felt that the statistical data that a questionnaire would generate would complement the large amount of predominantly qualitative data from previous studies (Cameron, Moss and Owen 1999). I also thought that if young people had negative views about men working with young children, they would be more likely to express these in an anonymous questionnaire, rather than face-to-face with an interviewer or within a focus group. As the project relied solely on the results of the questionnaire, the data was a little inflexible and unsophisticated as it could not clarify the attitudes of the young people any further. The questionnaire consisted of mainly closed questions, including dichotomous questions, multiple choice and Likert rating scales. Closed questions were chosen as the sample was fairly large and as Cohen et al. (2000) argued, the larger the size of the sample, the more structured and closed the questionnaire would be. The benefits of the mainly closed questions in the questionnaire were that they made it fairly easy and quick for the young people to complete, they were simple to score and did not favour those school pupils who were more articulate. However, as Oppenheim (1992) stated, closed questions do not enable the participants to add explanations for their choices and there was the risk that the responses given would not be sufficiently thorough enough or could reflect my own bias.

The questionnaire consisted of eight questions. The pupils were asked to state their gender. Next they were asked to state how seriously they had considered their future career: they were then given a list of 42 careers and asked to select which of these they would be interested in following. These responses were later analysed by investigating whether pupils selected careers traditionally associated with their gender. The pupils were then given the same list of 42 careers and were asked to state whether they felt each one was more suited to a man, a woman or either gender. These responses were also later analysed by investigating whether the pupils had gender-biased attitudes towards careers and, if they did, whether this was towards all careers or specific types of work, such as childcare. The fifth and sixth questions asked the pupils whether they would like to work with children and which age groups they would prefer to work with. They were also asked to give reasons for their answers. The seventh question consisted of a list of 28 statements relating to careers involving young children and/ or men working with young children. These statements covered the four main reasons that have been cited in the literature for the low numbers of men in the workforce. They included both positive and negative statements. The school pupils were asked to rate how strongly they agreed or disagreed with each of the statements. The final two questions gave the school pupils an opportunity to obtain further information on careers involving young children and to receive the results of the study.

All twelve secondary schools within North East Lincolnshire were invited to take part in the study. Three schools actively declined to take part and consequently 895 questionnaires were distributed to the remaining nine schools. This represented 50% of their year 10 pupils. Only three schools actually took part in the study and returned 212 fully completed questionnaires. This represented a 23.7% return rate in terms of the 895 questionnaires that were originally distributed, but a 54.4% response rate from the 390 questionnaires sent to the three schools in the study. These schools covered the range of schools in North East Lincolnshire in terms of their size and the areas served, including the rural nature of the area and reflecting unemployment levels and other measures of disadvantage. The schools were also asked to distribute the questionnaires to an equal number of boys and girls and to pupils of varying abilities and to multi-cultural groups. Therefore, the pupils who took part in the study came from a wide range of social and economic backgrounds.

Findings

The questionnaires produced interesting results in relation to young people's attitudes towards careers but more importantly about young people's attitudes towards men working with young children. The results showed that the female pupils were much more likely to want to work with children than male pupils (66% of female pupils in the study said they would like a career involving young children, compared to a mere 12.5% of male pupils). The questionnaire also showed that more females than males wanted to work with children in all the age groups up to age eleven, but more male than female pupils wanted to work with children over the age of eleven. The main reason female pupils gave for not wanting to work with this age range was concerns over controlling children's behaviour.

Finally, the study showed some very interesting results about why men do not choose to work with young children. The study found that in general both males and females had positive attitudes towards the career issues of work with young children. Although male and female pupils both felt that early childhood careers were more suited to women, they still had a positive attitude towards men who wanted to work in the sector. Also, although slightly more male pupils than females thought that males working with young children would face discrimination, this difference was not found to be statistically significant and discrimination was not seen as a major barrier for men working with young children, for either the male or female pupils. This was also the case for the theory that men are in fear of false allegations of child abuse. No significant difference was found between the male and female pupils on the child protection statements within the questionnaire and on the whole both sets of students had positive attitudes towards them.

In conclusion, the study showed that far more female pupils wanted to work with children and that male and female pupils saw careers involving young children as being a 'natural choice' for women. The study also showed that young males would rather follow a different career as they find children stressful and annoying: they feel they don't have the patience to work with young children and they believe that young children prefer the company of women. However, the study showed clearly that males who do choose to work with young children are not considered to be abnormal in any way by young people, male or female. The study also suggested that certain career issues might have a slight affect on the number of men entering a career in the early childhood sector. These include pay, perceived career opportunities and the low status. The results also suggested that although fear of discrimination is not seen as a major barrier for young males wanting to work with young children, there were slight concerns regarding the discriminatory views that parents of children, colleagues and employers may hold.

Overall the results of the study suggested that attitudes towards men working with young children are changing and that more positive work with schools, colleges and early childhood settings could lead to a higher proportion of men working in the sector in the future. These results imply that professionals should encourage schools and colleges to provide young males with more positive experiences of young children and promote non-discriminatory policies to colleges and early childhood settings. Early childhood professionals also need to lobby central Government to try to increase the salaries of early childhood workers to reflect the immense responsibilities of workers. Professionals also need to raise the profile of the sector and promote all the new career opportunities, including those available through EYDCPs, Sure Start, Neighbourhood Nurseries and Children's Centres.

The main focus of the study

The main focus of the study was to investigate young people's general attitudes towards early childhood careers and, more specifically, towards men working with young children in the pre-school education/childcare sector. It was thought that male pupils would have more negative attitudes towards early childhood careers than females. It was also predicted that out of the four reasons identified for the low number of men in the early childhood workforce, stereotyped gender attitudes would be the most prominent amongst young people.

Attitudes towards working with young children

The study found that 37.7% of the sample wanted a career involving children. When these results were analysed more closely it was found that a massive 66% of the female pupils would like a future career involving children, compared to a mere 12.5% of the male pupils. It was interesting that although there were fewer males than females wanting to work with children, 12.5% was a much higher percentage than the current proportion of men in the workforce.

The reasons the pupils gave for either wanting or not wanting to work with children are illustrated in tables 1 and 2, below.

Table 1 Reasons given by male and female participants for wanting to work with children

Reason	Males	Females
Like children	5.4%	40%
Would like to help children learn	0.9%	11%
Would like to make a difference to a child's life	2.7%	3%
Fun	0.9%	3%
Useful experience when having own children	0%	4%
Can learn from children	0.9%	1%
Total	**10.7%**	**62%**

Table 2   Reasons given by male and female participants for not wanting to work with children

Reason	Males	Females
Want to follow a different career	20.5%	9%
Children are annoying	13.4%	3%
Working with children would be stressful	15.2%	1%
Dislike children	9.8%	5%
Lack of patience	9.8%	4%
Concerns over naughty behaviour	4.5%	6%
Hard work	2.7%	2%
Would put me off having my own children	2.7%	1%
Find it difficult to get on with children	0.9%	1%
Children are messy – changing nappies	0.9%	0%
Don't want to conform to stereotypes	0%	1%
Total	**80.4%**	**33%**

The most common reason for wanting to work with young children was liking children, followed by a desire to want to help children to learn. An interesting finding from this section of the questionnaire was that some of the female participants commented that working with children would be a useful experience when they became parents themselves. These comments, which included 'They are a good experience for you when you have a child of your own' and 'It would give me a head start for when I have a child', support the view that early childhood careers are seen as an extension of mothering.

It was found that male pupils were much more likely to express negative views about young children, whereas female pupils were more likely to have specific concerns over controlling 'naughty' behaviour. Another interesting view from a female participant was that she would not want to conform to stereotypes. She stated 'It is so stereotyped that all women aged fifteen plus want to work with children, just because women are capable of having children.' Other interesting comments included those that implied that working with children might put the participant off having their own children, which was expressed by both male and female pupils. The most common reason cited by male pupils for not wanting to work with children was that they simply wanted to do something else. However, more male pupils than females stated that they found children annoying, or that they believed that a career with children would be stressful, or that they would lack the patience to deal with children. This might suggest that young male pupils do not have enough positive experiences with young children, which engenders negative views.

When the pupils were asked about their views about early childhood careers in terms of the type of work it involved: pay, status, and promotional opportunities, there were small differences between the views of male and female pupils, with females being slightly more positive. However, on the whole both males and females tended to be more positive than negative. This can be seen in Table 3 below. (An average score of 1 denotes a very positive attitude towards early childhood careers and a score of 7 denotes a very negative attitude, with a score of 4 being neither positive nor negative.)

Table 3 shows that male and female pupils tended to have positive attitudes towards early childhood careers. The statements that caused the most negative views were those regarding:

- promotional opportunities (they were more likely to believe that there were few opportunities)
- whether teaching young children is easy (they were more likely to think that it was easy)
- pay (they were more likely to believe that it was not well paid).

The biggest differences between the male and female pupils were about career opportunities, whether nurseries are important and whether teaching young children is about just keeping them safe and happy and not educating them, with the female pupils having a more positive view in each case. These findings support earlier research by Seifert (1984), who argued that men have more complex career aspirations, Penn and McQuail (1997), who found that women are more likely to be content with jobs with poor promotion opportunities, and Moss and Penn (1996), who found that childcare is often perceived as an extension to the care provided by the family, rather than an education service. Although pay scored the most negatively, there was no significant difference between male and female pupils on this issue, which suggests that although all pupils recognise that early childhood careers are lowpaid, females are more willing to accept this (Penn and McQuail 1997).

Table 3   Attitudes of males and females to early childhood careers

Statement	Average male score (mean)	Average female score (mean)	T score (x denotes no significant difference)
There are few opportunities for promotion	4.80	4.81	0.4
You don't need qualifications	3.09	3	0.5
Teaching young children is easier than teaching older children	4.38	4.49	0.5
There are lots of career opportunities	4.07	3.24	0.001
It's about keeping children safe and happy not education	3.66	3.6	0.01
It can be rewarding	2.96	2.43	x
It's hard work	3.02	2.69	x
It's well paid	4.41	4.51	x
It can be challenging	3.05	2.68	x
Nurseries are important	2.58	1.84	0.01
Overall career issue score	**3.60**	**3.32**	x

Gender-biased views

The study found that both the male and female pupils were more likely to believe that careers involving young children were more suited to women than men. As can be seen from Table 4, the early childhood careers that created the most

Table 4   Gender-biased attitudes towards careers involving children and young people

Career	Gender Bias	Males	Females
Nursery Teacher	Suited to a woman	69.6%	65%
	Suited to a man	0.9%	0%
	Suited to either	29.5%	35%
	Don't know	0%	0%
Infant School Teacher	Suited to a woman	55.4%	40%
	Suited to a man	0%	0%
	Suited to either	44.6%	59%
	Don't know	0%	1%
Junior School Teacher	Suited to a woman	20.5%	11%
	Suited to a man	3.6%	0%
	Suited to either	75.9%	88%
	Don't know	0%	1%
Secondary Teacher	Suited to a woman	2.7%	1%
	Suited to a man	10.7%	2%
	Suited to either	85.7%	96%
	Don't know	0.9%	0%
Child Support Assistant/Teacher's Aid/Nursery Assistant	Suited to a woman	69.9%	57%
	Suited to a man	0%	1%
	Suited to either	26.8%	39%
	Don't know	3.6%	3%
Nanny/Nursery Nurse/Childminder	Suited to a woman	92%	84%
	Suited to a man	0.9%	0%
	Suited to either	7.1%	16%
	Don't know	0%	0%
Midwife	Suited to a woman	87.5%	78%
	Suited to a man	3.6%	2%
	Suited to either	8.9%	19%
	Don't know	0%	1%
Health Visitor	Suited to a woman	21.4%	19%
	Suited to a man	1.8%	0%
	Suited to either	69.6%	78%
	Don't know	0.9%	0%
Youth Worker	Suited to a woman	12.5%	10%
	Suited to a man	6.25%	4%
	Suited to either	79.5%	83%
	Don't know	1.8%	3%

gender-biased views were nursery and infant teachers, child support assistants/ nursery assistants, nannies/nursery nurses/childminders and midwives (with the vast majority of participants believing that these jobs were more suitable for women). It was apparent that careers involving young children caused the most gender-biased attitudes, whereas careers involving older children, such as junior and secondary school teachers and youth workers, were more likely to be seen as suitable for either gender.

The small differences between the male and female pupils' scores were not statistically significant.

The pupils' views regarding early childhood careers were further examined for gender bias by analysing their answers to the eight statements on the questionnaire that measured gender-biased attitudes. The results can be seen in Table 5 below.

Table 5   Gender attitudes of males and females towards early childhood careers

Statement	Average male score	Average female score	T score (x denotes no significant difference)
More women than men want to work with young children	6.10	6.02	x
It is natural for a woman to want to work with young children	5.04	4.6	x
Young children prefer the company of women	5.15	4.74	x
Young children can be frightened of men in the nursery	4.10	4.29	x
There should be more men in the nursery so that children have male and female role models	3.19	2.7	x
Men don't have as much knowledge about young children as women	4.12	4.21	0.5
Men who work with young children are not masculine	3.38	3.1	x
Careers with young children are for women	3.76	3.31	x
Overall gender-biased score	**4.35**	**4.12**	**x**

Table 5 shows that although females were less likely to express gender-biased views, this difference was not statistically significant. On average, the views were fairly balanced, without a majority in either direction. Therefore, although the study found that both the male and female pupils thought that careers involving young children were more suited to women than men, on further analysis it was found that males and females had fairly non-gender-biased views about men working with young children. This contradiction shows the complexity of gender attitudes and how they are affected by the question asked. When individual statements were analysed those which evoked the most gender bias were:

- that more women than men want to work with young children (which was in fact a reality)
- that it is natural for women to want to work with young children (supporting earlier finding from Penn and McQuail (1997), who found that female childcare workers perceived their job to be intrinsic to being a woman)
- that young children prefer the company of women (supporting the views of Jefferies (2001), who claimed that children who have only ever experienced women can find it difficult to accept men in their lives).

Interestingly, two statements showed that female pupils had a more negative view than males. These were:

- that men don't have as much knowledge about young children as women (which was a statistically significant difference)
- that young children can be frightened of men in the nursery.

These views support earlier findings by Niva (1996) who found that female childcare workers doubt men's 'natural ability' to look after young children. This could be a potential source of discrimination against men in the early childhood workforce of the future. However, a positive finding was that pupils did not see men who want to work with young children as being 'unnatural', which contradicts evidence provided by Yelland and Grieshaber (1998), who argued that men who work in early childhood settings are not considered normal. This finding was very encouraging as it suggests that although a significantly lower number of men are choosing to work in the early childhood sector than women, men who do choose to work in the sector are not considered to be abnormal.

Fear of discrimination

There were only very small differences between the male and female pupils in terms of whether they thought that men working in the early childhood sector would face discrimination and these were not statistically significant. Fear of discrimination was not found to be a major barrier for men entering early childhood careers: the responses to the discrimination statements on the questionnaire were fairly positive. The individual scores on these statements of both can be seen in Table 6.

Table 6   Attitudes of the male and female pupils to discrimination faced by men working in the early childhood sector

Statement	Average male score (mean)	Average female score (mean)	T score (x denotes no significant difference)
Men who work in nurseries are often made fun of by family and friends	4.05	3.77	x
Parents would rather have women working in the nursery	4.91	4.44	x
Men can feel alone working in a nursery because most of the staff are female	4.60	4.60	0.4
Headteachers and nursery managers would rather have women working in the nursery	4.61	3.98	x
As nursery work has traditionally been a woman's job it should stay that way	3.72	3.00	x
Women feel that men are a threat in nurseries because men are more likely to get the senior positions	3.96	3.5	x
Overall discrimination score	**4.30**	**3.87**	x

Boy pupils were shown to believe that children's parents would be the biggest source of discrimination for male childcare workers which supports anecdotal evidence provided by Wallace (2001), whereas females seemed to believe that female colleagues would be the biggest source of discrimination. The only significant difference between the male and female pupils was discrimination by female colleagues: interestingly, more females agreed with the statement. The mean scores for males and females were the same for this statement, which was due to rounding, which highlights the importance of undertaking statistical tests. The study did not find any hard evidence to suggest that males who want to work with young children would fear discrimination from their own family and friends (contradicting Cameron, Moss and Owen 1999). This reinforces the idea that attitudes are changing and that society is becoming more accepting of men in these roles

Fear of false allegations of child abuse

No significant differences were found between boys and girls on the statements regarding child protection issues around the topic of men working with young children. Both the males and females scored positively on these statements, indicating that most of them disagreed with these statements. The individual scores can be seen in Table 7, below.

Table 7 Attitudes of male and female pupils to men working with young children and child protection

Statement	Average male score (mean)	Average female score (mean)	T score (x denotes no significant difference)
Men should not be left alone with young children in a nursery	2.69	2.2	x
It is unnatural for a man to want to work with children under the age of 5	3.92	3.12	x
Young children's health and safety are at risk if men are present in the nursery	2.84	2.29	x
Men may feel uncomfortable when children need a cuddle or need to go to the toilet	5.14	4.73	x
Overall child protection score	**3.65**	**3.11**	x

The only statement which stood out among this category was the one which mentioned men feeling uncomfortable cuddling children when they were upset or taking them to the toilet, which all pupils tended to agree with to some degree. However, it could be that all the pupils would have felt uncomfortable with these tasks and not just the males. This statement could have been worded more effectively by asking whether males would feel more uncomfortable than females about carrying out personal care for children. I felt that there were not enough statements on the questionnaire regarding child protection. This was because there were concerns that a questionnaire may not have been the most appropriate method for collecting data on such an emotive subject.

The most pertinent reason

Finally, the study investigated whether there were any significant correlations or differences between the four reasons for the low number of men in the early childhood workforce. The average scores for each of the reasons can be seen in Table 8.

Table 8 Average scores for the reasons identified in the literature for the low number of men in the early childhood workforce

Average career issue score (mean)	Average gender attitude score (mean)	Average discrimination score (mean)	Average child protection score (mean)
3.47	4.24	4.10	3.39

Significant positive correlations were found between each of the reasons, which meant that the pupils who had a positive attitude to one of the reasons were more likely to have a positive attitude to the other reasons. This was no surprise, as there is a great overlap between each of the four reasons. Out of the four reasons, stereotyped gender attitudes were found to be the most prominent. However, there was no significant difference between gender attitudes and discrimination, which implies that fear of discrimination is equally prominent. Pupils, however, did not score highly on any of the four reasons. This suggests either that there are other factors to explain the low number of men in the workforce or that the way the data was obtained was not quite sensitive enough to reflect young people's attitudes accurately. Any research undertaken on this topic in future would really need to have a mixture of quantitative and qualitative methods, so that specific issues can be explored in more detail.

Areas for further research

One of the major limitations of this study was that it relied solely on the results of a questionnaire. If further research was undertaken on the views of young people about men working with young children, qualitative methods, such as interviews or focus groups, should be used in addition to a questionnaire.

One major finding was that although far more girls than boys were interested in careers involving young children, and although all the pupils thought that these jobs were more suited to women than men, none of them had negative feelings towards men wanting to work in the sector. Boys were far more likely to want to follow a different career: they found children stressful and annoying, they felt they lacked the patience to work with young children and believed that young children preferred the company of women. This lead to a theory that young males may have not have had enough quality experiences with young children and a suggestion that schools should actively provide all pupils with some positive experience in this field. This could involve work experience in infant or nursery schools or older pupils mentoring and providing support to younger children in the feeder primary schools. This might enable male pupils to discover that they are able to communicate effectively with younger children and that working closely with a young child can be extremely rewarding.

Another suggestion was that all secondary school pupils should receive unbiased careers information positively promoting the early childhood sector which might include experienced male early childhood workers coming to talk about their work.

A future study could collect the views of young males about work with young children, using sensitive research methods such as interviews and focus groups, and discuss the implementation of suggestions from this survey in their schools. The views of male pupils could be measured again after these suggestions had been implemented. These young people could also be monitored to find out which careers/college courses they decide to follow. Maybe this study would need to be longitudinal, as an immediate change may not take place, but it may when pupils have received positive experiences and unbiased information over a number of years.

References

Cameron, C, Moss, P and Owen, C (1999) *Men in the nursery: gender and caring work.* London: Paul Chapman/Sage.

Cohen, L, Lawrence, M and Morrison, K (2000) *Research methods in education: 5th edn.* London: Routledge Falmer.

Department for Education and Skills (DfES) (2002) *Childcare workforce surveys 2001: overview.* London: DfES.

Ghedini, P, Chandler, T, Whalley, M and Moss, P (1995) *Fathers, nurseries and childcare.* Brussels: European Commission Equal Opportunities Unit/EC Childcare Network.

Gold, D and Resis, M (1982) Male teacher effects on young children: A theoretical and empirical consideration, *Sex Roles,* 8(5), 493–513.

Jefferies, T (2001) Why children need more male role models. *Early Years Educator,* 3(4).

Jensen, J J (1996) Men as workers in childcare services: A discussion paper. *European commission network on childcare and other measures to reconcile employment and family responsibilities for women and men.* Brussels: European Commission Equal Opportunities Unit.

Lee, A (1993) Gender and geography, literacy, pedagogy and curriculum. Unpublished PhD thesis. Western Australia: Murdoch University.

Men and Childcare Scotland (2000) Working Paper, January (Online at: http://www.international.mibnett.no/country/scotland/men_and_childcare_scotland.htm).

Moss, P and Penn, H (1996) *Transforming nursery education.* London: Paul Chapman Publishing.

Nilsen, T and Manum, L (1998) Masculine care: the nursery school as a man's workplace. In C. Owen et al. (eds) *Men as workers in services for young children: Issues of a mixed gender workforce.* Bedford Way Papers. London: Institute of Education, University of London.

Niva, L (1996) Professional male child caregivers: A pilot study in the Adelaide metropolitan area. Unpublished paper for the Graduate Diploma in Social Science (Child Development), The Institute of Early Childhood and Family Studies, University of South Australia, Magill, Adelaide.

Oppenheim, A N (1992) *Questionnaire design, interviewing and attitude measurement.* London: Pinter Publishers.

Penn, H and McQuail, S (1997) *Childcare as a gendered occupation, Department for Education and Employment Research Briefs, Research Report No: 23.* London: DfEE.

Seifert, K (1984) Some problems of men in child care centre work. In S Pleck and J Sawyer (eds) *Men and masculinity.* Englewood Cliffs, NJ: Prentice-Hall.

Wallace, W (2001) Men Wanted, *Nursery World,* 24 May.

Williams, F (1998) Troubled masculinities in social policy discourses: Fatherhood. In J Popay, J Hearn and J Edwards (eds) *Men, gender divisions and welfare.* London: Routledge.

Yelland, N and Grieshaber, S (1998) Blurring the edges. In N Yelland (ed.) *Gender in early childhood.* London: Routledge.

(*Source:* Cook, 2005)

Responding to Cook (2005), Marlene, a sociology student interested in gendered responses to employment decisions, wrote:

> Cook (2005) makes a good job of summarising the literature. This is useful to me in my study of gender and career choices. My interest is broader than the childcare field but the overview is useful. The focus of the study is justified, Cook has given a clear statement of why she is focusing on the target group of Y10 pupils as research participants. I'm not sure I agree with this reasoning but it is still apparently justified. The questionnaire method is justified, a biggish sample and fairly factual, broad sweep sort of data which have resulted in some generalisable findings. The analysis is clear, though I would have liked to have been able to dig under the surface of the percentages! (A drawback of using questionnaires). The tables are very clear and highlight the issues – what is also useful to me is the way the analysis of this study comments on other relevant literature.

Activity 5.8

Before you leave this chapter on critical reading, you may wish to consider the points we have discussed in relation to your own work. It may be useful to revisit the 'questions to "ask" the author' in Figure 5.3 and try to respond to them. Respond to them as they relate to a piece of your own writing.

We shall return to the issue of critical research writing in Chapter 8 which focuses on the research report.

Ethics: pause for reflection

We suggest that criticality – 'being critical' – is a matter of ethical practice and that a diligent and thorough critical review of the literature is in itself an ethical act.

Consider the ethical issues at work in the act of radical reading to justify the critical adoption or rejection of knowledge and practices. To what extent is the need for theory in research a matter of ethics?

What are the ethical implications of 'taking readings' from noticeboards and other documentation and events in institutions and public places?

What are the particular ethical implications around researching gender, or age, or 'race', or disability (or any aspect of human difference)?

Criticality – 'being critical' – is an ethical act because it is part of the duty of any academic to demonstrate the earlier work on which his or her study builds. It is important to acknowledge the work that others have done which makes it possible for the academic to embark on his or her present study. This does two things: it recognises the intellectual ownership of others' ideas; and it demonstrates a level of rigour for the basis of the new study. A study without a critical literature review is not an ethical study because it leaves unacknowledged earlier work and fails to build on established work. In the act of *radical reading* it is possible to take issue with, or agree with, literature in the public domain – to ask questions of the authors who have written earlier work and to point up places where such work might be better justified.

Building on exisiting theory is a matter of ethics because, again, it is a demonstration of the frameworks in which new studies are located and an indication of the ideas and positions which underpin and drive new work – making one's theoretical position clear is a matter of ethical report and a facet of practical research design.

When it comes to taking data from the workplaces (or other public or restricted spaces) the ethics of this is a matter for debate. Researchers who plan to engage in copying or photographing the surroundings of others need to consider the extent to which they are open about their study – or whether they are engaging in a level of covert research. Whichever it is, there is still a need for permission from an Ethical Review Committee to carry out the study, and sensitivities to the rights of others and to the moral integrity of the findings of the study must surely still apply.

When a researcher focuses on issues around what might divide people or focuses on difference and difficulty, the particular ethical implications need to be considered, with high sensitivity regarding the intention to affect the situation for good, and remembering the rubric that one should 'do no harm'. Focusing on difference, and with sensitivities, can support cohesion and understanding. The main ethical issues remain the same, whatever the focus.

CHAPTER SUMMARY

In this chapter we have:

- *Defined and demonstrated our view of radical reading in research and argued the importance of radical reading in the research process*
- *Outlined the place of criticality in radical reading of texts and practices*
- *Discussed how research questions can be used to define and refine the focus of a literature search*
- *Demonstrated, through two examples of research, different dimensions of 'radical reading'*
- *Drawn together the practices of radical reading of the texts of others with the need to adopt such a response to your own research writing*
- *Reflected on the ethical issues arising from the chapter contents*

FURTHER READING

Hart, C. (1998) *Doing a Literature Review: Releasing the Social Science Research Imagination.* London: Sage/The Open University.

>   Contains useful ideas and strategies for planning and carrying out a literature search.

Hart, C. (2001) *Doing a Literature Review: A Comprehensive Guide to the Social Sciences.* London: Sage/The Open University.

>   Contains useful guidance on designing and developing a literature review.

Pink, S. (2006) *Doing Visual Ethnography.* London: Sage.

>   This book offers a critical response to the 'visual' research methods with some suggestions about analysis and the ethical considerations of visual research – usful for taking 'visual readings'.

Pink, S. (2006) *Doing Sensory Ethnography.* London: Sage.

>   The companion to *Doing Visual Ethnography,* this book provides a further view on 'taking readings', using all the senses to 'read' and understand situations.

6 Questioning: The Focus of Research

CHAPTER CONTENTS

Introduction   140
Asking questions   140
How to ask – issues of method: using interviews and questionnaires   140
Future research questions   169
Ethics: pause for reflection   170

LEARNING OBJECTIVES

By studying and doing the activities in this chapter you will:

- consolidate work covered in Chapter 2
- reflect on several examples of research involving interviewing and questionnaires
- be able to write a critical response to a section of a research report (which justifies the use of a questionnaire survey)
- have an understanding of the multilayered functions of questions and questioning in research studies
- have an awareness of the importance of stating future research questions.

Introduction

> *Radical questioning* reveals not only gaps in knowledge but why and how answers might be morally and politically necessitated. *Radical questioning* lies at the heart of a research study, and brings together the earlier notions of *radically attending* to a topic or situation of events.

In this chapter we shall develop further the idea, introduced in Chapter 2, of *radical questioning*. We shall first reflect on issues already raised in earlier parts of the book in relation to research questions before we move on to discuss the questioning tools often used to collect data – interviews and questionnaires. We follow this discussion with some examples from our own work and from work by students to demonstrate the use of interviews and questionnaires in the context of the research questions they address. We also note the importance of concluding a research report with a statement of any further research questions which have arisen from the study.

Asking questions

In this chapter we emphasise the multilayered functions of questions and questioning in research studies; from the generation of research questions, to the decision to ask questions of research participants, to the devising of interview or questionnaire schedules, to questions about the researcher him or herself and the motivation for undertaking the study. In Chapter 2 we suggested that research methodology involves at least four kinds of questions: self-questioning, research questions, field questions and ethical questions. In this chapter we further discuss the functions of these four kinds of questions. As you will have noted from your reading of earlier chapters, the most important question is 'why?': *Why* this topic? *Why* this method? *Why* this setting? *Why* these participants? *Why* this question? These are central questions of *justification* and our reason for investing in *radical questioning* the moral and political roots of research studies.

How to ask – issues of method: using interviews and questionnaires

In this section we focus on two of the most popular methods for collecting data from research participants: interviews and questionnaires. We shall raise a number of questions to help you to clarify your use of these methods if you choose to use them in your own study.

Interviews

> Asking questions and getting answers is a much harder task than it may seem at first. The spoken or written word has always a residue of ambiguity, no matter how carefully we report or code the answers. Yet interviewing is one of the most common and powerful ways in which we try to understand our fellow human beings. (Fontana and Frey, 2000: 645)

The first question to ask when considering using interviews to gather data is whether this is the best method for your purposes. You need to think about the kind of data you want, and how much you want to control the interview. You need to decide whether you want to structure the interview so that you set the agenda, whether you simply want to listen to the interviewee's ideas on a particular issue or topic, or whether you want a bit of both. You will also need to decide whether you carry out the interviews face to face, by telephone, using web-cam or other internet communication methods, such as Skype, and whether interviews take place with individuals or in a group. In the example we shall look at later, participants preferred to be interviewed using their usual form of communication via internet chatrooms or email. This is becoming an increasingly popular method of interviewing and results in a script which does not need to be transcribed, although, as we shall see, there is still a need for some element of 'translation' or 'interpretation'. Answers to these questions will influence your later research decisions.

For example, let us imagine that you want to find out about people's use of social networking sites. You would need to consider a number of questions. You will need to decide who you are going to interview – this itself generating a number of questions:

- Who to interview – anyone who uses social networking sites or a particular group?
- How many interviewees?
- Which social networking sites fit into your study?
- Do age, profession, gender, social class influence your ideas of the sample?
- Will you interview people who don't use social networking sites?
- Will you choose people from a particular place or region or from anywhere in the world?
- Will participants be volunteers?
- Will you choose participants from a range of cultural and racial groups? How will you know and decide?
- Will you interview male and female participants or one gender group?
- Will you have upper and lower age limits?
- How will the interviews be conducted? Via the site? By email? By webcam/Skype? By post? Face to face?

As you can see, the questions could be endless but, whatever you decide, you need to be able to provide a rationale for those decisions. They must be explained and justified. For example, whether you decide to interview three people in depth and at length or, say, 50 people chosen at random very briefly, you must say *why* you made those choices and *how* you selected them for interview.

Then there are more questions:

- Should you produce a list of specific questions?
- Should you simply begin by turning on a recorder and saying, 'Could you tell me about your use of social networking sites?'
- Should you devise an interview schedule which includes some very open questions, such as 'What are your thoughts on the use of social networking sites?', and more closed questions, such as 'How much time each day do you spend on social networking sites?' and 'What do you use social networking sites for?'

These and many other questions, and their resolution, will depend on the reason for your carrying out the study, your research question or questions, and the extent to which you want the ideas of research participants to emerge from the study and influence its direction.

It is always good practice to pilot your interview ideas first with a small number of people who are similar to your sample. Try out your equipment, your technique, your questions and your ability to probe further, and then ask the pilot interviewees to tell you how the interview felt for them, whether they understood the questions, whether you could have done anything else to obtain better data and put them at their ease if they are nervous or anxious for any reason. It is important to remember that the actual interview can generate a large amount of data so you will need to consider how you will handle this.

Audio or video recording is by far the best way to record interview data – relying solely on handwritten notes inevitably means that some comments are lost. If you audio-record, or make a digital web recording of your interviews (this is by far the best way to obtain the actual words interviewees have used), you may find that a recording of a 45-minute interview takes several hours to transcribe! Few students have the facility of transcription services to convert audio or film recordings to a 'word' transcript, so it will be important to think about how you will extract responses from a digital recording and how you will use the data collected. Collecting data is one challenge but (as we see in Chapter 7) making sense of the growing amount of data is often the greater challenge!

The equipment needed to record a telephone interview is easily obtainable and relatively inexpensive; and web-based interviews are becoming very popular with people who already use such technology socially. Web technologies make it possible to interview people who live some distance away without the expense of travel. You must tell interviewees that you are recording them.

In some senses, research using the internet demands no different ethical integrity than face-to-face research. Issues of informed consent, safety, protection and well-being equally apply. So too, is the importance of confidentiality, anonymity and faithfulness in interpretation and reporting. However, because of the nature of the data which can be collected, and the potential for misuse, the integrity of the researcher and the scrupulous protection of those who use the internet to communicate is all the more important.

Sveningsson (2009) considers issues of privacy in qualitative internet research and argues that it is highly problematic for researchers to regard information which is accessible to the public – available on the internet – as a 'public place' (2009: 78). She suggests that:

> We have to consider not only whether the places we wish to study are public or private but also if the content of the communication is public or private. This consideration begins with the seemingly simple question: What kind of content can be considered public enough to be studied without informed consent? (2009: 80)

Whatever method is chosen to interview, there are decisions which need to be made and, importantly, carefully justified.

Activity 6.1   Thinking about your interviewees – justifying decisions

Imagine you are planning a project which involves you interviewing young people about their use of social networking sites. Consider how you would plan and conduct the interviews with the young people.
You may need to ask yourself a series of questions such as:

- What do I mean by the term 'young people'?
- Do I interview young people in small groups – hold a kind of focus group?
- Do I interview young people together or separately?
- Am I interested in becoming part of any conversations held through social networking sites myself?
- How many young people should I interview?
- Where should I interview the young people? Should I interview them online?
- What should I ask the young people?
- What assurances can I give about confidentiality, anonymity, safety, and so on?

Write about 250 words which list the questions you need to ask yourself and how you would resolve them. Make sure you know *why* you make the decisions you do. For example, why would you decide to interview, say, six young people instead of 25 or 100? This is an important element of methodology. It is an exercise in the justification of your research decisions.

The following is an example of a student response to Activity 6.1.

What I want to understand more about is the way young women (13–15) use the internet for social communication and what their main uses and practices are. This interests me because I teach in a comprehensive school and the girls seem so clued up on web technology. Sometimes their web chats, or the consequences of them, spill over into the classroom. I'd really like an insight into what they do, how they use *Facebook*, the kinds of protocols they have (if any), what sorts of 'unwritten rules' they create and adhere to. I want to run a short 'finding out' sort of pilot survey with a few girls and then perhaps look in more detail at some of the issues that come out of the survey. I'll try talking to three or four girls first of all, and use that as a way of finding out the best ways to investigate my topic. I'll draw on my own social use of *Facebook*, though I suspect that my uses and practices are different.

The researcher identified people willing to be involved in a pilot survey. She then sent the following questions to the participants by email, after some online face-to-face discussion of what was involved, how the data would be used, confidentiality, etc. The email looked like this:

@   Hi
Thank you for agreeing to answer a few questions about how you use the www to get information and to chat with your friends.
Please reply, by email to the questions below.
Thanks
Oh, and would you let me know what name you would like me to use instead of your real one? Thanks
Here goes!

1 What sort of technology do you have, e.g. laptop, web cam etc.?
2 Do most of your friends have this sort of technology at home?
3 Where/how did you learn how to use web-based communication systems? School? Home?
4 Do you use email, private internet chatrooms, what else?????
5 What sorts of things do you use internet chatrooms for?
6 How often would you say you use them?
7 Do you use chatrooms or Facebook to sort out school work or do internet searches for school work?
8 What kinds of things do you search for on the www?
9 Do you think a web cam is a good idea?
10 Do you think your personality can really come through to people when you talk on the internet or is it better meeting them face to face in person?
11 Have you ever experienced anything worrying when using social network sites or other www facilities?

12 Are you willing to tell me the kinds of things you chat about on the www?

Anything else you'd like to tell me?

Thanks

Following the responses, a further email was sent with two follow-up questions:

@   Hi

Thanks for answering me so quickly.

Would you answer two more questions for me please?

Do you ever worry that other people could see what you are writing or see your web cam conversation?

How do you know that the person you are talking to really is the person you think they are?

Thanks

This email exchange produced useful responses and also indicated the appropriateness of the form of data collection for the participant. The following extract from the data (which we shall see more of later) shows how the 14-year-old female respondent chose to write in txt/email/chatroom style which she used online with her friends:

@   **8 What kinds of things do you search for on the www?**

8 WWW thts a funny way of putting it lol i search for websites of bands i like, and anything i want to find out. also i look for film websites and just generally things im interested in. songs lyrics, free song downloads, record labels of bands, guitar/bass tabs...and then theres random stuff i search for thts just a thing of the moment thing. lol

9 Do you think a web cam is a good idea?

9 Yh its reli gd. you can see who it is, if its someone you met on the internet, or a friends friend. you can also have a laff wen on web cam. me and my best mate just do daft things on web cam. were always in hysterics. you can also c a persons emotions so you sorta no how theyre feelin.

Such a pilot can help to develop the best way of collecting data, provide insights into refining questions and point to issues that may arise in coding, interpreting and reporting the data as well as identify ethical issues which will need to be addressed. Davies' (2004, 2006) research into young people's use of online spaces shows how young women used such spaces for informal learning and to negotiate gender identities and femininities.

Devising interview questions

Having made those crucial research decisions about whether to interview and whom, the task then is to devise the interview questions and make decisions about the style and tone of the interview. We can best discuss this through a recent example of our own work. We interviewed five teachers who were working in schools using the *Index for Inclusion* (Booth et al., 2000).

The first set of interviews was carried out face to face; the second set of interviews – following up the experience some 14 months later – was done by telephone using the schedule in Figure 6.1. The questions are fairly open and were designed to elicit teachers' responses, asking them to address the issues on which we were trying to focus. The teachers were sent the interview schedule beforehand so that they were familiar with the questions and could, if they wished, prepare their responses. The schedule *guided* the interview but did not *dictate* the path. That is to say, if there were other issues the teachers wanted to raise they were encouraged to do so. (This decision relates to the discussion on 'voice' in Chapter 4.) Data collection for this small study took some eight hours in total, but it took an experienced secretary using a transcribing machine more than 30 hours to produce transcripts of all five telephone interviews. Transcripts were then sent to the interviewees for amendment before we began any analysis. Figure 6.1 shows our interview schedule, the bold headings being the categories we planned to adopt at the first level of analysis. We will turn to the final report of this piece of research later in this chapter but first we want to focus on the questions themselves.

Activity 6.2

We wanted to find out about the personal experiences of people using the *Index for Inclusion*; the impact on their work and on their thinking. We needed short prompts to make sure that we did not forget important things during the telephone calls. We also needed space to make brief notes as the interview proceeded. Look through the questions in the interview schedule.

Do you think the questions were likely to generate the data we needed? What about the introductory words and the closing statement?

If you use interviews, think about the design of your own interview schedule. Do the questions you ask help you to respond to your research questions? Does the schedule itself enable you to conduct the interview (whether by telephone or face to face) appropriately?

Make some notes in your research journal of the things you need to remember when you are designing an interview schedule.

Interviewing, as with any research method, takes practice. All researchers have to find their own style and their own approach to interviewing, and this will vary from researcher to researcher, and will sometimes be dependant upon the nature of the study and the ages and dispositions of the participants. The following hints may be helpful.

Name..

School...

Telephone number...

Email...

Date of interview..

[name] ... thanks for agreeing to talk to us again. As you know we're interested in what has happened in your school since you've been using the Index for Inclusion. There are just five questions, and perhaps there may be other things you want to add. So shall we begin with the first? I'll jot down some notes while we're talking but I'll also record the interview, so I'll turn on the recorder now, OK? Let's begin.

1   **You first saw the Index for Inclusion when it was launched in March 2000. What were your first impressions of the Index?**

2   **Now you've been working with it for 14 months. Did the Index change your practice?**

3   **What about other changes? Did using the Index change your thinking?**

4   **In the time you've been using it: what have you learned by working with the Index?**

5   **My last question: would you recommend the Index to other early childhood education settings?**

Thanks, [name] is there anything else you want to say about the *Index*, or working with it?

We really appreciate your help with this study. We will send you the transcript in the next week.

Figure 6.1   Interview schedule: Index for Inclusion (Nutbrown and Clough, 2002)

Interviewing: some hints

- Do your interview questions help you to respond to your research questions?
- Have you carried out a pilot run of your interview schedule?
- Make sure the questions are clear.
- Generating data can be easy. Be sure you can handle it all!
- Get parents' permission to interview children as well as permission from the young participants themselves.
- Give people time to respond – don't rush.
- Make it easy for interviewees to respond.
- Listen.
- Make audio or visual recordings of your interviews.
- Test your equipment before each interview.
- Think about the arrangement of the room and seating for face-to-face interviews – make sure interviewees feel comfortable.
- Make 'at a distance'/web-based interviews as comfortable as possible for the participants.
- Give your interviewees the opportunity to choose the time and location for interviews, but be aware that busy places can result in poor quality audio recordings and can be distracting for you and your interviewees – and difficult to transcribe.
- Tell participants why you are interviewing them.
- Explain what will happen to the recordings and transcripts – how they will be stored, used, made public and (ultimately) disposed of.

What do I do when I've done my interviews?

Once you have carried out your interviews you have a wealth of data which you must process and analyse. In fact, you must generate another set of questions with which to interrogate the data. There are many ways to do this but, however you approach the task, you need to ensure that you are remaining true to the voices of the research participants and developing responses to your research questions. You will need to become familiar with your interview recordings, transcripts and notes, get a 'feel' for the data and perhaps create an overview of what people have told you – your 'impressions' and 'intuitions' (we shall return to this theme in Chapter 7).

You will perhaps want to draw together comments on a particular theme, or you may wish to collate the very different responses to the same question. You may want to use a quantitative approach to analyse some of the data, counting up how many people said 'x' or how many said 'y', though of course this will depend on the research questions and on the number of people in your sample. Quantitative responses to the data in our study (Nutbrown and Clough, 2002) would be quite inappropriate for two reasons: the small sample and the focus of the research. If you do decide to carry out some quantitative analysis, there are now a number of computer packages you can use. This may or may not be a useful way to proceed if it suits your study. You may be able to add up the various responses yourself and draw meaning from it without the use of a statistical package. You will find helpful suggestions in the chapter on Interviews by Cohen, Manion and Morrison (2011: Ch. 21).

Interviewing: an example

One of the best ways to learn about the appropriate use of various methods is to read journal articles which report research carried out using the methods in which you are interested. We have included here a short article we wrote in 2002, which uses interview data collected both in person and using the telephone. We suggest that you first read the article and then try the activity that follows it.

'The Index for Inclusion:
Personal perspectives from early years educators', *Early Education*, January 2002

Cathy Nutbrown and Peter Clough
The University of Sheffield, School of Education

> *Respectful educators will include all children; not just children who are easy to work with, obliging, endearing, clean, pretty, articulate, capable, but every child – respecting them for who they are, respecting their language, their culture, their history, their family, their abilities, their needs, their name, their ways and their very essence.*

(Nutbrown 1996, p. 54)

The *Index for Inclusion* was launched in March 2000 and a copy was issued to every State school in England. Developed by eminent leaders in the field of inclusion, the *Index* maps out a process designed to lead to radical change through the development of learning and participation of all involved in the life of a school (Booth et al. 2000). For some schools the *Index* has proved to be precisely the tool for development which they were seeking, whilst for others it has become just another ring-binder housed on a shelf full of such ring-binders: full of good ideas, viewed with good intentions, 'if only we had the time'.

Arising from a number of research projects during the last two years, we have become very interested in the reaction of early childhood professionals to the *Index* and how it influenced their personal responses to issues of inclusion. In this article we draw on interviews with five early years practitioners to examine the concept of Inclusion in general and their response to the *Index* in particular. We interviewed five practitioners in March 2000 and again (fourteen months later) in July 2001 after they had used the *Index*. This is a small study which focuses on the *experience* of participants, thus uncovering those personal reflections which, though they often inform the outcomes of larger evaluations, are less frequently reported. We are seeking here not to evaluate the *Index for Inclusion*, but rather to report the experience of a small number of people who have worked with it.

Why are we talking about 'inclusion'?

Constructions of difference and difficulty

It has been argued that Early Education at its best *is* Inclusive Education (Nutbrown 1998), because it is often the experience of those who work within the Foundation Stage that children with learning difficulties and/or disabilities are included *as a first option*. In such settings we would argue that Inclusion is as much about *attitude* as it is about *response*. Educators, managers of settings and parents (among others) make decisions about children and their difficulties, and behind every decision made in response to an instance of educational difficulty, there lie traditions of practice that more or less evidently affect outcomes. As Herbert demonstrates in the case of Steven:

> *'This was the first time in her short career that Steven's reception class teacher had had a child with a statement in her class. She was conscious that by choosing the inclusive option Steven's parents had accepted that he needed to interact with his peer group and not become, once more, dependent upon adults. She was reassured by the head that it was not a scenario of 'success or failure' and was given support to evaluate her own practice in a way which led her to believe that her established skills of providing a well structured and stimulating learning environment for all children were particularly relevant for Steven. She realised that it was her duty to attend not only to what was 'special' about Steven but also to what was 'ordinary' and that there was no mystique to analysing tasks. She was already doing this and making them accessible to all children, including children with learning difficulties.'*

(Herbert 1998, p. 103)

The decisions made by parents and teachers in the case discussed above by Herbert pointed to an outcome of *inclusive* practice. How an individual educator, an early years setting, a local authority or service *constructs* both a problem and its solution is determined by their characteristic habits of interpretation. In the example above, Herbert draws attention to the transferable skills of a teacher of five-year-olds to 'analyse skills' and present learning situations to children in ways which fit their own individual needs. It goes without saying that other interpretations may well be made, dependent upon experience and upon cultural determinants.

Roots of inclusion: routes to inclusion

It is worth taking a moment to consider how we have come to use the term 'Inclusion' and to explore the roots of our present policy response to the education of young children with a variety of curricular, physical, emotional and social needs.

Inclusive ideology and practice has emerged – in only 50 years – from within a situation of statutory, categorical exclusion. *Special education itself has been transformed from the outside* by civilising forces which have deconstructed and reconstructed its meanings and effects. The move – from segregated Special Education in special schools, to Integration and the development of 'units' within schools, to Inclusion of pupils in 'mainstream' settings – has been fuelled by the various ideologies and perspectives which marked their 'moments' in history (Clough 1998). It is possible to sketch out a rough history of the development of inclusive education which identifies five major perspectives (Figure 1). Though never wholly exclusive of each other, they demonstrate historical influences which shape, in part, current views and practices.

By looking 'back' through the disability studies critique of the 1990s at influences of the psycho-medical model, the sociological response, curricular approaches and school improvement measures, it is possible to look *forward* to the emergence of a more homogeneous response to inclusive education where individual children's *rights* to inclusive education (as well as *needs for* individually appropriate education) are at centre stage *from the start of their educational career*. Looking back we can see how tests, labels and deficits dominated the identification of children's learning needs – a legacy from the psycho-medical model dominant in the 50s. As Sebba and Sachdev (1997) point out, educational 'labels' rather than categorisation 'labels' (for example: 'reading difficulties' rather than 'Down's Syndrome') lead to more inclusive responses to children's learning needs. In the move towards inclusive education, recent developments have hinted at a convergence of thinking about inclusion and about how best this can be achieved. The *Index for Inclusion* is one example of such convergence, an outcome of a particularly fruitful collaboration which is designed to help schools understand what they *mean* by inclusion as well as to identify their inclusive practices and blocks to those practices.

The psycho-medical legacy (1950s →)
This is understood as the system of broadly medicalised ideas which essentially saw the *individual* as being somehow 'in deficit' and in turn assumed a need for a 'special' education for those individuals.

The sociological response (1960s →)
This position broadly represents the critique of the 'psycho-medical legacy', and draws attention to a social *construction* of special educational needs.

Curricular approaches (1970s →)
Such approaches emphasise the role of the *curriculum* in both meeting – and, for some writers, effectively *creating* – learning difficulties.

School improvement strategies (1980s →)
This movement emphasises the importance of systematic organisation in pursuit of truly *comprehensive* schooling.

Disability studies critique (1990s →)
These perspectives, often from 'outside' education, elaborate an overtly political response to the exclusionary effects of the psycho-medical model.

Figure 1   Five key perspectives on educational inclusion (Clough 2000, p. 8)

Perspectives on inclusion

From the 'academy'...

> Some continue to want to make inclusion primarily about 'special needs education'
> or the inclusion in education of children and young people with impairments but that
> position seems absurd. ... If inclusion is about the development of comprehensive
> community education and about prioritising community over individualism beyond
> education, then the history of inclusion is the history of these struggles for an
> education system which serves the interests of communities and which does not
> exclude anyone within those communities.

(Booth 2000, p. 64)

Tony Booth's position here, then, is that inclusive education is about education for *all*
members of the community – all minority and oppressed groups. From this broad
definition of inclusion it could be argued that *Sure Start* initiatives and *Early Excellence
Centres* are – in effect – projects of Inclusion in the Early Years.

From practitioners...

We asked five early childhood educators what they meant by the term *inclusion*. Here
they talk about their own understanding of inclusion and what their settings do to
develop inclusive practice.

It's about letting children with Special Educational Needs come to the school in their
neighbourhood. I think that's right, but it doesn't always work out.

Kay
Nursery Nurse
Nursery Centre 2–5 years

It's political. It's about social justice – giving every child the right to an education in their
own community – which enables them to reach their full potential. For me, that means
doing a lot of work to make sure that the staff here is aware – but also arguing for
resources. Managing that is a challenge. The greatest need is for personal awareness –
so I need money for staff development – installing ramps is easy – changing attitudes –
challenging prejudice – that's the real issue of inclusion – it is a huge issue.

Sue
Head Teacher
School 3–10 years

Well, I think inclusion is really about equality. About not shutting children out. If children are kept out of the system at this stage they'll always be different – seen as different. It's easy to say that though – not always so easy to include children, especially

some who are very disruptive. Children with disabilities aren't a problem – I don't worry about them – they usually fit in well – toilets are a problem sometimes but we get round that! It's children who can't behave – can't fit into the group – mess up the equipment, slop paint everywhere – throw things – bite – I tear my hair out over them. They're the ones that are in danger of exclusion and being separated off at 5 years old – that's terrible isn't it? But I can't help it – I have to survive, and I have to think about the rest of the children.

Helen
Reception Class Teacher
School 3–7 years

A lovely idea – inclusion – and when it's good, it's great! I have been able to have children in the nursery with Down's Syndrome and children with various emotional difficulties – abused children – but when they (the LEA) asked us to take in a child with Autism, well, we had to say 'no'. Too risky – I was frightened that if we did something terrible would happen and it would be my responsibility. So yes, lovely idea, but it really is an ideal that will never be achieved – total inclusion is impossible.

Janie
Nursery Teacher
School 3–10 years

I spend my life arguing for extra support for children with SEN who we're trying to keep in our school rather than send them to 'Special'. Inclusion of all children in the community would be so much easier if it were the norm – the first resort – that's usually the case in the nursery, but as children go on into school that philosophy seems to fade and the first move seems to be 'how can I get rid of this one'.

Pauline
SENCO
School 3–10 years

So, how typical are these voices on inclusion? To what extent can the political ideal of social justice be realised in practice in the early years of education? How far are these *ideals of equity* and *fears of risk* shared by early childhood educators generally? A recently published 'snapshot of practice' includes many examples of work with children with special educational needs in the early years (Wolfendale 2000). This collection demonstrates the diversity of experience and attitude towards *needs* and to the concept of *inclusion*. Wolfendale presents many positive accounts of including young children with identified learning needs in nurseries or other early education settings; but there is another side to the coin – as our interviewees alert. The failure of inclusion hurts. Nutbrown (1998) gives an account of a nursery teacher who, reluctantly, tried to include a child with Autism into her nursery. Things went badly wrong because of endemic difficulties within the setting itself:

Martin was admitted to a nursery full of children with damage and dislocation in their lives – physical and sexual abuse, overwhelming poverty, disproportionate ill-health, numerous wet beds, and no end of broken hearts.

Martin stayed for two weeks. Each day his teacher talked with his mother. Each day she told her what Martin had enjoyed, and of the struggle he had with his peers in the nursery. There were many troubled children in Martin's company, and though Martin was interested, bright and he was able, the nursery disabled him. In that setting he was not being included in a calm, ordered society. He was not a member of a predictable community, he was appended into a community of children and adults in chaos.

After two weeks Martin left. His teacher hoped he had not been harmed, but she knew the harm it had caused his mother. Martin went to a nursery a few miles away which had a special unit for children with special educational needs and which worked to include children from that unit into mainstream classes once they had become established in the school community.

(Nutbrown 1998, p. 170)

Martin's story is a warning that early years settings must be fit to include, and educators equipped with appropriate professional development and management support. Berry's (2001) study of four children indicates that inclusion *can* work for some children and the factors for success depend upon the children's responses as well as those of educators and parents and on the ability of the adults so involved to listen, really listen, to the children's voices.

How do we know inclusion when we see it?

The *Index for Inclusion* is a tool for school development. It is summarised as follows:

The *Index* is a set of materials to guide schools through a process of inclusive school development. It is about building supportive communities which foster high achievement for all students. The process of using the *Index* is itself designed to contribute to the inclusive development of schools. It encourages staff to share and build on existing knowledge and assists them in a detailed examination of the possibilities for increasing learning and participation for all their students.

The *Index* involves a process of school self-review on three dimensions concerned with inclusive school cultures, policies and practices. The process entails progression through a series of school development phases. These start with the establishing of a co-ordinating group. This group works with staff, governors, students and parents/carers to examine all aspects of the school, identifying barriers to learning and sustaining and reviewing progress. The investigation is supported by a detailed set of indicators and questions which require schools to engage in a deep, and challenging exploration of their present position and the possibilities for moving towards greater inclusion.

(Booth et al. 2000, p. 2)

So, the *Index* is intended to enable schools to 'sample' their cultures, policies and practices to see how they measure up to the view of inclusion articulated above by Tony Booth, a view which embraces inclusion of *all*, and addresses aspects of gender, class, race, religion, sexuality, social class as much as learning difficulty or disability.

Of course, we know from our research that some early childhood settings and providers have not encountered the *Index*. Because of the diversity of provision, some – non-school – settings may well have missed the launch of the *Index* and have not (as yet) been able to work with it, or judge its usefulness to their setting. The *Index* is not 'just' about SEN and is distinct from statutory frameworks and structures such as the SEN code of Practice 2001 (see Roffey 2001 for discussion of the legal context).

Using the *Index for Inclusion*

Some Local Education Authorities and some schools have used the *Index for Inclusion* to great effect as an instrument of school change (Clough and Corbett 2000). But we were interested in how the *Index* made a difference to individual professional responses to inclusion; we wanted to know whether using the *Index* affected the personal 'routes to inclusion' of early childhood educators. After they had used the *Index* in their own schools and centres we returned to the five early years practitioners and asked them to reflect on their experience, and to talk about their own learning. We asked them five questions:

1 What were your first impressions of the *Index*?
2 Did the *Index* change your practice?
3 Did using the *Index* change your thinking?
4 What have you learned by working with the *Index*?
5 Would you recommend the *Index* to other early childhood education settings?

Here is a flavour of their responses:

Fantastic – a real eye opener. I never thought about some of the dimensions as being part of inclusive practice. I realise how inclusive we are! Of parents, of children from ethnic minority groups – It made me think – 'Am I being inclusive – as a professional?' Yes – I've really learned quite a bit – about me and my own attitudes – and about what other people who work here know too – and have shared.

Kay
Nursery Nurse
Nursery Centre 2–5 years

It suggests setting up a co-ordinating group. That's important for large schools, but it works equally well in small settings where there are not large numbers of staff. We used it in a series of staff meetings. Got the children as well as staff to do questionnaires. It really raised awareness, among staff, children and also with parents. My Governors were interested too – even when it came to spending money! There's very good practice – and positive will – it is such an effective process – takes some sustaining though! We were encouraged to realise that we had many aspects of inclusive culture and our main task was to extend and develop what we did.

Sue
Head Teacher
School 3–10 years

When they said we were going to do this I thought 'another initiative in another glossy folder'. I was sceptical – I admit – I wondered what the point was of doing another audit when we could have spent the time and money on a part-time support assistance for my class. But it was interesting – made me think – but whether it will make a difference in the end – well, we'll see.

Helen
Reception Class Teacher
School 3–7 years

I learned loads just by reading through the folder – thinking about the questions posed under the different dimensions – there's so much to think about – mind-blowing! It's a process that's never actually finished – but it feels very good. It is really about developing relationships – that's what it's about – valuing people enough to make relationships with them and then finding ways of working in that richness of diversity.

Janie
Nursery Teacher
School 3–10 years

He [the Head] said 'We should do this – take it home and see what you think'. As I worked through it, it all made sense – cultures, policies and practice – really obvious but it had to be laid out for us. So I took the folder back and said 'Yes – good idea – we should do this'. And the Head said 'Great! Will you set up the group?' It's been a lot of work but getting the children involved and the parents was really good – made a difference to the way we think about things now – I think. I would say that we – most of us – are at the point where we 'think' inclusion now – first.

Pauline
SENCO
School 3–10 years

We have been at pains here to let the voices of those people we interviewed speak for themselves, to convey – largely unedited – their experiences, excitements and reservations. In conclusion, we return to our five questions and ask why the index is necessary.

Why do we need an *Index*?

It seems that it is not uncommon to greet yet another development initiative with scepticism; as Helen said: '*another initiative in another glossy folder*'. Yet the five people we spoke to have conveyed something of a personal response to the *Index* which suggests a change *in themselves*. We are left with the impression that there is a great deal of personal interrogation, personal learning, personal change which results as an outcome of engaging with the index. As Pauline says: we '*think*' inclusion now. Can such changes in thinking, in attitude, in realisation fail to result in changes in practice? If our five participants are in any way typical, we have something to learn about the capacity of the *Index* to bring about personal/professional change. As Kay told us:

> That whole idea that 'Inclusion' isn't just the latest PC term for SEN – that was really refreshing.

A key point in the interviews was the development of a shared language for discussion. Sue commented: 'We've got a language now to discuss things within the school' and this change in language resulted in Pauline negotiating a change in her title as Special Educational Needs Co-ordinator: I've asked to be called the 'Learning Support Co-ordinator' now. It doesn't really fit, being a SENCO, in an inclusive school!

Their work with the *Index* in their settings, they told us, made a difference to them as individuals. It was not always easy, as Helen admitted: It was painful at times. I had to confront and admit some personal prejudices. But it seems that these early childhood professionals would want to recommend the *Index for Inclusion* to others, in other settings so that they can find out for themselves.

> It's not something you can get second hand, you have to be part of the thinking, part of the change.

Acknowledgements

We would like to thank Kay, Sue, Helen, Janie and Pauline for sharing their experiences and perspectives with us. Thanks also to Sue Webster for her comments on an earlier draft of this article.

References

BERRY, T. (2001) 'Does inclusion work? A case study of four children', unpublished MA in Early Childhood Education dissertation. Sheffield: University of Sheffield.

BOOTH, T. (2000) Reflection. In P. Clough and J. Corbett (2000) *Theories of Inclusive Education: a students' guide* London: PCP/SAGE.

BOOTH, T., AINSCOW, M., BLACK-HAWKINS, K., VAUGHAN, M., SHAW, L. (2000) *Index for Inclusion: developing learning and participation in schools* Bristol: Centre for Studies in Inclusive Education. The *Index* is available from: CSIE 1 Redland Close, Elm Lane, Redland, Bristol BS6 6UE.

CLOUGH, P. (ed.) (1998) *Managing Inclusive Education: from policy to experience* London. PCP/SAGE.

CLOUGH, P. (2000) Routes to inclusion. In P. Clough and J. Corbett (2000) *Theories of Inclusive Education* London: PCP/SAGE.

CLOUGH, P. and CORBETT, J. (2000) *Theories of Inclusive Education: a student's guide* London: PCP/SAGE.

HERBERT, E. (1998) Included from the street? Managing Early Years Settings for All. In P. Clough (ed.) *Managing Inclusive Education: from policy to experience* London: PCP/SAGE.

NUTBROWN, C. (ed.) (1996) *Respectful Educators: capable learners* – children's rights and early education London: PCP/SAGE.

NUTBROWN, C. (1998) Managing to include? Rights, responsibilities and respect. In P. Clough (ed.) *Managing Inclusive Education: from policy to experience* London PCP/SAGE.

ROFFEY, S. (2001) *Special Needs in the Early Years: collaboration, communication and coordination* (2nd Edn) London: David Fulton.

SEBBA, J. and SACHDEV, D. (1997) *What Works in Inclusive Education?* Ilford: Barnardo's

WOLFENDALE, S. (ed.) (2000) *Special Needs in the Early Years: snapshots of practice* London: RoutledgeFalmer.

Source: This article was first published in *Early Education,* the Journal of the British Association for Early Childhood Education, in January 2002. It is reproduced here with permission.

Activity 6.3

Having read this article, list the questions you would want to ask Nutbrown and Clough, the authors, about this piece of research.

Do you think they chose the right method to collect the data?
Were they justified in selecting a small number of their sample of people to interview?
How else might such a study have been designed?

Using questionnaires

The questionnaire is a widely used and useful instrument for collecting survey information, providing structured, often numerical data, being able to be administered without the presence of the researcher, and often being comparatively straightforward to analyse. ... These attractions have to be counterbalanced by the time taken to develop, pilot and refine the questionnaire, by the possible unsophistication and limited scope of the data that are collected, and from the likely limited flexibility of response, though ... this can be an attraction. The researcher will have to judge the appropriateness of using a questionnaire for data collection, and, if so, what kind of questionnaire it should be. (Cohen et al., 2011: 377)

Generally speaking, questionnaires allow researchers to survey a population of subjects, with little or no personal interaction, and with the aim of establishing a broad impression of their experiences or views. The important term here is *broad*, for it is unlikely that a questionnaire will reveal the *depth* of those views and experiences in any of their rich detail. This distinction is essentially what separates qualitative and quantitative approaches to enquiry, and in Chapter 7 we pursue that distinction at greater length. Here, however, we are concerned with what any and all research methods have in common in their generation of *radical questioning*.

Some see questionnaire methods as being at the 'hard' – the arguably more scientific – end of the spectrum of social science enquiry. Perhaps more than any other method of enquiry in social science, there are techniques of questionnaire design which are not specific to given topics but which apply across all instances of use. These concern procedures such as the construction of questions, the anticipation of a frame of analysis, and claims to significance. In these and other cases, there are some well-understood and accepted rules of design conventions of the practice and administration of questionnaires (see Cohen et al., 2011: 377). The examination of how such conventions have been observed is a key feature of a qualitative methodology. The significance of a large-scale study which seeks to create *generalisations* from its data rests crucially on its observance of these rules.

However, the most important of these 'rules' are also reflected in small-scale studies, too, even where generalisation is not an aim. Although they are not applied – and 'policed' – in the same detail, many of these same rules are to be found implicitly in a persuasive research account, whatever methods it employs. This is because its methodology – *its claim to significance* – addresses the same radical questions which are made more technically explicit in the quantitative study. These are:

- What are my research questions?
- What sort of, and how much, information do I need to answer my research questions?
- What field questions do I need to ask to get this information?
- What method/s should I use to pose these field questions?
- Have I made my purpose clear to participants? Have I made their right to respond or not clear to them?

These are questions which can be applied to all methods; what really matters, then, in choosing to use a questionnaire is the precise understanding of what it can and cannot reveal in terms of the central research questions.

Questionnaires: some examples
In this section we draw on two studies, carried out by our former students, to illustrate how questionnaires can be used to generate data in research. The first,

by Al Kaddah (2001) examined students' motivation for learning English as a second language; and the second (Raymond, 2001) explored students' perceptions of 'excellent teaching'. A brief overview is given of each study followed by the authors' rationale for using questionnaires.

Example 1: Motivation and learning a second language

Discussing the aims of her study, Al Kaddah states that she wanted to explore the 'social, historical and cultural factors that affected the motivation to learn English of students at a women's tertiary college in the United Arab Emirates (UAE)'. Al Kaddah surveyed different students at three stages in their three-year course. She also carried out some follow-up interviews to explore further the issues arising from the questionnaire survey. she summarises her approach to some of the methodological issues:

> My research took the form of a case study. Data were collected by questionnaire survey and follow-up interviews. Students in Terms 2, 8 and 10 of a twelve-term Diploma course were surveyed; that is, at three separate points within their three-year course. This made it possible to explore the differences in motivational factors at different points of the program. The information was gathered using self-completion questionnaires, the use of standard questions making it possible to draw comparisons between responses. As with the work of Schmidt et al. (1996), a variety of concepts were examined tentatively rather than a few concepts thoroughly.
>
> The questionnaires asked respondents to indicate the degree to which they agreed or disagreed with a list of statements and to provide a small amount of biographical information. Pilot interviews using an interview schedule were carried out to 'explore the origins, complexities, and ramifications of the attitude areas in question', and to elicit 'vivid expressions of such attitudes from the respondents, in a form that might make them suitable for use as statements in an attitude scale' (Oppenheim, 1992: 178). The language used was as simple as possible and the questionnaires for Term 2 were translated into Arabic, as the students' level of English was not as advanced as those of the students in Terms 8 and 10. I piloted the questionnaires with a Term 4 class to check that students were able to understand and respond to the questionnaire without difficulty.
>
> This study was, in effect, a 'mapping exercise' rather than a measuring exercise and, as a result, attitudes were identified and explored rather than measured or assessed. As such, I chose not to score responses but to analyse them qualitatively.
>
> A pilot questionnaire was trialled with a group of my students and, as a result of that trial, the questionnaire was significantly added to in order to reach the final form. After obtaining necessary permissions the questionnaires were distributed to the English-speaking teachers of the classes chosen (with a covering letter explaining the purpose and instructions for completion). I chose to ask English teachers to distribute the questionnaires because they were in a position to help with any language problems the students might have had in completing the questionnaires. This also overcame one of the problems of non-response, as it was made easy for the teachers to administer and return the questionnaires and many expressed their support for this research. Students could choose not to fill in the questionnaire and whether or not to add their name. (Al Kaddah, 2001: 35–6)

In the above extract Al Kaddah explains why certain decisions taken in the development and distribution of her questionnaires were necessary to the execution of the study. She justifies changes to the questionnaire following the pilot, the use of Arabic for relatively new students and English for students in the latter half of their course and the use of other teaching colleagues to distribute the questionnaires.

Example 2: Excellent teaching – perceptions of Arab, Chinese and Canadian students

In her study Raymond (2001) sought to 'identify, describe and analyse the characteristics of exemplary post-secondary teachers as perceived by Chinese, Arab and Canadian students'. Raymond surveyed 150 ESL/EFL first-year post-secondary students and used quantitative and qualitative methods to analyse the data generated to respond to the following research questions:

1 Are there differences amongst Arab, Chinese and Canadian students in their perceptions of characteristics associated with excellent teaching?
2 Are there universal attributes associated with exemplary teachers, regardless of differing cultural backgrounds?
3 Do Arab, Chinese and Canadian students have different preferred learning styles?
4 How do Arab, Chinese and Canadian students independently rank, in order of importance, a number of characteristics associated with teaching?
5 Is the notion of the excellent teacher culture bound? That is, is it limited to one country? (Raymond, 2001: 19)

In her summary of methodological issues Raymond states that:

> This was a descriptive study using multi-method research procedures with both quantitative and qualitative components. Data were collected in order to accurately describe the characteristics of exemplary teachers from the customers themselves (the students). The sample population was drawn from 150 ESL/EFL first-year post-secondary students and distributed equally to three distinct cultural groups: Arab, Chinese and Canadian. The characteristics of the excellent teacher as perceived by these three groups of fifty students were assessed through a researcher-designed, field-tested questionnaire instrument. The self-reported survey instrument consisted of twenty-five closed-choice questions and one open-ended question. In addition, recorded interviews were conducted with a sample from each population group.
>
> I collected the data, examined it for usability and entered details into an MS Excel spreadsheet. Bar charts and tables were constructed for analysis.
>
> Scoring of each questionnaire item by each population group was ranked by descending order. Using the data generated by the questionnaire, the top five and bottom five scored items were identified and analyzed. The quantitative data were displayed in tables and charts and accompanied by narrative text.
>
> The qualitative data from the open-ended question and interview questions were categorized into ten emergent themes and entered into sub-categories. Frequency counts were determined and the emergent themes were ranked in descending order

by population group. This data was then displayed in tables and charts, and accompanied by narrative text.

Statistical analyses such as ANOVA, Chi Square, or Standard Deviation were not applied to any of these data. For future research purposes statistical analyses of the data would yield a more scientific, accurate interpretation of the data. (Raymond, 2001: 4)

In both of the above examples, various methodological decisions are reported and justified. They are designed to persuade the reader that questionnaires – in the context of the given studies – were the right tools for these particular research purposes.

Activity 6.4

If you are considering carrying out a questionnaire survey in your own research, think about the summary you might write to explain and justify your decision. Try writing it in your research journal. Use some of the factors discussed in the two preceding accounts as prompts for your own.

Questionnaire design takes some skill. While general conventions apply, the phrasing and presentation of questionnaires will depend on the participant audience and the topic. Levels of literacy may be an issue, the understanding of the participants may affect the questions asked or the way they are expressed. These will vary from study to study, though the following general hints may be helpful.

Questionnaires: some hints

- Do the field questions help you to respond to your research questions?
- Have you carried out a pilot run of your questionnaire?
- Are the questions clear? (You will not be there to clarify them.)
- Are you excluding any participants by requiring a particular level of literacy or using a particular language?
- Questionnaires can quickly generate a large amount of data. Do you know how you will use it?
- Make it easy to respond: include a stamped addressed envelope or administer the questionnaire electronically.
- Think about offering anonymity.
- How can/will you guarantee anonymity and/or confidentiality?
- Set a timescale for returns.
- What ethical issues do you need to address?

Questionnaires may well be an efficient way to generate data, but they can take some time to design so that the responses received are of the kind you hope will help you answer your research questions, and the questions are clear to the respondent. Nutbrown and Hannon (1997) carried out a questionnaire survey of 25 teachers asking for their views on a theoretical framework which they had earlier developed in a research project focusing on work with parents on children's early literacy development (see Nutbrown and Hannon, 1996). The questionnaire was piloted by three teachers who were not part of the sample, revised, and then sent out by post to the teachers to be surveyed. However, an electronic survey system, such as Google Docs[1] or Survey Monkey,[2] could also be used to the same end. A report of the study is available (Nutbrown and Hannon, 1997) but at this point we are interested in the design of the questionnaire which follows on pages 164–167.

[1] http://www.google.co.uk/
[2] http://www.surveymonkey.com/

During the REAL Project Seminars held at the start of the Project we have been discussing and working with the ORIM Framework. We have considered various strands of literacy:

- Environmental Print,

- Book Sharing,

- Early Writing

  and

- Developing Language for Literacy.

We have asked four main questions in relation to each of these strands:

- How can we help parents provide **OPPORTUNITIES**?

- How can we enhance parents' **RECOGNITION** of early achievement?

- How can we support/extend parents' **INTERACTION** with their children?

- Can we suggest how parents could provide a **MODEL**?

Having shared some of our ideas with you throughout the Seminars, we now want to evaluate the usefulness of the ORIM framework for work with parents and their young children. We need to know whether to modify the framework, drop it, or stick with it. Your views can help us decide. Please answer each of the questions on the inside pages and write any further comments on the back page.

Please return this completed questionnaire in the SAE provided to:
Cathy Nutbrown, REAL Project Office, Education Building, University of Sheffield, 388 Glossop Road, Sheffield, S10 2JA

It would be helpful if you could return your completed questionnaire before 12th July – but better later than never!

I Does the idea of different strands of literacy make sense?　　Yes [　] No [　]

Please explain your answer:

2 Have you found the ORIM framework to be a useful way of thinking about the things parents do to promote children's literacy?　　Yes [　] No [　]

If yes, in what way?

3 Has ORIM changed the way you think about early literacy development and work with parents?　　Yes [　] No [　]

4 Looking at children's literacy, can you think of any other aspects of the parent's role you might add to the framework (in addition to Opportunities, Recognition, Interaction and Model)?　　Yes [　] No [　]

Could you give an example and say why you think these additional aspects are important?

5 Are there any of the four elements (Opportunities, Recognition, Interaction, Model) that you disagree with or would like further clarification of?

Yes [　] No [　]

If yes, please say which and if possible, what is unclear or wrong.

6 Has the ORIM framework helped you in your work with parents?

Yes [   ] No [   ] Partly [   ]

---

7 Have you, in the past, made use of any other practical frameworks or guidelines in any work with parents and children on early literacy?

Yes [   ] No [   ] Partly [   ]

Please give some details of what you have used.

---

8 If you were explaining ORIM to someone new to the idea, what would you say
was its main value?

---

9 Similarly, if asked to be critical, what are the main disadvantages or weaknesses
of ORIM?

---

10 If you plan future work with parents, will you use the ORIM framework?

Yes [   ] No [   ]

Please explain the reason for your answer:

Please use this space for further comment if you wish.

One last question:

Which REAL Project seminars did you attend? Please tick:

1. Introduction [   ]

2. Environmental Print [   ]

3. Sharing books [   ]

4. Early writing [   ]

5. Developing Language for Literacy [   ]

6. Parents as adult learners [   ]

We may wish to talk with you further about some of your responses and ideas. It will be useful to us to know who has given which responses so we have included your name and address below. If you wish to return an anonymous questionnaire please remove or delete the label. If the information is incorrect please let us know. While we may quote from the responses, we will not attribute them to named individuals or schools.

Name and address:

Thank you. Your co-operation can help make the Project more effective.

Activity 6.5 Critiquing questionnaires

Look at the questionnaire on pages 164–167 devised by Nutbrown and Hannon (1997) and then write a sentence or two in response to the following questions:

- Are the questions phrased in helpful ways?
- Do they make it easy for respondents to give negative responses?
- Does the design make response easy?
- How would you respond to the request from researchers to complete such a questionnaire?
- Do you think a questionnaire was the best tool to use to obtain the kind of data needed for the study?

Make some notes on what you have learned about questionnaire design which will be useful in your own research.

In this section we have discussed the use of interviews and questionnaires as a research tool. The examples provided in this chapter have been chosen to help you reflect on the use of interviews and questionnaires in your own research, and of the need to justify these as the 'right' research decisions for the studies under discussion.

Asif, a student of musical psychology, was interested in investigating the effects of music on the emotions. He planned to use a web-based questionnaire with the aim of having over 100 respondents. After discussion with his supervisor, he decided to redesign his study to take a more qualitative approach – asking a small number of people to talk him about some of their favourite pieces and why then liked them. Which design do you think would result in a study which answered his research question: How does music affect people's emotions?'

Albrecht, a student of architecture, was interested in how the design of housing could facilitate community involvement. He planned to post a survey questionnaire through the letter boxes of two differently designed housing estates. During a group seminar discussion, his fellow students suggested that he would be better inviting residents of each estate to a series of meetings to gather their views and to take their views as starting points rather than generating questions for them to respond to. Which approach is likely to generate meaningful answers to Albrecht's question 'How can housing design enhance community engagement?'

Activity 6.6

If you are planning to use either interviews or questionnaires to collect data, you may wish to write your own summary of the usefulness and disadvantages of using questionnaires and/or interviews in the context of your own research.

Such a discussion may well feature in your submitted work, so it is as well to begin rehearsing the arguments 'for' and 'against' in your research journal.

Future research questions

Much research generates further questions for future investigation. This takes us back to the students' discussion in Chapter 1 where one student concluded that there were 'more questions than answers'. It is often the case that research generates new questions and it is important to state these in a concluding section of your study. Such questions can be raised in various ways – as a general statement about what is needed next in the field of enquiry or as specific questions or areas of concern which your own study did not address. For example, Raymond (2001: 27) concluded a summary of her research study on 'excellent teaching' by saying that: 'further cross-cultural studies are needed which focus also on biography and teaching strategies', whereas Al Kaddah chose, in the conclusion of her report, to identify four key areas for future research, stated thus:

Areas for further study

In conclusion, it is important to say that though the study uncovered many issues which help me to understand the motivation of many of the students I teach, it has also, inevitably, identified areas and issues for further research. I conclude this chapter with a summary of four key areas for future research:

- It would be useful to learn more about integrative motivation in connection with the role and status of the English language and how it affects motivation and SLA.
- The research suggests that students' motivations may change over time, but the study focused on different students at different stages of a course, rather than a longitudinal study of the same students. Much useful insight might therefore be gained from a longitudinal study of student motivation.
- The research did not attempt formally to assess the strength of student motivation but rather accepted the self-report data from students. Further research using different types of observation methods could be beneficial in order to explore the relationship between motivation and success at SLA.
- This study suggests that goals and motivation are strongly linked. There is much scope for research in this area. The students' long-term goals were identified in this study but the ability of students to set short-term goals needs further research as well as the role of the teacher in setting such goals. (Al Kaddah, 2001: 41)

However expressed, it is important that there is some acknowledgement that any given study has not and cannot provide *all* the answers, yet has played a part in offering some answers and generating new avenues for research. You may not yet be at the point of concluding your study, but bear in mind the importance of raising new questions as well as responding, throughout your empirical work, to those questions you generated as the basis for the study. New questions can arise at any point in any research project, and these should be noted and acknowledged as an important outcome, along with other findings of the study.

We shall return to the theme of concluding questions in Chapter 8 when we focus on writing the research report.

As you carry out your own work it is possible that further avenues for research may well come to mind. Record these in your research journal – they may well provide the seeds of future research questions.

Ethics: pause for reflection

Radical questioning reveals not only gaps in knowledge but why and how answers might be morally and politically necessitated. What are the ethical implications of interviewing and other forms of questioning of research participants?

What are the ethical decisions which have to be taken when deciding on a sample of research participants?

What are the particular considerations around ethical practices in research using the internet?

How does the application of ethical research practices vary across cultures, generations and intellectual capacity? Does 'one size fit all'?

Whenever we ask questions of our research participants we need to be aware of what drives the questioning and the motivations behind them. There will be situations where it is important, from the researchers' viewpoint, to ask particular questions on a particular topic and these questions may well be underpinned by a moral or political position (or both). An important ethical protocol of interviewing is that interviewers are clear with their participants about the area of questioning and what will happen to the responses, how they will be used and in what arenas and contexts they will be reported. Israel and Hay (2006) provide a thorough discussion of the ethical issues that social scientists may have to face and resolve.

When it comes to choosing research participants, it is important to be clear as to the grounds on which they have been chosen, and this will depend on the research design and the research questions. Volunteer interviews or interviews with family members raise a different set of issues from those that might arise when interviewing people chosen at random. Clough and Nutbrown (2011) discuss the particular circumstances and issues which can arise when including family members in research.

The internet provides its own specific ethical issues and dilemmas, with decisions to be made around informed consent, what is personal and what is public. The discussions in Markham and Baym (2009) are helpful in pointing up (if not resolving) specific ethical issues in relation to internet inquiry.

There is no doubt that ethical research practices vary across cultures, generations and individual knowledge and understanding, and in this respect there cannot be a case of 'one size fit all'. All research studies bring and generate specific ethical issues, and while some might be common to many, their resolution and idiosyncratic nature often demand specific, bespoke responses.

CHAPTER SUMMARY

In this chapter we have:

- *Further developed our theme of radical questioning*
- *Reflected on issues raised earlier about research questions, developing and consolidating this aspect of methodology*
- *Discussed the questioning tools often used to collect data – interviews and questionnaires*
- *Presented some examples of research using interviews and questionnaires*
- *Examined the importance of closing a research report with a statement of further research questions*
- *Reflected on the ethical issues arising from the chapter contents*

FURTHER READING

Hannon, P. and Nutbrown, C. (1997) 'Teachers' use of a conceptual framework for early literacy education involving parents', *Teacher Development*, 1 (3): 405–20.

> Describes a questionnaire survey.

Nutbrown, C. and Hannon, P. (2003) 'Children's perspectives on family literacy: methodological issues, findings and implications for practice', *Journal of Early Childhood Literacy*, 3 (2): 115–45.

Hannon, P., Morgan, A. and Nutbrown, C. (2006) 'Parents' experiences of a family literacy programme', *Journal of Early Childhood Research*, 3 (3): 19–44.

> Both describe interview surveys.

Clough, P. and Nutbrown, C. (2004) 'Special Educational Needs and inclusion: multiple perspectives of pre-school educators in the UK', *Journal of Early Childhood Research*, 2 (2): 191–211.

Nutbrown, C. and Clough, P. (2004) 'Inclusion in the early years: conversations with European educators', *European Journal of Special Needs Education*, 19 (3): 311–39.

These texts describe two surveys carried out by mixed methods of questionnaire and interview.

Cohen, L., Manion, L. and Morrison, K. (2011) *Research Methods in Education* (7th edn). London: RoutledgeFalmer.

Key chapters in this book provide a general overview on interviewing and questionnaires.

Part 3 Making Research Public

7 Research Design: Shaping the Study

CHAPTER CONTENTS

Introduction	176
Developing questions	176
'Being radical' in research planning	178
Developing and critiquing research plans	179
Ethical issues in research design and development	187
Critical relationships in methodology	188
Design and interpretation: drawing meaning from the questions – an example	189
Ethics: pause for reflection	195

LEARNING OBJECTIVES

By studying and doing the activities in this chapter you will:

- have an understanding of how research questions can be designed and how their design influences the shape of a study
- develop an awareness of the place of radical looking, radical listening, radical reading and radical questioning in the research planning process
- have an understanding of a strategy for developing and critiquing research plans
- be aware of ethical issues in research design and development and ways of resolving them
- be aware of the critical relationship between research questions, research plans and the justification of research decisions
- be aware of how research design influences the interpretation of research data.

Introduction

In this chapter we bring together work covered in Part 2 of the book. Our starting point is the series of 'radical' actions which we have already discussed. Here we shall see how *radical looking, radical listening, radical reading* and *radical questioning* can underpin and inform research design and planning, and how they can be used to critique new research plans. First, we shall review the four statements of radical action. Second, we suggest ways of designing research questions. Third, we introduce a *research planning audit* as a tool for developing and critiquing research plans. Fourth, we examine the critical relationships in methodology between research questions, research design and planning and field questions. We conclude the chapter with an example of a study which operated at several layers of policy development and implementation.

Developing questions

There are many ways in which research questions are constructed. We showed (in Chapter 2) how our students refined some questions for the *Hoywell* study and (in Chapter 5) we showed how research questions (developed using the same technique) were used to plan the literature search and focus the literature review for another study, *Crowsfoot*. With our focus now on research design, we want to demonstrate the vital relationship of the research question (or questions) to the research design. Figure 7.1 shows how research questions in the social sciences can be plotted along two axes: *general–specific* and *breadth–depth*.

We have indicated the 'type' of some of the studies at the extreme points in cells 1, 3 and 4 in Figure 7.1. The scattered xs indicate that a study could fall anywhere in much of this framework. There will be nothing at the extreme point in cell 2 because it is not realistically possible to carry out a study which covers everything in great depth and with a large enough focus to allow generalisability.

Activity 7.1

With your own study in mind, try to position your enquiry in the diagram shown in Figure 7.1.

Use this to identify the main features of the study.

Will your enquiry include a large enough sample to be generalisable (in which case you will have made the decision to sacrifice some depth of detail)? Or will your study focus on a single individual (so giving you great depth into this one case but forgoing the potential for generalisation)?

Of course, your study may well be plotted at a different point in cells 1, 3 or 4 – not all studies take place in the extreme parameters!

Some studies can be designed to achieve *breadth and generalisability,* featuring a large sample and a broad coverage of the chosen topic, while at the same time including an element of *depth and specification* by focusing in on a small number

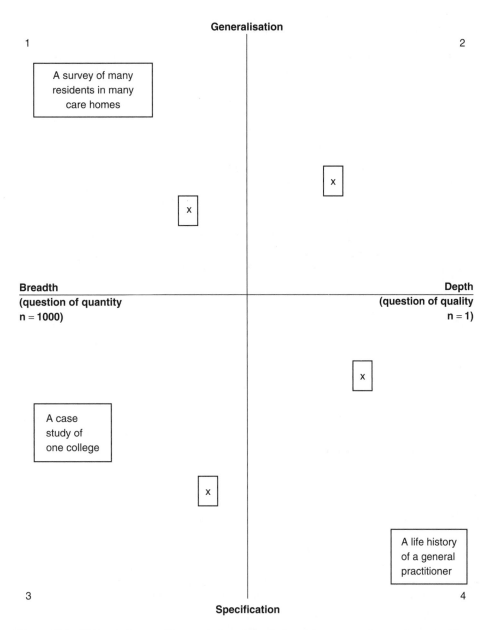

Figure 7.1   Research questions can be placed along two axes: general – specific and breadth – depth

of the participants to follow up in greater detail. Thus a study which examines social care policy may involve many residents in many care homes but may also include a single life-historical study of a carer in those homes. We will provide an example of what we mean by this in the final section of this chapter.

'Being radical' in research planning

Throughout this book we have been arguing and demonstrating the need for 'radical enquiry' throughout research processes. In this section we wish further to develop your awareness of the place of *radical looking, radical listening, radical reading* and *radical questioning* in the research planning process. We have said that:

Radical looking is the means by which research process makes the familiar strange, and gaps in knowledge are revealed.

Radical listening – as opposed to merely hearing – is the interpretative and critical means through which 'voice' is noticed.

Radical reading provides the justification for the critical adoption or rejection of existing knowledge and practices.

Radical questioning reveals not only gaps in knowledge but why and how answers might be morally and politically necessitated in practices and lies at the heart of a thesis, bringing together the earlier notions of *radically attending* to a topic or situation of events.

Additionally, we have argued (in Chapter 1) that social research is:

persuasive;
purposive;
positional;
and *political*.

> All social research sets out with specific *purposes* from a particular *position*, and aims to *persuade* readers of the significance of its claims. These claims are always broadly *political*.

We have invited you, in the earlier part of the book, to reflect on these statements:

- Those who carry out social research aim to persuade readers of the significance of their claims.
- What is often forgotten (as too obvious) is that any piece of research in the social sciences emerges from a distinct purpose (whether or not this is apparent to the reader).
- Since research is carried out by people, it is inevitable that the standpoint of the researcher is a fundamental platform on which enquiry is developed; all social science research is saturated (however disguised) with positionality.
- Research which changes nothing – not even the researcher – is not research at all. And since all social research takes place in policy contexts of one form or another, research itself must therefore be seen as inevitably political.

What we want to demonstrate in this chapter is how our definition of social research as *persuasive, purposive, positional* and *political* together with our four processes of *radical enquiry* are integral to research design and planning, and how, if these are held central in the researchers' thinking, they will act as 'prods' for ongoing critique of any research plan *as it is being developed.*

Activity 7.2

You may find it useful at this point to look through any notes you have made about the above ideas. There may be issues and questions you have noted in your research journal which are relevant to the following discussion and to the development of your research plans.

Developing and critiquing research plans

In this section we suggest a process which you might use in order to develop and critique your research plans. The *Research Planning Audit* is a tool designed to help you devise your research plans and then subject them to some critical reflection. The *Research Planning Audit* suggests that you focus first on your reasons for choosing your research topic, first stating those reasons and then justifying them. The process then moves on to the expression of research questions and their origins in literature, experience or some other source of stimulation. Practical issues, such as research location and timetable for completion, are also asked, alongside the details of research methods to be used to gather data. Research questions are then revisited in the light of practical and ethical considerations and reframed if necessary.

We suggest that you work through Activity 7.3, which has been designed to help you become familiar with this instrument, as you think critically about your own research design and planning.

Activity 7.3   The Research Planning Audit

Look through the *Research Planning Audit* on the following pages. The version that follows includes (in italicised script) our own notes, which provide a rationale for its construction and the specific steps included.

Following this version, you will find an example of how one student used the audit to plan her research. We have also included notes by her supervisor in response to her work by way of critique.

A blank version of the *Research Planning Audit* has been included in Appendix 1. We suggest you use a version of this in relation to your own research study.

You may wish to use this as a discussion tool with your own research supervisor or with fellow students. Our students tell us that it is worth taking time over this exercise. It requires a good deal of thought and revision, but the impact on the quality of written methodological discussion is testimony to time well spent!

Research Planning Audit

Name ....

Date ....

What is the topic of my research?	*At this stage the topic can be fairly broad. In choosing a topic, bear in mind that social research sets out to achieve something. Does your topic enable you to make a difference to something or someone?*
Why have I chosen this topic?	**Previous research (the literature)** *Have you reviewed the literature sufficiently to know where your chosen topic is positioned within the field? Which particular literature has stimulated your choice of topic?* **Professional relevance (my current work)** *Are there particular personal/professional or policy contexts which simulate this research? What will your study achieve in this respect?* **Other reasons (such as ...)** *Is the study commissioned by funders or an agency/employer paying your course fees? If so, clarity about this is important. Do you still need to identify other stimuli and a research/professionally related rationale? Does your reason for choice of topic seem sufficient to sustain you through to completion of the study?*
Are my reasons good enough?	**Yes, because ...** *Interrogate your reasons for your above choice. Check that they are good enough reasons to proceed.* **No, because ...** *Nothing is perfect. Even if you're satisfied with part of your rationale, you may still have to manage elements which are not so good. Be clear about the negative aspects and decide whether the 'pros' outweigh the 'cons'.*
What are my research questions?	*State your research questions clearly and precisely. Remember the Russian doll principle and the 'Goldilocks' test. Do your research questions stand up?* I. 2. 3. **Are there more?** *Be clear about how many research questions you are addressing. Keep control of your study. If there are more than three questions, state them as clearly as you can at the outset.*

Where do these come from?	**(Literature, practice, other? ...)** *Identify the relationship between your questions and existing work in the field as well as professional stimuli.*
Can I justify the research questions? How can I do this?	*Draw on your research journal, the literature and your professional/personal contexts to write a strong justification for each of your research questions. If you find it difficult or impossible to justify a question, then consider revising or rejecting it.*
Where will I do the research?	*Practical questions are important. Choose a location where you will be able to respond to your research questions. If you have to make changes due to the setting you choose, be clear that you want to change your research in this way. If you are not content to change your research, you may need to change your research setting.*
Have I negotiated access to the research setting? How? What?	*Be clear with everyone involved what access you have negotiated. Ensure that key people know about your work and that you understand the conditions under which access has been granted. If you are carrying out your research within your own professional context ensure that you are clear about any boundaries between research and professional work, the ethics of your role as researcher, and the expectations and understandings of others working within the setting.*
When will I do the research? Is my timetable realistic? What methods will I use to investigate the research questions?	*Create a timetable – to suit you, your academic study plan and your research participants. Check out your timetable – are your plans achievable? At this point, think about the four forms of 'radical enquiry': radical looking, radical listening, radical reading and radical questioning. Remember that methods are created for particular research tasks, not simply lifted from a research methods manual and replicated. Your study is unique and your research methods will be moulded to enable you to respond to your research questions.*
How can I justify these methods?	*This is a crucial question. Research methods are justifiable only in so far as they help you to respond to the research questions. Do your chosen methods help you to do that? What have other researchers done in the past? How have other similar issues been investigated? Does the literature help your justification? Will your methods enable you to conduct a study which is persuasive, purposive, positional and political?*
What are the ethical considerations? How will I address these?	*This is a further question of justification. As you judge it at this point, can you see any danger of your research doing harm to participants in the study either in the process or in*

(Continued)

(Continued)

Does the study need ethical approval?	*its report? Have you weighed your research plan against various codes of practice for the conduct of ethical research? If you are planning to include the voices of others in your research report, do you have their permission? What guarantees have you given them?*
Is there anything I need to rethink?	**The topic? The methods? The timetable? The location?** *Pause now and reflect on the issues raised by carrying out this planning audit. What, if anything, do you need to rethink? Are your research questions sufficiently clear? Are they robust? Do they reflect previous research in the field? Are your methods appropriate to the study? Will they enable you to respond to the research questions? Can you fulfil your research plan in the timescale available? Are you planning to locate your study in an appropriate setting? Are you clear about any ethical considerations within your study?*
Do I need to revise the research questions? Are they clear? Are they researchable?	*In the light of the above reflection, undertake one more review of your research questions. This is an opportunity to check that your research questions are expressed in the clearest possible terms.* **1.** **2.** **3.** **(Others?)**
Where have I got to in my research?	*Review your research journal and your research timetable to create a brief synopsis of progress to date.*
What is my first/next step?	*Action! What, in the light of your research questions, your timetable and your progress, do you need to do next?*
What help do I need?	*You do not have to carry out the whole of your study in solitude. Make a list of those who can help you, including your supervisor, and be sure to contact them when you need them.*

Karen, doing an MA in Early Childhood Education, worked through the *Research Planning Audit* as she planned her own dissertation. Her example shows the kinds of issues which arise and the sorts of responses that might help at this stage of the research planning process.

Karen's Research Planning Audit

What is the topic of my research?	This study will involve observing a child under the age of two years old. It will focus on social/emotional development. As many children now spend long periods of time in a day care environment from a very young age, I want to research the effects (if any) this environment has on social/emotional development. The study further aims to explore the views of Piaget, who suggested that children under the age of three years are unable to take the viewpoint of another and were therefore 'egocentric'. During the course of the research, I aim to consider whether this is still the case for a child attending a day care setting, and experiencing regular social interactions with peers and significant adults.
Why have I chosen this topic?	**Previous research (the literature)** Piaget, Vygotsky, Bruner, Bowlby, Elfer, Golschmied, Jackson, Buddulph **Professional relevance (my current work)** I work as an Under Threes Officer supporting practitioners in childcare settings with the implementation of the Birth to Three Matters Framework (DfES, 2003) to help them meet the care and educational needs of children under three. **Other reasons** I feel passionately that young children in a day care setting should have access to the same quality and continuity of care that they would receive in a home environment. By choosing this topic, I feel it will enable me to follow a young child's day care experiences and look in some depth at how everyday interactions help to shape their social/emotional development.
Are my reasons good enough?	**Yes, because ...** The study will incorporate my professional experiences to date, and further aid my professional understanding. I feel my experiences (and deeper understanding) after completion of the study will benefit the practitioners to whom I offer guidance and support.

(Continued)

(Continued)

	No, because ... I cannot think of any negative reasons, although it will be hard to observe and not intervene if standards of the care in the setting do not meet my expectations. I will need to think carefully about if and how this can be addressed (if the situation occurs); I will need to discuss any issues with my dissertation supervisor before taking any action.
What are my research questions?	1. Can a child under two years old socially interact with others? 2. Does this interaction involve peers and adults? 3. Can a child under two years old demonstrate empathy towards others? 4. In what way (if any) does the early years environment support the child's social/emotional development? **Are there more?** Yes, I feel the study will generate further questions.
Where do these come from?	**(Literature, practice, other? ...)** They come from past theorists and current literature in the field, including: Piaget and Vygotsky, and more recently The Birth to Three Matters Framework (DfES, 2003). I have also been particularly influenced by the work of Elfer, Goldschmied and Jackson. However, I have recently been worried by the findings of Biddulph, and would therefore like to look (through my observations) at how the day care environment can support or hinder social/emotional development. I feel the questions are also relevant to my working practices as an Under Threes Training and Quality Officer.
Can I justify the research questions? How can I do this?	I will be discussing the questions in detail with all the respondents, including parents/carers on behalf of the child. I have carried out the 'Goldilocks Test' and 'Russian Doll Principle' to ensure the questions are not leading or biased in any way. I must also be aware that any preconceived ideas may influence my responses, and acknowledge that I need to remain impartial throughout the course of my study.
Where will I do the research?	It is important that I choose a setting which has children under the age of two years, so that I can answer my research questions. I feel it would be best to approach some settings which I have already worked with, as I feel strongly that staff and children will be relaxed while I am present, and this will enable me to correlate accurate information through my observations. It is important to me to ensure my observations remain as naturalistic as possible.

Have I negotiated access to the research setting? How? What?	I have approached two settings which I have previously been working with. At this stage I have discussed an outline of my study with the managers, and have agreed that I would contact them if and when I know my study can go ahead. I intend to speak initially with the manager, and then meet with parents/carers if they are agreeable to their child taking part in my study. I will also arrange to meet with the child's key person, so she/he will also be very clear about what I want to do. I will develop participant information sheets to clarify their understanding, and ask them to sign the relevant consent forms, before undertaking any observations. As I have previously visited these settings in a professional capacity, I will need to be clear about the boundaries between the research and my professional work, the ethics of my role as a researcher, and the expectations and understandings of other staff working in the setting.
When will I do the research? Is my timetable realistic?	Although it will be quite demanding, I feel I will need to ensure that I keep up to date with the timescales I have planned, if I am to carry out the ten observations which form the basis of my research. I will be evaluating each one as I go along, so this should also help me to correlate relevant literature, etc. to support my arguments.
What methods will I use to investigate the research questions?	Radical looking, listening, reading and questioning. To carry out ten observations using different observational techniques, including narrative, sociogram, tracking, time sampling and anecdotal. I will also complete two recorded interviews: one with the parent/carer, and one with the child's key person.
How can I justify these methods?	I think the observations will provide me with lots of relevant information relating to the child's social/emotional journey since joining the nursery setting (during the time the study takes place). I have carried out structured interviews before and feel that although I recognise the need to be sensitive, and on occasions 'read between the lines', these methods will help me to 'radically look and listen'.
What are the ethical considerations? How will I address these? Does the study need ethical approval?	I will need to ensure that I am aware of all the ethical issues relating to using children as research participants in my study. I will need to ensure that all adult participants are happy about the methods I will be using, and that I have parents/carers' written permission for their child to be included in the study. I will also need to guarantee all subjects anonymity/confidentiality at all times.

(Continued)

(Continued)

	Finally, I will need to clarify any issues which might arise while undertaking the research, between my role as a researcher and my professional role. I will also need to apply for ethical review and achieve approval for my study.
Is there anything I need to rethink?	**The topic? The methods? The timetable? The location?** I know there will be things which I will need to change or adjust as I go along, but for now I think I am clear about what I need to do next. I am happy regarding my chosen methods. I have carried out the 'Goldilocks Test' and the Russian Doll Principle' to clarify my research questions (although I feel these may still need some refinement – I will need to seek the views of my dissertation supervisor regarding this). I may also need to review the timescale as I go along.
Do I need to revise the research questions? Are they clear? Are they researchable?	I have already carried out the 'Goldilocks Test' and the 'Russian Doll Principle' on my research questions, but feel this might be an area I need to discuss with my dissertation supervisor. I have not as yet prepared the questions for the structured interviews, as I want to relate these to the findings of my observations. When I do prepare them, I am intending to 'trial' the questions to ensure that they provide me with accurate data relevant to my study.
Where have I got to in my research?	Discussed possible access with two settings. I know who my supervisor will be. Planned a timetable. Begun researching literature review. Prepared ethical review forms and participant information sheets.
What is my first/ next step?	To commence in-depth reading for literature review. To contact setting and agree access. To arrange meetings with the Nursery Manager, Key Person and parent (before next study school) to get permission forms signed, so I can begin research as soon as possible. To attend next study school which focuses on dissertation (February).
What help do I need?	I will need ongoing help and support from my dissertation supervisor and also my line manager at work. I will also need the support and help of my family to enable me to keep on task and stick to my research timetable so that I can submit the dissertation on time.
Who do I call?	My supervisor My manager My sister (she is a good listener).

Ethical issues in research design and development

Ethical review and ethical practice in research

Research involving human beings being carried out by students and staff in universities must obtain ethical approval in order to ensure it meets minimal required ethical standards. Such standards are designed to ensure that enquiries are conducted in ways which:

- provide the best possible protection for researchers and their participants;
- ensure that data are collected with the informed consent of participants;
- protect participants' personal details, identities and well-being.

Such requirements for studies to be ethically reviewed are not simply a way of ensuring that university research meets necessary ethical standards but are also a beginning point for securing a value base which ensures that research is conducted in ways which have moral integrity, and hold the rights and dignities of the research participants in high regard.

Ethical practices are central to social science research, and decisions about research questions, participants, publication, methods, analysis and so on are all taken with due regard to ethical judgements about what is 'right' and the importance of avoiding harm to participants or as a result of the study. While procedures for the ethical review of students' research will vary from institution to institution, the *ethical practices* of all research will take similar issues into consideration and take account of legislative frameworks involving data protection, human rights, the Freedom of Information Act, and so on. Ethical issues are central to the methodology of any social science study, however large or small. Take, for example, the following study by Kwaku, a third-year, full-time PhD Medical Education student, who, in group discussion, reflected:

> I don't think I realised what it [methodology] really was, what it meant until I was well into it [the project*]. I had worked out a tight scheme – had it agreed by my Supervisor and everything – I told you all that … but it was only when I was in the thick of it and like literally I was despairing and I had to think the whole thing through again… It was a case of 'Whose life *is* this anyway'? – [because] I had this lad, Simon's permission to tell his story but like his story was lots of other people's lives – like his father, and I certainly did not have his permission and in fact he'd tried to get me banned from going to the unit. Because he said I was upsetting Simon. But he knew that Si was telling me things that he [the father] would rather have kept way in the dark… Anyway I had some really very hard thinking to do about the very point of the study mostly to do with the ethics of making data from people's lives… Even though I had got all the permissions etc. … I wasn't sure they held water – true – any more or did they? So, like I said, I had thought of methodology as just decisions about instruments, but those are

---

*An ethnographic study of an adolescent psychiatric unit: the initial design anticipated, among other measures, in-depth, life-historical interviews with five patients.

the tip of the iceberg, eh? What's beneath the water is a whole massive complex of things about ethics and ownership and... that's really methodology – the real justifications that you make for this or that piece of ... of... human action. D'you know what I mean?

Critical relationships in methodology

In this section we bring together some critical research relationships: research questions; research design and planning; and field questions. In so doing we shall demonstrate how the fundamental research questions influence both the shape of a study and the formulation of field questions. Figure 7.2 illustrates the ways in which these three (research questions; research design and planning; and field questions) are connected in any empirical work.

Figure 7.2 shows how *research questions* influence the *design and planning* of the study. Bearing in mind Figure 7.1, the question of *purpose* is fundamental here, for it is clear that the research questions influence the sample size and the breadth of the study. 'What must the study achieve?' is a question to be asked at this intersection.

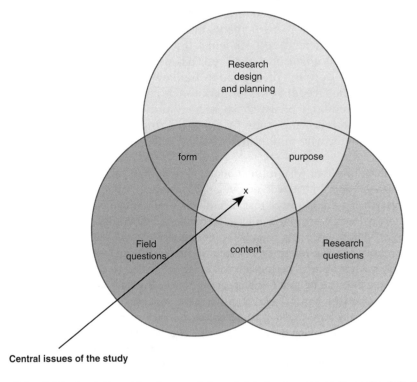

Figure 7.2 Critical relationships in special social science research methodology

If we examine the relationship between *research questions* and *field questions* we can see that they are connected and that this is a question of *content*. 'How should the questions be phrased?' and 'What shall I ask them?' are the key questions at this intersection. Field questions must be phrased so as to respond eventually to the original research questions. Where *field questions* and *research design and planning* coincide, it becomes a question of form. How shall I go about this? What scheme, what methods, what words?

Clearly, every study will be different, but the understanding of these three relationships, as expressed in any specific study, will lead critically to the central issues of the study (point x in Figure 7.2). And the issues which lie here are central to the research design, the ethics of the methodology and its findings.

Before we leave this discussion it is important to clarify the ways in which *field questions* can be generated from the refined *research questions*. Figure 7.3 shows how field questions can be generated from research questions, and the form and content of these questions will depend upon the design of the study.

In this chapter we have demonstrated the relationships (and mutual dependency) of research relationships. In the next section we provide an example of a research design which takes account of these various relationships.

Design and interpretation: drawing meaning from the questions – an example

Introduction: getting to the point

> Analysis is the act of stripping away whatever clothes or disguises an object, so that we can see it in its simplest form.

All analyses – chemical, economic, literary or whatever – share a common feature: the resolution of something complex into its simplest elements for a particular purpose. In this sense, to analyse anything is to strip away from it properties which may be part of the character of something, but which are not essential to the specific task in hand. The aim, then, is to get to the object in its purest form.

This is probably easier for the natural scientist (though some might disagree), who works within a community where notions of objectivity and scientific impartiality are an important part of what defines the community and its work. In such research, though the judgement of scientists is vital, their values and ideology are – as far as possible – set aside, and there is broad consensual agreement about the construction and policing of method.

In social science, however, the situation is radically different, and few social scientists would want to insist that their work is neutral, value-free or uninfected

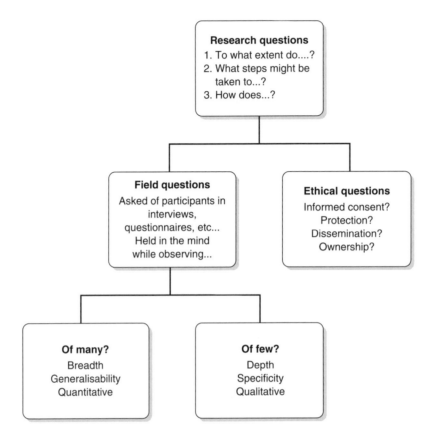

Figure 7.3 The generation of field questions from research questions and their relation to research design and planning

by personal and political ideology. On the contrary, in fact, many would see their work as failing to have meaning apart from its political engagement (see Chapter 1 and our discussion of the 4Ps of social science research). Mertens and Ginsberg (2009) highlight the range of issues likely to arise in social science research, and the very many concerns to which research involving other human beings might give rise.

And so, for many, the adoption or construction of method for a particular study is in itself a political act: at its simplest, the way you choose to view an object – your distance from it, 'where you're coming from', the quality of your vision – effectively creates that object. In this sense, *methods make objects.*

We do not come innocent to a task or a situation of events; rather we wilfully situate those events not merely in the institutional meanings which our profession provides, but also, and in the same moment, we constitute them as expressions of our selves. Inevitably, the traces of our own psychic and social history drive us. (Clough, 1995: 138)

Situating a research design

Here we provide an account of a researcher's thinking which led to the design of a large-scale, ESRC-funded study. We begin with a brief overview of the study and this is followed by Clough's account of the experiences and decisions which led to the design of the study as it was eventually conducted.

The COSEN study: an overview

Known operationally as COSEN (Construction of Special Educational Needs), this project was funded by the ESRC between October 1989 and September 1991 as 'Teachers' Perspectives on Special Educational Needs Policy and Practice', award no. R000231910.

The main aim of the research was to document the experiences and effects of SEN and educational reform policies as they were expressed through local education authorities and schools, and realised in the daily lives of practitioners. This aim was realised through the following objectives:

The description and evaluation of the structures and experiences of SEN developments within four 11–16 schools in each of four LEAs.

- The exploration in depth of the experiences, attitudes and professional orientations of some 30 staff within these schools, with particular reference to the 1981 and 1988 legislation.
- The relation of teacher conceptions of SEN to policy realisation.
- The development of theoretical and methodological positions within an interactionist analysis of special education.

The schools which participated were identified so as to provide a range of LEAs and of broadly different contexts and systems. There were three overlapping phases of the data collection:

- Interviews with key policy framers in the LEAs and schools in order to build up a picture of the way in which SEN policy had developed and was constructed by those charged with developing and enacting policy.
- A questionnaire for all teachers in all participating schools, seeking information on their knowledge about and views on LEA, school and departmental policies, and about their experiences of those policies in action.

- Life-historical case studies undertaken with individual teachers to explore how their own life experiences, their beliefs, attitudes and values mediated the ways in which they interpret and develop policies.

(*Source:* Clough, 1995: 141–2)

Clough's account of the design processes of COSEN

COSEN started life as some idle hunches about what teachers thought Special Educational Needs were and, in particular, what *caused* them. Long before it became properly a topic for enquiry, I had found myself interested in the sorts of explanations and ascriptions that teachers made around kids with learning difficulties. I'd heard – and still hear – such clichés as 'Of course, he's just like his sister/mum/cousin...'; or 'Well, what d'you expect from a family like that?'; or, 'They're all like that on the Elswick Estate...'. Even more offensively, and no less current, are observations like: 'She's just plain thick – a complete waste of time trying to do anything with her'; or, 'But why do they come here if they just want to keep to their own way?'

This idea had been coming a long time. I had first noticed it in Croll and Moses' (1985) *One in Five*, where they talk about primary schoolteachers' preferences for different sorts of information about children with difficulties. I had worked as an educational psychologist years before, and saw often in teachers that barely contained need to know what was a child's IQ; not what the child could do, or had done in a previous school, but more: 'what's the raw material we're working with here?' This tendency to a ready causality issues in so many casual staffroom attributions. The drive, so often, is towards reaching to the shelf for so many ready-made, well-worn and superficial 'explanations'. And I wondered simply where these ideas – about what is 'wrong' with children – came from in the lives of these teachers.

To understand the particular significance of my early wonderings and hunches, it is necessary to know something of the policy contexts of the time. For this was in the mid 1980s at a time when UK public sector education was experiencing integration policies, which sought to 'mainstream' children in – a phrase borrowed from US legislation – the 'least restrictive environment'. And the question that arose from my hunches was about the very ideas of 'Special Educational Need' and 'Learning Difficulty' that mainstream teachers had. In the proposal for funding I wrote:

> The issues and practices of integration make many, often threatening demands on teachers, who may be required to develop new roles and ways of working within new and unpredictable systems. ... Such changes in policy clearly depend for their success to an important degree on the professional orientation and motivation of staff who are charged with realising them. If teachers are seen as mediators of policy in this way, then – both for the evaluation of that policy and for its development – we need to be able to identify and describe the ways in which teachers engage with and feel about their work; we need, that is, to understand what teachers' views are, how they are formed, and what influences they are susceptible to...

The *object* of the enquiry, then, becomes mainstream teachers' views of special educational needs. But how do we 'get to' that object? What analysis will help us to arrive at the 'simplest elements' of those views? What do we need to discard and what retain?

I realise – much later, of course, and with the sleight of hand of hindsight – that even my crude, early interest – though apparently inchoate – was in an important way already analytic. For I had found sufficiently significant – to pin on my wall – a suggestion made by Wilson and Cowell (1984) in a paper called 'How shall we define handicap?' There is the seed of a method in their call to

> ... find out what principles and assumptions control the thinking (and hence the decisions) of those concerned [with SEN]; and that means interacting with and conversing with them, not merely issuing them with questionnaires or seeing what they have to say in structured interviews. For ... the assumptions are often hidden; not only from the interviewer but from the person interviewed. Much time and effort is required to grasp *the shape and style of a person's deepest thoughts.* [Emphasis added]

And another burr had stuck to me: speaking of the relationship between the individual and society, Raymond Williams (1965) talks of the 'fundamental relation between organism and organisation', and a pointer to method is again evident in his occupation with one central principle:

> that of the essential relation, the true interaction, between patterns learned and created in the mind, and patterns communicated and made active in relationships, conventions and institutions. ... [And] we begin to realise, from experience, that [these] relationships are inherent, and that each organisation is an embodiment of relationships, the lived and living history of responses to and from other organisations. Organisation, that is to say, is enacted in the organism and *to know either fully is to know the other* [emphasis added].

There were others – like the broadly parallel echo in Wright Mills' relation of 'private troubles and public issues' – but in Croll and Moses, in Wilson and Cowell, and in Williams, I had a context and a glimpse, if not of the tools, of a method which would provide some answers to my early questions.

What did I do?

My early hunch about how to get to the core of teachers' thinking about SEN was simply to interview them, in the belief that sufficient purposive questioning would reveal what I wanted to know about the various aspects of their lives which had shaped their views and practices. I carried out three such pilot interviews, and it was from these that I noticed some common elements which were to influence not only the Field Questions but more radically the design of the study as a whole [see Figure 7.3]. My initial Field Questions helped me to gather information about teachers' thinking which, even at this early stage, seemed to be grouped analytically around a number of key constructs. These are represented schematically in Figure 7.4.

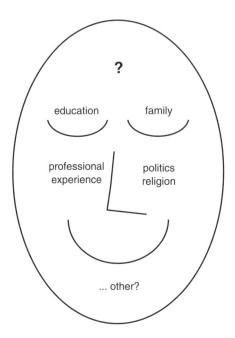

Figure 7.4   Key constructs for field questions for COSEN pilot

I have quite deliberately represented this part of the process in this way because I think it helps to reveal both what was 'wrong' with my early thinking, and also how it led to the final design of the study. For one of the things which my Pilot interviews showed strongly was how more and less directly the teachers' thinking could only be fully understood in the context of their workplace experiences; these, in turn, were expressions of given policies at both local and national level. My Research Questions emerged directly from this realisation of how intimately tied up are personal and professional experiences with their political contexts – how, to draw on Raymond Williams again, *organism* and *organisation* share structures such that 'to know either fully is to know the other'. I expressed the COSEN questions thus:

1   To what extent are teachers' perspectives on SEN key determinants in realising integration policies?
2   What are the major influences on the development of these perspectives?
3   How do these perspectives themselves influence policy and practice?

These research questions led to the design of a large study which embraced national, local and school policies as well as personal teacher perspectives (see Clough, 1997: 141–2). As Figure 7.5 shows, this involved samples of various sizes within each 'level' and a range of methods. The study included life histories of individual teachers (which, if we return to Figure 7.1, we could plot in cell 4) and a questionnaire survey of 984 teachers would lie in the extreme of cell 1 in Figure 7.1.

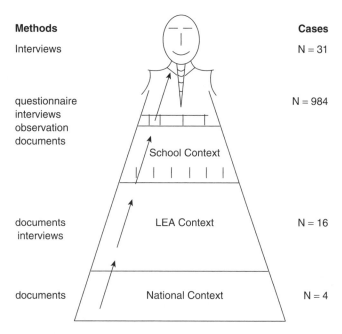

Figure 7.5 Scheme of contexts and methods of enquiry for COSEN project

In this chapter we have focused on research planning and design, demonstrating how some of the critical relationships in methodology coincide to create the shape of a study. In so doing we have emphasised the impact of research questions on research design and the importance of critiquing research plans at the outset of an enquiry.

Ethics: pause for reflection

Does the scale of a study carry with it different ethical considerations?
  What checks on the research design are needed at each stage of the study to ensure that ethical issues are fully identified and addressed?

Social science researchers must pay respect to the ethics of their inquiry, however large or small the study. In this respect, ethical considerations are of equal concern whatever the scale of design of the study. For example, it is likely that the ethical issues will be different for a life-historical study involving one single participant from those which appertain to a questionnaire survey of 5,000 participants. But the underpinning issues of consent, information, protection and well-being remain, whatever the scale.

One of the most important ongoing checks in any study is the protection and well-being of participants. Informed consent is not simply something that is obtained at the outset of a study. It is an issue which researchers must continually remain aware of. Participants have the right to withdraw at any point in the study, even if they have given their consent and regardless of the impact this might have on the study. Researchers need to design the impact and effects of attrition into their study and ensure that the starting sample is sufficient to withstand the effects of some participants withdrawing from the study.

CHAPTER SUMMARY

In this chapter we have:

- Discussed the importance of planning research studies
- Reviewed the importance of 'being radical' in research planning and the need to remain aware of the skills of radical looking, radical listening, radical reading and radical questioning in the research planning process
- Provided an instrument for developing and critiquing your research plans
- Examined some ethical issues in research design and development
- Reflected upon some critical methodological relationships between research questions, research plans and the justification of research decisions
- Provided an example of research design to demonstrate the features discussed in this chapter
- Reflected on the ethical issues arising from the chapter contents

---

FURTHER READING

Rossman, G.B. and Rallis, S.F. (2011) *Learning in the Field: An Introduction to Qualitative Research* (2nd edn). London: Sage.

See particularly Chapter 5, Conceptualizing and Planning the Research.

Demn, R. and Brehony, K.J. (1994) 'Why didn't you use a survey to generalise your findings? Methodological issues in a multiple site case study of school governing bodies after the 1988 Education Reform Act', in D. Halpin and B. Troyna (eds), *Researching Education Policy: Ethical and Methodological Issues*. London: Falmer.

Though not the most recent of sources, this is a good exposition of the need to justify enquiry.

Mertens, D.M. and Ginsberg, P.E. (2009) *The Handbook of Social Research Ethics*. London: Sage.

See particularly Chapter 1 by Kitchener and Kitchener, Social Science Research Ethics: Historical and Philosophical Issues.

8 Reporting Research: Telling the Story

CHAPTER CONTENTS

Introduction: making research 'public'   198
Two examples of research reports   198
Strategies for writing your research report   238
Ethics: pause for reflection   243

LEARNING OBJECTIVES

By studying and doing the activities in this chapter you will:

- have an understanding of the importance of forms of writing and dissemination in research reports
- be able to evaluate two research reports in terms of their qualities of *persuasion, purpose, position* and the extent to which they are political
- have an awareness of the skills and structures you might use in writing your own research report.

Introduction: making research 'public'

We argue throughout this book that social research is *persuasive, purposive, positional* and *political*. We also argue (in Chapter 2) that the *arrest of experience*, which is present in all research studies, can be characterised by four forms of *radical enquiry*, these being *radical looking, radical listening, radical reading* and *radical questioning*. Through these themes we have demonstrated and discussed the essential methodological constructs of any successful piece of social research. In this chapter we focus on how the above themes might pervade the writing of a research report; how they might be useful in deciding its specific genre and in planning its structure.

'Systematic, self-critical enquiry – made public'

It was Stenhouse (1975) who wrote that: 'Research ... is systematic and sustained enquiry, planned and self-critical, which is subjected to public criticism and to empirical tests where these are appropriate.' In other words, research is not complete until it finds an audience. In the case of award-bearing courses, research reports may have a limited audience of tutors, examiners and those who peruse the shelves of academic libraries. But, increasingly, students' work is published in academic journals and books, thus widening the audience. In this chapter we want, through demonstration, to continue our argument that the dissemination of research must *persuade*, must be *purposive*, must represent a clearly articulated *position* within the field, and that it must have (or seek to have) some *political* impact. We show, too, how in making research public it is necessary also to express the ways in which the four processes of *radical enquiry* (*radical looking, listening, reading* and *questioning*) have shaped the study. Ultimately, the research report should not only tell the story, but also *justify* the enquiry.

Two examples of research reports

In this section of the book we ask you to read two research reports. *Example 1* reports a study of family literacy practices from the perspectives of 5-year-old children drawn from areas of social and economic deprivation in an English city (Nutbrown and Hannon, 2003). *Example 2* is a story which grew out of a larger research study into educational difficulty and constructions of special educational need, but which – in its published form – stands alone (Clough, 2001). We suggest that you first read both examples and then turn to the activity which follows them.

Example I

Children's perspectives on family literacy: Methodological issues, findings and implications for practice

Journal of Early Childhood Literacy
Copyright © 2003
SAGE PUBLICATIONS
London, Thousand Oaks, CA and New Delhi
VOL 3(2) 115–145
[1468-7984(200308)3:2;
115–145;034597]

CATHY NUTBROWN   *School of Education, University of Sheffield, UK*

PETER HANNON   *School of Education, University of Sheffield, UK*

Abstract This article reports a study of family literacy practices from the perspectives of five-year-old children drawn from areas of social and economic deprivation in an English city. Methodological and ethical issues of interviewing young children are discussed. An interview survey (N = 71) found literacy activity reported in all homes; fathers involved in literacy with their children; and boys (as well as girls) involved in literacy activity. Findings were compared with those of a further randomly selected sample (N = 77) whose parents had participated in a family literacy programme. The comparison showed a modest, but consistent, increase in child-reported family literacy activity in the programme group, and concludes that the impact of a family literacy programme is discernible through children's perspectives. Implications for family literacy practices and the need for further research, including measures of children's literacy achievement and views of parents and the teachers participating in the programme, are identified.

Keywords children's perspectives; family literacy; methodology

Introduction

'Family literacy' is a term used to refer to the interrelated literacy *practices* of parents, children and others in homes (Barton and Hamilton, 1998; Hannon, 2000; Heath, 1983; Hirst, 1998; Taylor, 1983; Taylor and Dorsey-Gaines, 1988; Teale, 1986; Weinberger, 1996). It is also used to refer to certain kinds of educational *programmes* that recognize the importance of the family dimension in the literacy learning of children or parents or both (Cairney and Munsie, 1995; Dickinson, 1994; Hannon, 1995; Hannon and Nutbrown, 1997; Morrow, 1995; Wolfendale and Topping, 1996). This article is concerned with family literacy practices as viewed by children. Most interest in family literacy has focused on disadvantaged communities; this article reports data from five-year-old children from such communities in England just as they are starting formal schooling. The study focused on children's perceptions of their literacy interactions at home with family members. Family literacy practices in this article include writing, reading, aspects of oral language and engagement with environmental print. The article first considers families who were not involved in any family literacy programmes, then goes on to compare findings from such families to those from families who were involved in a family literacy programme.

Research into family literacy (*practices* and *programmes*) has, over the past two decades, involved three main approaches. First, researchers have found ways of observing and recording literacy practices in the home (Bissex, 1980; Clay, 1975; Moll et al., 1992; Nutbrown, 1999; Schickedanz, 1990; Tizard and Hughes, 1984). Second, they have solicited views and reports from parents (Hirst, 1998; Hannon and James, 1990; Parker, 1986; Weinberger, 1996). Third, they have evaluated learning outcomes for children and adults (Brooks et al., 1997; Brooks et al., 1996; Edwards, 1994; McNaughton et al., 1981; Tizard et al., 1982; Whitehurst et al., 1994). What has so far been rather overlooked has been the children's views of what is happening. It is unrealistic, of course, to expect young children to provide comprehensive reports of all the home activities that researchers and theorists now consider to comprise family literacy, but what may well be possible is for young children to tell us something about who and what is most *salient* in their literacy experiences.

The opportunity to study children's perspectives arose during the evaluation of a family literacy programme (described later) in which children had been randomly allocated to programme and control groups. The overall evaluation of that programme has included programme–control comparisons of measures of children's literacy development as well as studies of the perspectives of parents, children and teachers (Hannon and Nutbrown, 2001). This article, however, is solely concerned with children's perspectives.

An interesting issue from the point of view of programme evaluation is whether there are detectable differences between the perspectives of children in the programme and those of control groups. However, that is a subsidiary concern of this article. The control group on its own is the main interest because it constitutes a representative sample from the communities being studied. It is, in effect, a *survey* group and will be referred to as such from now on. Findings from that group offer insights into children's perspectives on family literacy – family literacy that exists independently of any programme. Later in the article, findings from the programme group will be compared to those from the survey group to see what impact, if any, the programme had on children's perspectives.

Before reporting any findings, it is necessary first to describe the methodological and ethical approach taken in studying young children's perspectives.

Methodological issues of conducting research with child participants

Children's perspectives are increasingly being seen as an important focus of educational research (Aubrey et al., 2000; Christensen and James, 2000; Greig and Taylor, 1999; Holmes, 1998; Lewis and Lindsay, 1999). Although recent studies have shown that exploring children's perspectives on their own learning can be illuminating, this approach does present methodo-logical challenges (Burnett and Myers, 2002; Critchley, 2002; Marsh and Thompson, 2001). Arguably, the involvement of children as research *partici-pants* rather than research *subjects* should be afforded them as a matter of right (Nutbrown, 1996) in order that their voices are heard and their viewpoints are taken into account in the development of policy and the evolution of practices which are designed to involve them. Some of the methodological considerations in this research can, therefore, be situated within the study of 'voice' in social science research in general which has emerged in recent years as a politically and morally positioned research response to issues faced by oppressed and silenced minorities: black women, people with AIDS, students with disabilities and learning difficulties, disaffected youths and parents with disabled children (Fine, 1994; Tierney, 1993; Clough, 1998; Pereera, 2001). Tierney writes that differences of (for example) race, class, gender and sexual orientation:

> ought to be honoured and brought into the centre of our discourses about education and its purpose. (Tierney, 1993: 111)

To Tierney's list of differences we could add 'age'. Perhaps educational research is one of the last arenas in society where it is still the case that children – especially *young* children – are seen but not heard? Including children as research informants brings them 'into the centre' of discourses about 'education and its purposes'. Research methods to understand children's learning have mainly relied on observation and techniques of

JOURNAL OF EARLY CHILDHOOD LITERACY 3(2)

observation have proliferated (Drummond et al., 1992; Nutbrown, 2001), but far less attention has been given to *listening* to children and soliciting their views on matters of daily life and learning. It is the case that the 'voices' of vulnerable children have sometimes been attended to with the pioneering of specifically designed interview techniques, mainly in areas of difficulty, such as child protection and child witnesses in court (thus reflecting the interest in 'voice' in relation to oppressed and minority groups). But until recently there has been relatively little interest in understanding the perspectives of children on what we might call the 'ordinary, everyday aspects' of their own lives (Dyer, 2002; Filippini and Vecchi, 2000). This study therefore asks: 'what do children say about literacy at home?'

Developing methods

Interviewing young children: some concerns

Given limited resources, constraints of time and a desire to survey a relatively large sample, there was no possibility of conducting lengthy case studies of the children. Detailed studies of this kind have been carried out (Bissex, 1980; Burnett and Myers, 2002; Kirkpatrick, 2002; Nutbrown, 1999; Schickedanz, 1990) but this study aimed to develop a broader picture of children's perspectives. The chosen method for obtaining their perspectives in this study was interviewing and it was clear that interviews would have to be brief, consisting of a few short, clear questions. A team of 10 early childhood professionals (7 teachers, 3 nursery nurses) worked with the research team to develop appropriate strategies for interviewing the children, and to devise an interview schedule. As part of their preparation, the concerns that some members of the team had about interviewing five-year-old children were considered. These could be summarized as: unreliability, misunderstanding and fear. Members of the team raised concerns such as:

'they may give you the answers they think you want'

'they may not understand the questions'

'they may feel overwhelmed by the situation'

It takes only a moment's reflection, of course, to realize that these are exactly the same concerns that need to be addressed when interviewing adults. Again, the literature on 'voice' and interviewing those who traditionally have not been heard in social science research encouraged the identification and resolution of difficulties by devising an approach that would best suit the young research participants. Such an approach is now well established in feminist studies with women participants (Oakley, 1993) and in advocacy work with adults with learning difficulties (Booth and Booth, 1994; Goodley, 2000). Thus it was decided to proceed on the assumption that the children would be willing to give their perspective on family literacy. It was also noted that five-year-olds can be much better at saying 'no' than many adults, should they not wish to proceed. It was concluded that children would know they were being asked questions and that interviewers could put children at their ease, just as they would if the interviewees were adults. Finally, the possibility that, despite all the thinking and planning, the children would not say anything at all was accepted from the outset.

Ethical considerations

The ethical considerations of this study centred largely on issues of informed consent – both from parents and children – and of ensuring that children were at no time uncomfortable or unhappy. The issue of taking up children's time for our own research purposes was also considered. The following steps were taken:

- parental permission to interview the children was obtained;
- interviewing protocols were developed that included a clear explanation to the children about the interview, and ensured that they understood that they did not have to participate. The children were also told that they could stop whenever they wished. No interview began until children's explicit agreement was given;
- children were interviewed in familiar surroundings;
- data remained anonymous by the allocation of an identification number, with the children's names known only to the interviewing team;
- interviewers worked with children in their usual roles of teachers and nursery nurses within the same LEA and had therefore undergone necessary legal checks in relation to child protection legislation;
- full briefing, training, debriefing and a telephone helpline was provided for all interviewers.

The interviewing team was sensitive to the needs and comfort of the children and prioritized the well-being of the children above data collection. Concerns about taking up or 'wasting' children's time were addressed by piloting the specifically designed interview schedule and finding out from children how it felt, whether they 'liked it', if they understood what they were being asked, and if they 'minded'.

The schedule was piloted by the team with 30 children (each member

JOURNAL OF EARLY CHILDHOOD LITERACY 3(2)

of the team interviewing 3 children). Children responded positively to being interviewed and the style and scope of the interview was broadly appropriate. The team reported that:

'No parent objected'

'Children seemed to enjoy the individual attention'

'Children liked the idea of talking to someone different who was interested in them'

'Children had no difficulty with being withdrawn from their larger group for the short period of the interview'

'Children understood the questions'

'Children said they "didn't mind" talking to the interviewers'

'Interviews took around 10 minutes to complete'

The interview questions, for the most part, appeared to be understood by the children, though some points of clarification were needed. Consequently some questions were rephrased to make them clearer and some additional prompt questions were added. Many aspects of family literacy could have been investigated but questions had to be limited, owing to constraints of time and concern to ensure that the experience was not too demanding of interviewees. There were difficult choices to be made and consequently some aspects of literacy were omitted (such as storytelling, talk about literacy, media literacy, computer use and ownership of books). Finally, six questions (with prompts) were chosen which focused on four strands of literacy (reading, writing, nursery rhymes and environmental print) that Nutbrown and Hannon (1997) have suggested are key in early literacy development work with parents. The term 'interview' is used throughout this article but, in reality, the experience for each child took the form of a one-to-one conversation about their views on family literacy. After a preamble, which followed the protocols detailed above, in which the interviewers explained about the interview and checked the child understood and was happy to participate, they asked the following:

1. Who do you write with? (Do you write at home?) (Who writes with you?)
2. Who do you read with? (Do you read at home?) (Who reads with you?)
3. What's your favourite book? (Is there one you like a lot?)
4. There is a lot of writing in books, but can you think of anywhere else where you see words? (Where is that?)

5. Have you got a favourite nursery rhyme? (What is it?)
6. Who sings rhymes with you? (Do you sing/say them at home?)(Who with?)

Where children only mentioned school and their teachers, the prompt questions (in brackets) were asked to focus children's thinking on home literacy interactions. Asking 'Who?' and 'What?' questions was not intended to uncover a full picture of children's literacy experiences. It cannot be relied upon to generate an exhaustive list of everybody involved in literacy practices with the child and what they do. But it seems reasonable to infer from their responses something about the *salience* of certain individuals, certain literacy interactions, and aspects of literacy from children's perspectives.

Children's responses were recorded in writing by interviewers and later coded into the self-evident categories listed in Figures 2–12. The figures also show comparisons between groups (in Figures 2–6, the comparison is between boys and girls; in Figures 7–12, the comparison is between the survey and programme groups explained below). Comparisons between groups of the frequencies shown were carried out separately for each category and the statistical significance of any differences assessed (by repeated chi-squared tests). Only a few group differences were statistically significant at $p< .05$; these will be referred to later.

The interviewing experience

Interviews were carried out at the children's schools after the children had been in their reception classes (the first class attended by children of statutory school age in England) for half a term (six weeks). The interviewing team found the experience interesting and reported that most of the children were happy to talk, responsive and not inhibited by the situation. Not all the interviews were completed in full. Interviewers never persisted if they felt the child showed the slightest sign of anxiety (two interviews were curtailed by the interviewers for this reason).

The groups studied

As explained earlier, two groups of children were studied. The main one, referred to as the 'survey group', was a control group in the evaluation of a family literacy programme; the second, referred to as the 'programme group', consisted of children in that programme. Originally, a sample of 160 families with three-year-olds had been drawn at random from the waiting lists of 10 schools in areas of social and economic disadvantage in a northern city in England. All schools were in areas (electoral wards) above

JOURNAL OF EARLY CHILDHOOD LITERACY 3(2)

the national median on the government's index of multiple deprivation and 5 were in the most deprived 2 percent of such areas nationally. At each of the 10 schools, 16 children aged around three-and-a-half were drawn at random from preschool waiting lists (virtually all families in the areas were on such lists). All the families were white monolingual. Families agreed to participate in a University research study on the understanding that half of them, selected entirely at random, would be invited to join a preschool family literacy programme (described later) with the remainder serving as a control group. There were 8 children in each school in each group. Both groups of families cooperated fully in the study and programme take-up was very high. Children were interviewed shortly after they reached their fifth birthday. Attrition in the two groups over the 18-month period of the programme was less than 10 percent. In the survey group, 3 children were lost to the study because families left the city; in the programme group 2 children were so lost. Seven children were absent from school on the day of interviewing (all but one from the survey group). Thus the survey group finally consisted of 71 children (31 girls, 40 boys) and the programme group consisted of 77 children (33 girls, 44 boys). In the survey group 14 (out of 71) families had lone parents, and there were 9 (out of 77) lone-parents in the programme group, all mothers.

Children's views of family literacy: Findings from the survey group

Each set of interview notes was reviewed and used to develop brief individual profiles of the children. The following examples of profiles use pseudonyms.

Philip

Philip was five years and two months old when he was interviewed. He had been in the first class of school, full time, for seven weeks, and prior to that had attended a nursery near his present school. Philip lived with his mother and father close to the school.

Philip reported that he wrote with his teacher at school and at home he wrote and read with:

'mum and dad and grandma and my grandad and uncles and aunties'.

Philip told the interviewer that you can also read at school with:

'Your friends who can read, or your teacher.'

The books he said were his favourites at the time were:

NUTBROWN & HANNON: FAMILY LITERACY

'*The Magic School Bus* and *The Times of the Dinosaurs*'

He gave some examples of print in school:

'On some boards, on charts that stick on the wall, and on cards.'

And he also said that there were lots of words '*at home*'.

Philip talked about singing rhymes at home, saying his favourite was 'Baa, baa black sheep', and he usually sang them with:

'Nobody. They only clap at me when I'm done. Sometimes they do sing with me.'

Juliet

Juliet was aged five years and one month when she was interviewed. She had been in the first class of school, full time, for six weeks, and prior to that had attended a nursery class in the same school. She lived with her mother and father and twin sisters.

Juliet reported that she wrote with:

'Lauren, my friend, at school – we write about things like animals'.

and she said she wrote at home too,

'sometimes . . . but I have two sisters who get the pen and write on the sofa'.

Juliet mentioned reading with several people:

'Lauren and Abbey, my friends. I read to Laura and Megan (my sisters – they're one)'.

She also told the interviewer something about busy family lives, saying that she read with:

'Mummy or daddy sometimes, mummy has to do the ironing and daddy has to paint the conservatory'.

Pocahontas was the book Juliet named as her favourite book at the time.

Juliet gave some examples of neighbourhood print:

'On a sign, in the middle of the street, and at the bus stop.'

At home, 'while mummy is making tea' Juliet and her sisters sang nursery rhymes, her favourite being *Humpty Dumpty*.

Fleur

Fleur was five years and two months old when she was interviewed. She had been in the first class of school, full time, for five weeks, and prior to

JOURNAL OF EARLY CHILDHOOD LITERACY 3(2)

that had attended the nursery class in the school, full time. Fleur lived with her mother and sister Collette close to the school.

Fleur reported that she wrote at home:

'with my sister Collie'.

She said she did not read at home, but at school, and she did not give a title of a favourite book but said that she liked:

'books about animals'.

Fleur thought about places where she would find words and suggested that there were some in:

'colouring books'.

When it came to rhymes Fleur thought her favourite was 'Jack and Jill'.

All the children had their own personal literacy stories to tell and the data were sufficiently rich to continue analysis for generalizable findings across the sample. Having achieved an overview of the children's perspectives from their individual profiles, the next stage of analysis was to explore what the 71 five-year-olds said about reading, writing and sharing nursery rhymes at home. A clear finding was that all children reported some literacy activity at home. From their perspectives, reading and writing were common activities at home (over 90 percent saying they read *and* wrote at home). Singing and saying rhymes was also seen as a home activity though less frequent than reading and writing, Figure 1 illustrates this graphically. It is interesting that virtually all of these young children, from poor areas of a northern English city, where school measures of literacy are low (as are expectations of parental involvement in school literacy), reported that they *did* engage in reading and writing at home. The fine detail of their responses is even more interesting.

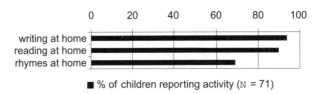

Figure 1 **Children's experience of writing, reading and rhymes at home**

Children's family experiences of writing

In response to the question, 'Who do you write with?', the children listed a variety of people known to them: mother, father, siblings, teachers, peers

NUTBROWN & HANNON: FAMILY LITERACY

at school, grandparents, other family members, and some also said that they wrote by themselves. Some responses to the question were:

'Andrew, my bestest friend'

'My dad'

'Mrs Hudson, my teacher'

'Mrs Aston, you put your hand up and she comes'

'My mummy and Ben'

'Lauren (my friend) at school. We write about things like animals'

'My nanan. We write numbers'

Figure 2 shows responses from all children, distinguished in terms of gender, to the question, 'Who do you write with?'. Findings in relation to gender were of interest because of continuing concern, in England, over the school literacy achievement of boys (Qualifications and Curriculum Authority, 1998; Frater, 2000). Figure 2 suggests some gender differences but, apart from girls' greater readiness to mention writing with teachers, none was statistically significant by the chi-squared analyses described earlier. This finding is consistent with Brooks et al. (1997) who found that girls outperformed boys in writing. The main interest in Figure 2 is the overall pattern of responses common to both sexes. Over 50 percent of children reported writing with their mothers, and around 25 percent of children said they wrote with their fathers. Lynch (2002) examined the role of gender in parent–child reading relationships, one of the few studies of family literacy to include separate discussion of 'parents' roles' as they relate

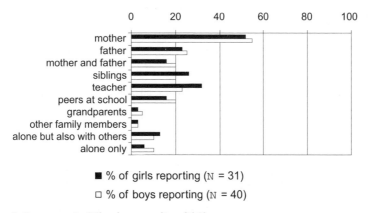

■ % of girls reporting (N = 31)

□ % of boys reporting (N = 40)

Figure 2 **Responses to 'Who do you write with?'**

JOURNAL OF EARLY CHILDHOOD LITERACY 3(2)

to *mothers* and *fathers*. Most research refers to *parents* (Benjamin and Lord, 1997; Brooks et al. 1997) even when the majority of participants appear to be women (McNaughton, 2001; Wood, 2002). It is therefore difficult to distinguish the specific roles played by mothers and fathers. However, it is acknowledged that mothers play a prominent role in literacy with their preschool children (Harrison, 1996) and are in the majority in family literacy programmes (Mace, 1998). The findings from this survey show that children see it this way too, but the survey also indicates that around a quarter of children mentioned that their father wrote with them. This, perhaps, provides some indication that, though relatively under-reported, fathers *are* involved in their children's writing at home. Grandparents and other family members seem to have less salient roles in the writing lives of these young children. A small number of children (8 percent) said that they only ever wrote alone, and 11 percent said they sometimes wrote alone but also wrote with others, perhaps indicating developing independence in writing.

Children's family experiences of reading

The children were asked, 'Who do you read with?', and again they listed a variety of people known to them: mother, father, siblings, teachers, peers at school, grandparents, other family members, and some also said that they read by themselves. Some responses were:

'Lewis, my friend from Scotland'

'Loads of books with daddy and mummy'

'Your friends who can read or your teacher'

'My teacher, Mrs Day'

'My sister Leigh, she's Y4'

'Mummy, my dad can read but I learn with my mummy'

'My brother Eric'

'Mrs Bingham, she's at school but she's not my teacher'

'Me grandad and me nanan'

Figure 3 shows the responses from all the children (again distinguished in terms of gender) to the question, 'Who do you read with?'. None of the gender differences was statistically significant. Seventy-two percent of children in the survey group reported reading with their mothers and 39 percent said they read with their fathers. Twenty-five percent of the children in the sample said they read with both their mothers and fathers. Again,

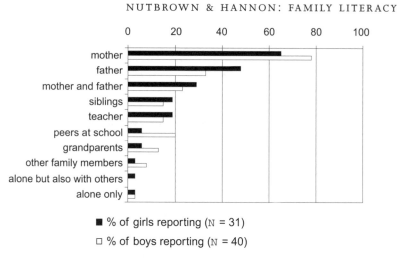

Figure 3 **Responses to 'Who do you read with?'**

the children's reports accord with the view that mothers play a prominent role in reading with their children but, as with writing, the reported involvement of fathers in reading activity provides much-needed evidence of fathers' involvement in their children's reading at home. According to the children, grandparents and other family members are minimally involved. The children were also asked to name a favourite book and responded with a variety of titles, including: *Aladdin, Toy Story, Bug's Life, The Little Mermaid, Go, Go Power Ranger, Fireman Sam, Spot, Barbie, Grandpa, Goldilocks, What a Mess!, Thomas the Tank Engine, Dumbo* and *Hansel and Gretel*.

Some children said:

'Can't remember the name of the story, I have the telly when I go to bed to – watch videos, Bambi'

'My reading book from school "The Sausage"'

'I spy with my little eye – a book beginning with the one about A for Alice'

'One that opens things up'

'That police book that makes a noise'

'One about a dog. It has a sheep and a dog that talks'

'Me and Eric like Baa Baa Black Sheep book best'

'Goldilocks and the 3 bears, I've got it at Nanny Anne's'

'Houses – it's a book at school'

JOURNAL OF EARLY CHILDHOOD LITERACY 3(2)

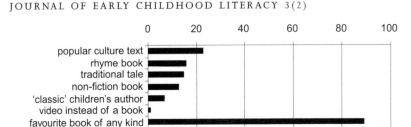

■ % of children reporting (N = 71)

Figure 4 **Children's favourite books**

They named various types of book: popular culture, rhyme books, traditional tales, non-fiction, books by a 'classic' modern children's author (for example, Shirley Hughes, Eric Carl) and one child named a video instead of a book. Figure 4 shows the percentage responses, with 89 percent of children naming a favourite book. Weinberger (1996) found that the ability to name a favourite book at age five was a predictor of later literacy achievement. The majority of children were able to do this and, in keeping with findings from studies of literacy and popular culture (Marsh and Thompson, 2001), the texts named most frequently were those relating to popular culture such as Disney films (for example *Toy Story* and *The Little Mermaid*) and children's television programmes (such as *Teletubbies* and *Fireman Sam*).

Children's family experiences of sharing rhymes and songs
When asked, 'Who do you sing or say rhymes with?', the children listed a variety of people. They said:

'Grandad'

'Nobody, they only clap at me when I'm done, sometimes they do sing with me'

'Mummy and on my own'

'I sing them on my own'

'I don't need anyone to help'

'Chelsea, my cousin'

'With our Toni'

'Mummy and daddy'

'My mummy and she likes Robbie Williams'

NUTBROWN & HANNON: FAMILY LITERACY

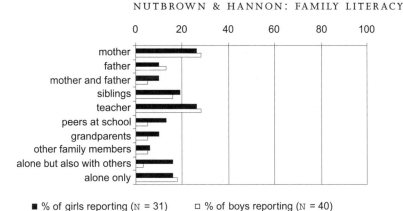

■ % of girls reporting (N = 31)   □ % of boys reporting (N = 40)

Figure 5 **Responses to 'Who do you sing or say rhymes with?'**

Figure 5 shows the responses from all the children and their responses to the question, 'Who do you sing or say rhymes with?'. Twenty-seven percent of children reported singing or saying rhymes with their mothers, and around 11 percent of children said they did so with their fathers. Seven percent of the children in the sample said they shared rhymes with both their mothers and fathers. From the children's perspectives, grandparents and other family members also appear to be involved in sharing rhymes at home. Twenty-seven percent of children report sharing rhymes with their teachers and 17 percent said that they enjoyed rhymes on their own.

Children's family experiences of environmental print

Finally, the children were asked about environmental print. They named a variety of examples of environmental print found in the community, school, home and on clothing. Their examples included:

'A list on the side of food'

'Sweet shop'

'Where you play football'

'Bus stop'

'On the wall at Manor Top – people draw on the wall – it's naughty'

'On the floor on my road'

'White board'

'Letters outside in the yard'

JOURNAL OF EARLY CHILDHOOD LITERACY 3(2)

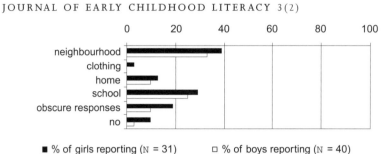

Figure 6 **Responses to 'Can you think of anywhere else you see words?'**

'Name cards'

'Charts on the wall'

'A poster on my wall'

'Colouring books'

'In my kitchen behind the fruit basket'

'My brother's clothes'

Figure 6 shows children's responses to the question, '(apart from books) can you think of anywhere else where you see words?'. Environmental print in the neighbourhood is mentioned most frequently with both boys and girls identifying some examples of print and only four children giving no examples. The lack of mention of print on clothing is surprising, especially given the fashion for the printed word on many items of children's clothing. Print in school was mentioned by some 27 percent of children: 'teddy words', 'words on drawers', 'labels on coat pegs' being typical examples of such print. 'Teddy words' relate directly to teaching strategies being promoted nationally as part of the 'literacy hour' (DfEE, 1998) and clearly had an impact on the children's concepts of print. There were no statistically significant differences in the responses of boys and girls regarding environmental print.

So far this article has reported findings from a survey of 71 five-year-old children who were selected at random from 10 schools in areas of social and economic deprivation and with low literacy achievement. It appears, from the children's perspectives, that much of their literacy took place in their homes and was supported by their families. The remaining question centred around whether it might be possible to add to such pre-existing literacy practices (as illuminated in this study) through a family literacy programme.

The family literacy programme

The family literacy programme, developed and implemented by teachers at the schools, was 'long duration' (18 months) and 'low intensity'. It was based on a conceptual framework developed by Hannon and Nutbrown (1997) in which parents are seen as providing opportunities, recognition, interaction and a model of literacy. The programme framework and examples of activities have been previously reported (Nutbrown and Hannon, 1997) and included the following five components.

Home visits by programme teachers; where teachers focused on a particular strand of literacy, loaned materials and made suggestions to parents about what they might do next to support their child's learning in this area of literacy. For example: a home visit that focused on print in the neighbourhood might include a walk to the local shop and the suggestion that the parent and child might make a collection of words they found on food packages to share on the next visit.

Provision of literacy resources; particularly books, but also writing materials, scrapbooks, glue and literacy games. Teachers identified, in discussion with parents, the literacy interests of the child and loaned parents literacy resources that would help to develop that strand of literacy. For example: a focus on playing with letters of the alphabet was developed by loaning parents play dough and alphabet cutters for children to use to make their names and those of others in the family.

Centre-based group activities; where a small group of parents involved in the programme might meet to talk about an aspect of literacy. For example: writing workshops were held to explain some theories of early writing development and help parents identify the 'stage' that their own child was at within the broad range of writing development which can be identified in three- to five-year-olds. Book parties were also held where food, games and activities were linked to a favourite book, or books.

Special events; which involved groups out of the home or centre included group library visits where families could join the library and enjoy especially planned activities for the children, print walks and rides where families took part in 'literacy treasure hunts' – spotting words and signs in the local community.

JOURNAL OF EARLY CHILDHOOD LITERACY 3(2)

Postal communication; between the child and the programme teacher which included: birthday cards, postcards, reminder notes. A collection of nursery rhyme cards was printed and sent to children by the teachers, so providing for the child and parent the words of popular rhymes. Such postcard collections were popular with the children and were often stuck on the kitchen wall or into scrapbooks and used on subsequent home visits.

In these ways the programme sought to promote children's experience with family members of four strands of early literacy development: writing, reading and rhyming at home and greater awareness of environmental print. There was also an optional adult education component where parents were given information about local adult education classes and the opportunity to develop a portfolio of the work they had done with their child for accreditation.

As well as the ethical issues discussed earlier around children as interview participants, there was a further ethical concern to be addressed by the researchers and schools. The programme outlined above had been offered only to one group of children, not both. However, it should be recognized that no children were deprived of anything, all children accessed their regular educational provision. The programme families were offered something extra that would not have been available without research funding.

What difference does a family literacy programme make?

The findings reported were next compared to findings from the programme group of children attending the same schools as the children in the survey, to determine what difference, if any, children's experience in the programme made to their perspectives on family literacy. As the children had been allocated strictly at random to two groups, there was no difference between them in relation to geographical area, school placement, age, gender or pre-programme literacy achievement. The only difference was that children in the programme group had been part of a family literacy programme for the previous 18 months, and their parents had worked with teachers, both in their own homes and in occasional small group sessions, on aspects of children's literacy development. The interview schedule used for the programme group was the same as that used in the first survey and the interviewers did not know which children had been involved in the family literacy programme. None of the teachers involved in the programme was involved in interviewing the children.

Figure 7 shows the proportions of children in each group who said that

NUTBROWN & HANNON: FAMILY LITERACY

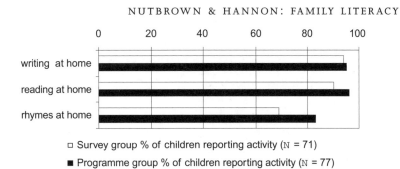

Figure 7 **Children's reported experience of reading, writing and sharing nursery rhymes at home**

they wrote, read or said nursery rhymes at home. The children's responses indicate that they experienced literacy with a range of family members. A greater proportion of children in the programme group mentioned that they wrote, read and shared rhymes at home but the differences were not statistically significant. It is worth probing a little deeper, however, in comparing the two groups.

Comparing children's family experiences of writing

In response to the question, 'Who do you write with?', children in both groups listed a variety of people known to them: mother, father, siblings, teachers, peers at school, grandparents, other family members, and some also said that they wrote by themselves. Figure 8 shows the responses from all the children (survey and programme) to the question. Responses from children in the survey group were reported earlier; some responses from children in the programme group when we asked, 'Who do you write with?' were similar:

'By myself, mummy watches me and helps me a little bit'

'I wrote loads of things with my mum and once I wrote loads by my own – even one big page'

'My mummy, she doesn't know how to write so I help her out'

'Sometimes on my own, my mummy, dad, friends, sister and brother'

'My nannan when my mum goes to the pub'

Children in both groups report active engagement in writing with others at home, with a slightly greater proportion of programme children reporting writing with their mother, father, siblings and grandparents, and a slightly higher percentage of children in the survey group reported writing

JOURNAL OF EARLY CHILDHOOD LITERACY 3(2)

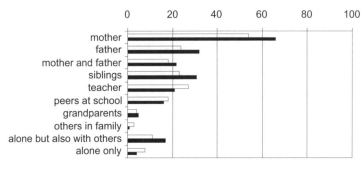

□ Survey group % of children reporting (N = 71)

■ Programme group % of children reporting (N = 77)

Figure 8 **Responses to 'Who do you write with?'**

with their teachers and peers at school. None of these differences, however, was statistically significant.

Comparing children's family experiences of reading

When asked, 'Who do you read with?' both groups listed a variety of people known to them: mother, father, siblings, teachers, peers at school, grand-parents, other family members, and some also said that they read by them-selves. Responses from children in the survey group were reported earlier; responses from children in the programme group were similar:

'Daddy and mummy'

'Upstairs with my sister Emma'

'My brother, Aaron, my little brother'

'My teacher'

'Mummy at bedtime'

'I've got a big story book with Snow White in it and on my video and my mum and me Nanan reads it me'

'My mum and Niall, yes, at night, and sometimes in the afternoon. That's when I go to my caravan on holiday to Skegness'

Figure 9 shows the responses from both groups to the question, 'Who do you read with?'. Children reported active engagement in reading at home with others but – as with writing – a greater proportion of programme children mentioned reading with their mother, father and siblings. The only differences, however, to be statistically significant at p< .05

NUTBROWN & HANNON: FAMILY LITERACY

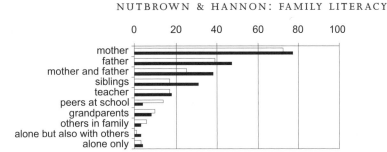

□ Survey group % of children reporting (N = 71)

■ Programme group % of children reporting (N = 77)

Figure 9 **Responses to 'Who do you read with?'**

(again, according to chi-squared tests) were programme children's greater likelihood of mentioning reading with siblings at home and their lesser likelihood of mentioning reading with peers in school.

The children were also asked to name a favourite book and responded with a variety of types of book as shown in Figure 10. None of the differences between groups was statistically significant although programme children appeared slightly more likely to name a favourite book, and to name rhyme books, non-fiction books and books written by well known modern classic children's authors (such as Shirley Hughes or Eric Carl). In the survey group, the percentage response appeared slightly greater for popular culture texts (such as those produced to accompany Disney films, or TV programmes) and traditional tales (such as *The Three Bears*) but the difference was not statistically significant. Some of the titles reported by children in the programme group were: *Tom Kitten, The Dream, Thomas the Tank*

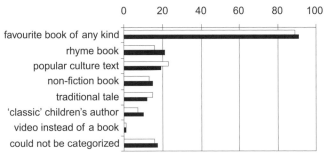

□ Survey group % of children reporting (N = 71)

■ Programme group % of children reporting (N = 77)

Figure 10 **Children's favourite books ranked in order of the Programme group**

JOURNAL OF EARLY CHILDHOOD LITERACY 3(2)

Engine, Butterflies, Three Little Pigs, Humpty Dumpty, Go, Snow White and the Seven Dwarves, Mickey Mouse, Spot, Jack and Jill, Peter the Tractor, We're going on a Bear Hunt, Teddy Bears' Picnic, Bug's Life.

Comparing children's family experiences of sharing rhymes and songs

Children listed a variety of people known to them: mother, father, siblings, teachers, peers at school, grandparents, other family members when we asked them 'Who do you sing or say rhymes with?'. Responses from children in the survey group were reported earlier, some responses from children in the programme group to the question, 'Who do you sing or say rhymes with?', were:

'Mummy, daddy, brother and Jakey the dog'

'Emma, my sister, my big brother Joe'

'My teacher, Mrs Hatton'

'My grandad'

'Teachers and everybody'

'Nanan Shirley, Grandad One'

'Nile does and Nanan when she comes up'

Comparing children's family experiences of environmental print

Finally, when children were asked about environmental print, children in both groups responded with examples from four print domains: the neighbourhood, school, home and on clothing. Responses from children in the survey group were reported earlier, examples of responses from children in the programme group are listed in Table 1 and include:

'Tesco'

'At the shops, my big brother lifts me up'

'On your credit card'

'On a newspaper'

'MacDonald's'

Figure 12 shows responses of both groups to the question 'Apart from books, can you think of anywhere else where you see words?'. Although the programme group children provided more examples of family literacy in their neighbourhood, on clothing, in their homes and in school, and

NUTBROWN & HANNON: FAMILY LITERACY

Table 1 **Children's comments in response to the question 'Can you think of anywhere else you see words?'**

	Survey group	*Programme group*
Neighbourhood	on my road where I live	Tesco
	at shopping	crisp packets
	down the street	bread in the shop
	a list on the side of food	at shops
	on tins	at the bank
	outside the shop	at the shops, my big brother lifts me up
	shop sign	at the library
	in the car	shops have words
	sweet shop	on your credit card
	where you play football	on a poster
	Netto	at Asda
	newspaper	on a newspaper
	on my wall	at the pictures
	on my bike	on windows
	Co-op	in signs
	bus stop	in town
	signs	MacDonald's
	toyshop	KFC
	television	on a roof
	on the wall at Manor Top – people draw on the wall – it's naughty	on a lollipop (crossing)
	on the floor on my road	on a shop poster
	outside Crystal Peaks	on birthday cards
	Asda	on letters and envelopes
		on food tins
		on ingredients
		on the road and the path – I writed it and I got done but me Mam don't know
		work signs on the road side
		on the road
		on walls near my house
		on boxes, shops, baskets, trolleys
		on lolly sticks I can read it and it might be a joke
		video shops
		sweets
School	ABC on my classroom wall	on the walls
	in the corridor	in 'words and pictures' letters
	on the wall	on a board
	at school when it's someone's birthday	on a drawer
	labels of drawers	on our meal boxes
		on the box of letters

JOURNAL OF EARLY CHILDHOOD LITERACY 3(2)

Table 1 **Continued**

	Survey group	Programme group
	white board	on doors at school
	letters outside in the yard	on paper
	name cards	on the floor in the hall
	milk label box	on work
	on a jigsaw	playground
	on the door at school	tuck shop
	on paper at school	
	on the calendar at my school	
	on pencil cases	
	charts on the wall	
	labels on paintings	
Home	I have a number on my door	in an envelope
	a poster on my wall	in the cupboard
	colouring books	I've got a poster that says words
	in letters	my dad put words on the back gate
	in my kitchen behind the fruit basket	in a letter
	Action Man pad and pencil	on a cake
		we've got a sign up because we're moving house
		on my walls in my bedroom
		on my jumper
		in my bedroom
		newspapers
		magazines
		on an invitation sometimes
Clothing	my brother's clothes	on clothes
		school uniform

survey group children were less likely to give examples of environmental print or provided obscure responses, these differences were not statistically significant.

The quality of children's responses in the two groups is worth further comment. Table 1 lists the responses from children in each group in each of the categories of print reported in Figure 12. Although many children gave similar responses, each is listed here only once. Table 1 suggests a more diverse set of responses from children in the programme group who tended to give more examples of print in the neighbourhood and in their homes. Children in the survey group, however, appeared to draw on a wider variety of print in the school environment.

NUTBROWN & HANNON: FAMILY LITERACY

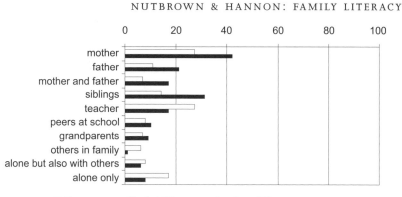

☐ Survey group % of children reporting (N = 71)

■ Programme group % of children reporting (N = 77)

Figure 11 **Responses to 'Who do you sing or say rhymes with?'**

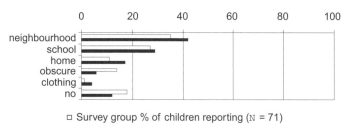

☐ Survey group % of children reporting (N = 71)

■ Programme group % of children reporting (N = 77)

Figure 12 **Responses to 'Can you think of anywhere else where you see words?'**

Overall comparison of survey and programme groups

Responses of children in the two groups to questions about writing, reading, rhymes and environmental print have been compared. The findings suggest that there are differences in so far as children in the programme group were slightly more likely to mention literacy involvement at home, and slightly less likely to mention school literacy than their survey group peers. Taken singly, these differences were not statistically significant. Taken collectively, however, a pattern may be discerned.

Table 2 presents 43 different family literacy activities in two columns: those more often reported by survey group children and those more often reported by programme group children. Table 2 further distinguishes literacy activities promoted by the family literacy programme from activities that were not actively promoted by the programme (not because they were

JOURNAL OF EARLY CHILDHOOD LITERACY 3(2)

Table 2 **Comparison of family literacy activities reported by children according to whether or not promoted in family literacy programme**

	More often reported in survey group	More often in programme group
Promoted in family literacy programme	writing with others in family reading with grandparents reading with others in family naming a traditional tale rhymes with others in family rhymes alone (and with others) rhymes alone (only)	writing at home reading at home rhymes at home writing with mother writing with father writing with mother and father writing with siblings writing with grandparents writing alone (and with others) reading with mother reading with father reading with mother and father reading with siblings reading with teacher reading alone (and with others) reading alone (only) naming a favourite book naming a rhyme book naming a non-fiction book naming book by 'classic' author rhymes with mother rhymes with father rhymes with mother and father rhymes with siblings rhymes with grandparents print in the community print on clothing print in the home print in school
Not promoted in programme	writing with teacher writing with peers at school writing alone (only) reading with peers at school named a popular culture book rhymes with teacher	rhymes with peers at school

felt inappropriate, simply because they fell outside the conceptual framework on which the programme was based). It can be seen that over three-quarters (29 out of 36) of the activities promoted by the programme were cited more often by the programme group. As this difference is statistically significant, $\chi^2(1) = 16.0$, p< .001, it indicates that there was an overall programme effect in terms of children's perspectives on family literacy. Given that the two groups of children were equivalent as a result of random allocation with the only difference being that children in the programme group were participants in a family literacy programme, one is forced to conclude that the family literacy programme had a discernible impact from the children's perspective.

Conclusions

This study has demonstrated that young children *can* give their perspectives on family literacy. Findings suggest that such perspectives are worth listening to and that what children have to say is illuminating. There are four specific findings.

First, *all* children do some literacy at home. The children in this study were attending schools in very deprived areas of a poor northern English city in the UK where it would not be surprising to find low levels of literacy activity. If deficit assumptions about such family literacy practices are held by some educators, it is perhaps because home literacy is not as clearly visible (in school contexts) as school literacy. Studies such as this are needed to make visible home literacy practices. Family literacy practices are also sometimes different from school literacy and so there is the possibility that such literacy is not always recognized and valued as the kind of literacy that holds currency in school.

Second, the study provides some evidence that fathers *are* involved in literacy at home. Relatively little is known about fathers' roles in their children's preschool literacy, but – according to their children – the fathers in this study appeared to play an important role. Further research into fathers' roles would illuminate this neglected aspect of family literacy *practice* and could influence the development of family literacy *programmes*.

Third, *boys* are involved in literacy at home. At the age of five, these boys say that they are active in literacy, even if studies and national testing raise concerns about literacy not being a masculine pursuit and boys' lower achievement in literacy later (Office for Standards in Education, 1993; Qualifications and Curriculum Authority, 1998; Frater, 1997, 2000).

Fourth, a programme *can* make some difference to family literacy activities as perceived by children.

There are perhaps three implications from this study for the future development of family literacy programmes:

1. As has been previously argued (Auerbach, 1989; Hannon and Nutbrown, 1997; Taylor, 1997), family literacy programmes need to

JOURNAL OF EARLY CHILDHOOD LITERACY 3(2)

start from a positive position that they are building on existing knowledge and skills, not starting with 'blank slates'. Programmes can maximize children's literacy repertoires by offering a broad range of literacy activities continuous with – but also extending – those they experience at home.

2. Family literacy programmes need to be reviewed in order to maximize the involvement of fathers. For example where home visiting forms part of the programme, fathers may become more involved than they would in programmes that *require* regular group attendance. Emphasis on the roles both parents can play to support their children may well help fathers to enhance their roles in their children's literacy. Such interactions may be hidden, taking place in the home and not observed by family literacy workers who run group sessions, but just because it is not witnessed it does not mean that it does not happen.

3. The capacity of family literacy programmes to make some difference, across strands of literacy, to children's achievement may, again, point to the need to review the *content* and *delivery* of programmes to maximize the benefits. The content of family literacy programmes may need to be adjusted to focus on particular strands of literacy and parents' roles in developing their children's early literacy. The delivery of the programme may need to include flexible home visiting (which can reach both fathers and mothers) as well as group sessions and optional adult learning opportunities.

These findings and suggested implications emanate from analysis of the reports from the children in the study. A fuller picture of family literacy practices and the impact of family literacy programmes needs to incorporate the voices of parents and teachers and measures of children's literacy development. Meanwhile, this study shows that young children are able to share their perspectives and their voices deserve to be heard in the future development of family literacy programmes.

Acknowledgement
We wish to acknowledge the cooperation of the children, parents and schools in the project of which this study was a part. We are grateful to the team of interviewers and to the schools who facilitated communication with parents and interviews with children. We are also grateful to Judi Duffield, Heather Scott and members of the Literacy Research Centre at the University of Sheffield School of Education. The research was part funded by the Nuffield Foundation.

References
Aubrey, C., David, T., Godfrey, R. and Thompson, L. (2000) *Early Childhood Educational Research: Issues in Methodology and Ethics.* London: Routledge Falmer.

NUTBROWN & HANNON: FAMILY LITERACY

Auerbach, E.R. (1989) 'Toward a Social-contextual Approach to Family Literacy', *Harvard Educational Review* 59(2): 165–81.

Barton, D. and Hamilton, M. (1998) *Local Literacies: Reading and Reading in One Community.* London: Routledge.

Benjamin, L.A. and Lord, J., eds (1997) *Family Literacy: Directions in Research and Implications for Practice.* Washington, DC: US Department of Education/Office for Educational Research and Improvement.

Bissex, G. (1980) *GYNS AT WRK: A Child Learns to Write and Read.* Cambridge, MA: Harvard University Press.

Booth, T. and Booth, W. (1994) *Parenting under Pressure: Mothers and Fathers with Learning Difficulties.* Buckingham: Open University Press.

Brooks, G., Gorman, T., Harman, D. and Wilkin, A. (1996) *Family Literacy Works: The NFER Evaluation of the Basic Skills Agency's Family Literacy Demonstration Programmes.* London: The Basic Skills Agency.

Brooks, G., Gorman, T., Harman, J., Hutchison, D., Kinder, K., Moor, H. and Wilkin, A. (1997) *Family Literacy Lasts: The NFER Follow-up Study of the Basic Skills Agency's Demonstration Programmes.* London:Basic Skills Agency.

Burnett, C. and Myers, J. (2002) '"Beyond the Frame": Exploring Children's Literacy Practices', *Reading* 36(2): 56–62.

Cairney, T.H. and Munsie, L. (1995) *Beyond Tokenism: Parents as Partners in Literacy.* Portsmouth, NH: Heinemann.

Christensen, P. and James, A. (eds) (2000) *Research with Children: Perspectives and Practices.* London: Falmer Press.

Clay, M.M. (1975) *What did I Write?* Auckland, New Zealand: Heinemann Educational.

Clough, P. (1998) *Articulating with Difficulty: Research Voices in Inclusive Education.* London: Paul Chapman Publishing.

Critchley, D. (2002) 'Children's Assessment of Their Own Learning', in C. Nutbrown (ed.) *Research Studies in Early Childhood Education*, pp. 53–66. Stoke-on-Trent: Trentham.

DfEE (1998) *The National Literacy Strategy.* London: The Stationery Office.

Dickinson, D., ed. (1994) *Bridges to Literacy: Children, Families and Schools.* Oxford: Blackwell.

Drummond, M.J., Rouse, D. and Pugh, G. (1992) *Making Assessment Work: Values and Principles in Assessing Young Children's Learning.* Nottingham: NES Arnold/National Children's Bureau.

Dyer, P. (2002) 'A Box Full of Feelings: Emotional Literacy in a Nursery Class', in C. Nutbrown (ed.) *Research Studies in Early Childhood Education*, pp. 67–76. Stoke-on-Trent: Trentham.

Edwards, P.A. (1994) 'Responses of Teachers and African-American Mothers to a Book-reading Intervention Program', in D. Dickinson (ed.) *Bridges to Literacy: Children, Families and Schools*, pp. 175–208. Oxford: Blackwell.

Filippini, T. and Vecchi, V., eds (2000) *The Hundred Languages of Children: Exhibition Catalogue.* Reggio Emilia: Reggio Children.

Fine, M. (1994) 'Dis-stance and Other Stances: Negotiations of Power Inside Feminist Research', in A. Gitlin (ed.) *Power and Method: Political Activism and Educational Research*, pp. 49–62. London: Routledge.

Frater, G. (1997) *Improving Boys' Literacy.* London: Basic Skills Agency.

Frater, G. (2000) *Securing Boys' Literacy: A Survey of Effective Practice in Primary Schools.* London: Basic Skills Agency.

Goodley, D. (2000) *Self-advocacy in the Lives of People with Learning Difficulties.* Buckingham: Open University Press.

JOURNAL OF EARLY CHILDHOOD LITERACY 3(2)

Greig, A. and Taylor, J. (1999) *Doing Research with Children.* London: Sage.

Hannon, P. (1995) *Literacy, Home and School: Research and Practice in Teaching Literacy with Parents.* London: Falmer Press.

Hannon, P. and James, S. (1990) 'Parents' and Teachers' Perspectives on Preschool Literacy Development', *British Educational Research Journal* 16(3): 259–72.

Hannon, P. (2000) 'Rhetoric and Research in Family Literacy', *British Educational Research Journal* 26(1): 121–38.

Hannon, P. and Nutbrown, C. (1997) 'Teachers' Use of Conceptual Framework for Early Literacy Education Involving Parents', *Teacher Development* 1(3): 405–20.

Hannon, P. and Nutbrown, C. (2001) 'Outcomes for Children and Parents of an Early Literacy Education Parental Involvement Programme', paper presented at the Annual Conference of the British Educational Research Association, Leeds, 5–7 September.

Harrison, C. (1996) 'Family Literacy: Evaluation, Ownership and Ambiguity', *Royal Society of Arts Journal* (November): 1–4.

Heath, S.B. (1983) *Ways with Words: Language, Life and Work in Communities and Classrooms.* Cambridge: Cambridge University Press.

Hirst, K. (1998) 'Pre-school Literacy Experiences of Children in Punjabi, Urdu and Gujerati Speaking Families in England', *British Educational Research Journal* 24(4): 415–29.

Holmes, R. (1998) *Fieldwork with Children.* London: Sage.

Kirkpatrick, A. (2002) 'Preschool Writing Development and the Role of Parents', in C. Nutbrown (ed.) *Research Studies in Early Childhood Education*, pp. 97–114. Stoke-on-Trent: Trentham.

Lewis, A. and Lindsay, G. (eds) (1999) *Researching Children's Perspectives.* Buckingham: Open University Press.

Lynch, J. (2002) 'Parents' Self-efficacy Beliefs, Parents' Gender, Children's Reader Self-perceptions, Reading Achievement and Gender', *Journal of Research in Reading* 25(1): 54–67.

Mace, J. (1998) *Playing with Time: Mothers and the Meaning of Literacy.* London: UCL Press.

McNaughton, G. (1997) 'Who's got the Power? Rethinking Gender Equity Strategies in Early Childhood', *International Journal of Early Years Education* 5(1): 57–66.

McNaughton, S. (2001) 'Co-constructing Expertise: The Development of Parents' and Teachers' Ideas about Literacy Practices and the Transition to School', *Journal of Early Childhood Literacy* 1(1): 40–58.

McNaughton, S., Glynn, T. and Robinson, V. (1981) *Parents as Remedial Tutors: Issues for Home and School.* Wellington: New Zealand Council for Educational Research.

Marsh, J. and Thompson, P. (2001) 'Parental Involvement in Literacy Development using Media Texts', *Journal of Research in Reading* 24(3): 266–78.

Moll, L., Amardi, C., Neff, D. and Gowzalez, N. (1992) 'Funds of Knowledge for Teaching: Using a Qualitative Approach to Connect Homes and Classrooms', *Theory into Practice* 3(2): 132–41.

Morrow, L.M., ed. (1995) *Family Literacy: Connections in Schools and Communities.* Newark, DE: International Reading Association.

Nutbrown, C., ed. (1996) *Respectful Educators – Capable Learners: Children's Rights in Early Education.* London: Paul Chapman Publishing.

Nutbrown, C. (1999) 'Learning about Literacy in the Earliest Years: Alex's Story', in E. Millard (ed.) *Enquiries into Literacy*, pp. 37–58. Sheffield: University of Sheffield Papers in Education.

NUTBROWN & HANNON: FAMILY LITERACY

Nutbrown, C. (2001) 'Watching and Learning: The Tools of Assessment', in G. Pugh (ed.) *Contemporary Issues in the Early Years: Working Collaboratively for Children*, pp. 67–77. London: Paul Chapman Publishing.

Nutbrown, C. and Hannon, P., eds (1997) *Preparing for Early Literacy Work with Families: A Professional Development Manual*. Nottingham/Sheffield: NES Arnold/REAL Project.

Oakley, A. (1993) 'Interviewing Women: A Contradiction in Terms', in H. Roberts (ed.) *Doing Feminist Research*, 2nd edn, pp. 89–98. London: Routledge.

Office for Standards in Education (1993) *Boys and English*. London: The Stationery Office.

Parker, S. (1986) '"I Want to Give Them What I Never Had." Can Parents who are Barely Literate Teach their Children to Read?', *Times Educational Supplement* (10 October), p. 23.

Pereera, S. (2001) 'Living with "Special Educational Needs": Mothers' Perspectives', in P. Clough and C. Nutbrown (eds) *Voices of Arabia: Essays in Educational Research*, pp. 62–9. Sheffield: University of Sheffield Papers in Education.

Qualifications and Curriculum Authority (1998) *Can do Better: Raising Boys' Achievement in Schools*. London: The Stationery Office.

Schickedanz, J. (1990) *Adam's Righting Revolutions*. Portsmouth, NH: Heinemann.

Taylor, D. (1983) *Family Literacy: Young Children Learning to Read and Write*. Exeter, NH: Heinemann.

Taylor, D., ed. (1997) *Many Families, Many Literacies: An International Declaration of Principles*. Portsmouth, NH: Heinemann.

Taylor, D. and Dorsey-Gaines, C. (1988) *Growing Up Literate: Learning from Inner-city Families*. Portsmouth, NH: Heinemann.

Teale, W.H. (1986) 'Home Background and Young Children's Literacy Development', in W.H. Teale and E. Sulzby (eds) *Emergent Literacy: Writing and Reading*, pp. 173–206. Norwood, NJ: Ablex.

Tierney, W.G. (1993) 'Self and Identity in a Postmodern World: A Life Story', in D. McLaughlin and W.G. Tierney (eds) *Naming Silenced Lives*, pp. 87–100. New York: Routledge.

Tizard, B. and Hughes, M. (1984) *Young Children Learning: Talking and Thinking at Home and in School*. London: Falmer Press.

Tizard, J., Schofield, W.N. and Hewison, J. (1982) 'Collaboration between Teachers and Parents in Assisting Children's Reading', *British Journal of Educational Psychology* 52(1): 1–15.

Weinberger, J. (1996) *Literacy Goes to School: The Parents' Role in Young Children's Literacy Learning*. London: Paul Chapman Publishing.

Whitehurst, G.J., Epstein, J.N., Angell, A.L., Payne, D.A., Crone, D.A. and Fischel, J.E. (1994) 'Outcomes of an Emergent Literacy Intervention in Head Start', *Journal of Educational Psychology* 86(4): 542–55.

Wolfendale, S. and Topping, K., eds (1996) *Family Involvement in Literacy: Effective Partnerships in Education*. London: Cassell.

Wood, C. (2002) 'Parent–Child Pre-school Activities can Affect the Development of Literacy Skills', *Journal of Research in Reading* 25(3): 241–58.

Correspondence to:

CATHY NUTBROWN and PETER HANNON, School of Education, University of Sheffield, 388 Glossop Road, Sheffield, S10 2JA, UK. [email: c.e.nutbrown@sheffield.ac.uk; p.hannon@sheffield.ac.uk]

Example 2

A version of the following story has been published in *Auto/Biography* – a well-known journal in the social sciences.

Auto/Biography 2001; 9: 65–70

Bev: an embodied theory of schooling?

Peter Clough
University of Sheffield, UK

Listen to this. It's a sort of poem:

> There is mess everywhere. Because he has tried to reach the bathroom there is mess in a trail across the carpet and – though she does not find this for several days – there is mess on a pile of folded curtains by the top of the stairs.

> There is a way of dealing with this mess; one thing is not to rub it into the carpet, but to pull what can be pulled with a cloth onto damp paper tissue and then to tamp towels hard down, pressing hard down as on dough. This takes ten or twelve minutes.
>   Matthew is wedged on the toilet; his shoulder is fallen hard against the wall so that his bottom is wedged in the ring of the toilet seat.
>   When Bev finishes the floor he is sleeping and he starts slightly as she touches his arm. She lifts him and puts his arm around her shoulder. There is nothing in the toilet bowl.
>   In her bed she arranges his bald head cradled in her armpit and when he turns slightly some minutes later his mouth takes her nipple through her nightdress.
>   It is 4.30 and there is no sound outside. At 5.10 a car can be heard some streets away and some minutes later the first bird starts. At 6.20 Bev turns off the alarm clock before it can start to ring.

Not that many years ago I watched a woman fall apart in a school. The school was falling apart, too, and I knew – without being able to name it at the time – that there was some connection between these disintegrations. The school recovered.

I was working as a researcher, and I'd been studying how schools dealt with kids with learning difficulties. Someone said: 'Oh, you should go to Whatsitsname Comprehensive, that's *very* interesting ...'

I phoned the Headteacher and was there within two days. It was clear I was welcome: yes, they would be happy for me to visit the school; and I could talk to as many of the staff as I wished, and in return I should do a 'sketch' for them.

It's timely. It will do us some good, said the Head. You can hold a mirror up to us. We run a good ship but it will do us good to see ourselves more clearly. We're in something of a Cretacean period *(whatever that meant)*.

I didn't like him. He was young for the job – forty, forty-three, maybe – and had a clearly expensive suit. He was tall and bald and his body was obviously trained firm beneath his shirt without jacket. At the time I thought that men like this should not be Headteachers of schools in Labour-controlled authorities. Waiting also in his office was Bev. Bev weighed – when I met her – some twenty-two stones, and was maybe five-feet-six. I learned as a fact later – though I could sense at the time – that she smoked forty cigarettes a day (which is quite an achievement on a full timetable); and certainly in all the time I knew her she seemed short of a decent breath.

She walked [it seemed] always with some difficulty – as if she suffered some continual agony – something which was apart from the weight-given gait.

- Bev will show you round – the Head said – Bev is my right-hand man, aren't you darling?
- There you go – all talk no action. What about my extra .5 teacher, then?
- Bev and I go back a long way, don't we? We've had some fights ...
- We have that ...
- ... but we come out of them, don't we darling?
- When I come round to your point of view we do!
- Don't believe her – it's Bev runs this show; I'm just a suit in Committee.

I was embarrassed for – as on a stage in front of me – they were quite clearly nibbling and nipping at each other beneath the banter, the banter oddly freighted with a sexuality. They contrasted so much, Giles spare and tall and somehow his very baldness was vigorous; Bev quite round and flushed and looking hard for breath. And he was at once her son, her lover and her boss; and Bev, too, played.

I couldn't name this sexuality at the time; I didn't know the name of my embarrassment until – in fact – I had written *'There is mess everywhere ...'*

Bev took me to the staff coffee-room and then to a small room off it, set aside for smokers. We smoked together.

- He's alright is Giles, I can handle Giles. We've had our ding-dongs but we know where we stand. He's given me a lot of head – he's given me a lot of stick, too – but we're alright. But that's Giles – if you show him what you can do he's behind you all the way.

We smoked again – cigarettes end-on – and I learned the first somethings of her life: she was single, fifty-one; she was Irish, she was diabetic, she lived with her Dad. This was a list – a sort of summary – which gave up no hint of difficulty. Later I would understand something of what held this list together.

I talked about my study.

- Well in some ways you couldn't have come at a better time; we're sort of in crisis – did Giles tell you? – well not crisis but – how shall I say? – in a melting pot. Giles's a pain but I love him – he's thrown up this plan where we re-make my department – he does this, I think, when he's bored; like, throws in a little grenade just to see what will happen. He's a rascal, he's infuriating but he's generally right, the rat.

I talked with Bev for an hour that day, and again two days later. She gave me a history of the department, and it was then she started to tell me how this history was involved with her own. *My dad became really sick that year and I had to take some time off.* But she did not speak further of him on this occasion, nor actually ever properly. This life and its sadness she hardly spoke of, as though I knew it all and so in the end, by another route, I did.

When we met the third time we talked for nearly two hours of Bev's life as a child in Dublin, a student in Liverpool; as houseparent in a Remand Centre, teaching in Africa, then social work here and there, and finally teaching here. And on this occasion, I remember a moment when she took her cigarette to her mouth, and as rapidly pulled her hand away again, and said: *I really stink.* I laughed and she said *I was up half the night, Dad's incontinent now.* And from this time I think I started to feel Matthew – the dying Matthew – watching.

Elsewhere – out of the immediate compass of Bev's life, that is – elsewhere, things were no better, possibly worse. In the fourth and last week of my visits, I was met by the School Secretary who said that Giles, the Head, would see me at 10.30. It was clear that this was not an invitation as such. He had a simple point to make, which you can hear being driven home in the tape-recording of our brief conversation. It goes something like:

– Bev is poorly
– Oh? Er ...
– Bev is sick; very, very sick
– I know that she ...
– and has been for a long time, for some long time actually
– I know her Dad's ill, I ...
– but short of actually forbidding her to come to work there's not much I can do well that's not true I did I did forbid her one week because she's no use to anyone – to anyone – in this state.

Giles asked me for my report, the 'sketch' I had promised.

– It'll take a week or two to polish, but ...
– Yes, but the gist. What d'you think of us? Of Bev's Department?

What did I think of Bev's Department? It was in chaos. It was falling apart and was become friable as its Head of Department. Few structures held the thing together, beyond those which organised Bev's own spirit. To be sure, there were timetables, a policy of sorts, schedules for staff to refer children for help. But these things were contingent, mere stuff that routed Bev's energy. My hunch was that when Bev was vigorous, the whole show thrived, was large with her presence and verve. But when Bev began to fall apart – as her dying Dad suffered on and on – the Department, too, sagged. So: lessons were missed, or started late; departmental meetings were cancelled without warning; vital case-conferences were ill-prepared. These were the things to point to later in the account when the infection of the Department needed a name in a report. But what really happened was a matter in the nerves.

For Bev sat the while holding court among the dozen or so smokers who had been granted a separate staffroom. A 15-minute break mid-morning is just long enough for two, sometimes three cigarettes end-on if you leave your lesson sharp enough on the bell, and will always be a few minutes late for the class at 11. If you really have to see Bev you must find her in this smoky room.

And I had met Ken, the 2nd in the Department, whom I knew had adored Bev; who indeed had come to the school just so as to work with Bev; but whose love is exhausted.

- I couldn't *start* to tell you, Ken said. I couldn't *start*/this for starters and he held up a file pinched at the corner between his thumb and forefinger,
- this is a ... a child ... a ... some *scrap* waiting desperately but *d*esperately for a Statement so he can have a Support Assistant, yeh? and where's the file and where's it been for the last five – five – months? *I*'ll tell you where it's been for five months: under Bev's fat arse in the Smoker's!

And – indeed – it seemed it had been under the crocheted red cushion of Bev's arm-chair. Ken's hair is sticking with sweat close to his head and his shirt is very wet around the armpits. Actually he is very close to tears. From the way he is holding the file you could think that it was soiled.

And every time we walked from Smokers' to classroom, children quite swarmed about her.

- Eh Miss! Miss, me Dad's out on Friday
- Miss! Miss! Look at me trainers!
- Miss will yer tell'im? Will yer miss? I aren't goin' to no bloody doctor
- Miss

But I had also seen her moving like a mayoress or a ship down the corridors, dealing out a word of warmth or counsel here, a cuff or a warning finger there. For all the world like some benign potentate entering court fat with bounty and swarmed with plaintiffs. And I once saw her lead a boy – a young man, some six or eight inches big-ger than her – I saw her lead this youth squealing by his ear the length of a corridor. We were passing him bent in menace over another boy – 'bring it tomorrow Paki or tha' dees ...' – and she led him squealing to her office.

- Ah! Gerroff! Bloody gerroff! Tha'rt bloody 'urtin' me!
- I'll hurt yer, Derek Turner
- Ah'll 'ave police on thee, whalearse, our kid'll pop thee! Ow! gerroff!

Once in her office, safe from other eyes, the boy's curses became tears, and Bev held him on her bosom.

- Yer a great daft thing, Derek Turner, what are you?
- Gret ... [sob] ... daft ... [sob] ... thing, miss

So ... the gist, Giles? The gist is a larger than life, smaller than data woman who made magic and chaos around her; loved children, lost files; breathed smiles into hopeless scraps; knew it was hopeless to try to teach Susan Elsworth to read just yet, so taught her to sew; sat on Ahmed Birham's doorstep until his father opened the door nearly five February hours later and just had to let her in; forgot to attend two tribunals, and brought the wrong notes to a third; neglected her body – abused it with excess of nicotine and sweet foods and sometimes alcohol and starved it of the routine health checks and daily blood tests and injections it needed to maintain some sort of existence. She ignored her own illness in the witness of her father's – doing just enough to keep going for another day – and another – and another – and another. What, Giles? This is sentimental? If it is, Giles, so be it.

Of course I didn't give Giles a report. I didn't need to, and he knew I wouldn't. And I only heard what happened to Bev some fifteen months later, when I met one of the teachers on holiday in Filey. Bev's Dad had died six weeks after I'd finished at the school. Bev had sold the house where they'd lived and moved to a modern flat – a-nice-neat-fresh-smelling-flat-for-one. Things at school had not improved, though Bev had by now exhausted the patience – the love, possibly – of everyone but the kids, who still mobbed her. Then a preliminary report by Government Inspectors found Special Needs wanting, and Giles got his licence to act as he had always wanted. He sent for her and suggested some leave; she refused, but he told her to go home and take a couple of weeks, really get over her father. Giles, I was told, 'explained' his long held concern for Bev at the next routine staff meeting. How he had worried about her health for some time – how he had insisted that she take time to recuperate.

I did not need to be at the meeting to know what happened. I had spent a month in the school; I knew Giles, the staff and their confusion of respect and disgust for Bev.

Neither was I there the day Bev left, of course, but I was told of how the bloated and gasping Bev was taken home that day; sent home, actually, by taxi, though Giles would have had an arm around her as she left by the back. And I have an image of her leaving Giles' office all puffed up with tears, all florid and a tiny forbearing smile slightly softening the rictus of her terror.

It is of course a fantastic indictment of us all that Bev's body – Bev's severely reduced body; Bev now livid and finally rigorous – was not found until eleven days after this day. Her new neighbours didn't know her, she bought milk from the super-market, had no routine callers. Oddly, she was discovered by a burglar who decently called the police (though – for she pungently had no further need of it – relieved Bev of her purse as his fee). It seems that in her anxiety she had forgotten to eat, or else had not eaten properly. Also she had fallen – a gash to her head had bled on to the carpet. Her ulcerous legs had borne the brunt of her illness. There could only be an open verdict. But – the teacher told me – there was enough cat food out for ten days, maybe two weeks.

I don't know what the real conclusion to this story is, for it's not a story simply exhausted by Bev's death. But with the passage of time the story has assembled itself from a clutch of data and – nude of any critical clothes – is simple enough. What is left when the data – the given – are returned to their owners is something simple and terrible; something grave and constant in human suffering. And schooling, it seems to me, is all but theorised by Bev's body.

> *Source*: Clough (2001). This story was published in *Auto/Biography* in November 2001. It is reproduced here with permission.

Activity 8.1

As you reflect back on each of these two contrasting examples, ask yourself: in each case:

- Has the author *persuaded* me?
- Is the *purpose* of the research (and its report) clear?
- How is the research *positioned*?
- What might be the *political* impact of this report?

Where would you position the research in terms of paradigm?
  Is the enquiry *justified* in its report?
  What have you learned from reading and reflecting on these two reports which will be useful in the writing and dissemination of your own research?

Reflections

The two examples are very different from each other in style, tone and objective, and they demonstrate diversity of style in research report. So, given this diversity, how does the notion of social research as persuasive, purposive, positional and political stand up? Is it possible to identify those characteristics within both reports? The following reflections give our perspective on this question in relation to the two examples.

Reflection on Example 1 (Nutbrown and Hannon, 2003)

This report is intended to *persuade* the reader of the importance of understanding children's perspectives on their literacy learning. Such persuasion is important for the impact of the findings of the survey will depend on the extent to which readers are persuaded by the 'voices' they hear. The *purpose* of the research is clear, to uncover the detail of *what* the children had to say and *how* the research was designed in order to best elicit their views. So, the *purpose* of the report itself is to *persuade* readers that this purpose is successfully executed. The literature review clearly establishes the researcher's *position* and the theoretical framework for the study, but the report makes reference to other chapters of the book (from which this chapter is taken) which makes its *position* clear. As for the *political* dimension to this study, it is a political position in itself to recognise that very young children can express views which are worthy of a research study, and their views contribute to the debate about families' roles in early literacy development. (Further exposition of the *positionality* and the *political* frame of the research is provided in the paper.)

Reflection on Example 2 (Clough, 2001)

This story is written to *persuade* the reader (among other things) of the connections between personal and professional life – between schools and teachers, of the impact of difficulty in one on the other. Its *purpose*? To report the difficulty of experience, and the suffering of teachers in the under-resourced, under-supported regime of its time – and the common occurrence of Ofsted inspections as the 'final blow'. There is (arguably) no need for further location of this story within the research literature of educational difficulty – the position of the author is made clear through the narrative – though the literature (and the testimony of experience) exists to allow this. Finally, what of its *political* impact? What does this story *do*? Does it provide 'evidence', whatever its form, to support its author's claim that 'What is left ... is something simple and terrible. And schooling ... is all but theorised by Bev's body'? (For further discussion of the contexts and motivations for reporting in this way, see Clough, 2002.)

Activity 8.2

You may wish to consolidate your evaluation of our two examples in terms of their demonstration of the four Ps of social science enquiry: *persuasive, purposive, positional* and *political*. Table 8.1 suggests how such reports can be interrogated to identify these four characteristics and their substantive content. The various cells can be used to add notes about the report. Try this with other examples of research report (or your own writing) using the format in Table 8.2.

Table 8.1 Analysis of research reports for their four key characteristics of social enquiry

	Is the report *persuasive*? In what ways?	Is the *purpose* of the research and its report clear?	How has the author demonstrated the *positionality* of the research?	In what way is the report *political*? What might be the *political* impact of the report?
Example 1 Nutbrown and Hannon, 2003	• Uses children's words to identify literacy practices • Large survey	• To add a child's perspective • To identify family literacy practices	• Identified through literature review and critical commentary	• Validation of children's perspectives • Challenges some accepted views
Example 2 Clough, 2001	• Narrative style • Appealing to the personal	• To tell a story • To connect with the lives of teachers? • To suggest the links between policy, institution and personal lives?	• Indicated through the language used – but no direct reference to other work in the field	• Its very existence is a political act. The publication of a story of a teacher's destruction within the colluding system is a political statement

Table 8.2 Framework for analysis of research reports for their four key characteristics of social enquiry

	Is the report *persuasive*? In what ways?	Is the *purpose* of the research and its report clear?	How has the author demonstrated the *positionality* of the research?	In what way is the report *political*? What might be the *political* impact of the report?
Reference				
Reference				

We asked our students to try the above exercise with two more papers. We asked them to read the following two papers:

Clough, P. (2009) 'Finding God in Wellworth High School: legitimations of story-making as research', *Ethnography in Education*, 4 (3): 347–56.

Nutbrown, C. (2011) 'Naked by the pool? Blurring the image? Ethical and moral issues in the portrayal of young children in arts-based educational research', *Qualitative Inquiry*, 17 (1): 234–67.

In the session, as a group, we asked them to identify any elements which related to the four Ps. They wrote various responses on post-it notes and added them to four sheets of paper headed with these four questions:

Is the report *persuasive?* In what ways?
Is the *purpose* of the research and its report clear?
How has the author demonstrated the *positionality* of the research?
In what way is the report *political?* What might be the *political* impact of the report?

Their analysis is summarised in Table 8.3.

Strategies for writing your research report

This section addresses the essentials in writing a research report. The focus here is on telling the story of the research. Both of the examples in the previous section are research stories, though they are accounts of different styles, and were constructed for different purposes. In the case of your own study, you need first to ask yourself, before you begin to write: *What is the research story I wish to tell?* Having decided this, the next question is: *How can I best construct my research account?*

Writing

Many people write obscurely because they have never taken the trouble to write clearly. This sort of obscurity you find too often ... even in literary critics. Here it is indeed strange. You would have thought that men who passed their lives in the study of the great masters of literature would be sufficiently sensitive to the beauty of language to write, if not beautifully, at least with perspicuity. Yet you will find in their works sentence after sentence that you must read twice in order to discover the sense. Often you can only guess at it, for the writers have evidently not said what they intended.

Another cause of obscurity is that the writer is himself not quite sure of his meaning. He has a vague impression of what he wants to say, but has not, either from lack of mental power or from laziness, exactly formulated it in his mind, and it is natural enough that he should not find a precise expression for a confused idea. This is due largely to the fact that many writers think, not before, but as they write. (*The Summing Up*, William Somerset Maugham, 1938)

Table 8.3 Group analysis of Clough (2009) and Nutbrown (2011) for their four key characteristics of social enquiry

	Is the report *persuasive?* In what ways?	Is the *purpose* of the research and its report clear?	How has the author demonstrated the *positionality* of the research?	In what way is the report *political?* What might be the *political* impact of the report?
Clough (2009) *Finding God in Wellworth High*	• This paper has the style of a play – and so 'carries you along' • It appeals to very personal things so 'draws you in' • You want to believe it. I wanted to ask 'did he do it?'	• It makes a point about vulnerability of teachers • It highlights the ways things can get twisted • It shows the vulnerabilities of students and teachers • It shows the power of religion and how it can be misused • Teenage fantasy and how it can be damaging	• Yes – linked to evidence of the instances of teachers accused of misconduct – and then found not to have • In terms of the difficulties and viewpoints it is very powerful and I think I can see where the author is coming from	• The issue is political in that it is controversial • Bringing it to the fore is a political act • Wanting to raise the issue and alert the dangers • This makes you think… was in my head for ages
Nutbrown (2011) *Naked by the pool...*	• The way it is written carries you into agreement • I was going along with the argument from the start • It draws on a large amount of literature to make the point so uses others to make the case as well as the author's own voice	• The purpose is very clear – there is a single argument about photos in research and the difference cases 'for' the argument are made systematically	• Her position is very clear because this paper is a position piece really • The whole point of the paper is stating the author's position on using photographs of children in research	• This could be quite political because it has to address the arguments about child protection • Because children are considered 'vulnerable' participants in research there are political elements to the argument • The part on 'risk' is taking a political position.

We suggest that an important purpose of writing is *thinking*; of course people do indeed *think* as we *write*. But more than that, many use writing as the tool and process by which we decide what it is – precisely – that we *are* thinking.

Writing is not merely the means by which we record and report our thinking, but a means by which we discover it. It is for this reason that a 'piece' of writing may go through several drafts before it is offered into the public domain. Writing as *process* must not be confused with writing as *product*. The task of committing our ideas to paper forces a permanence of articulation which the spoken word can sometimes evade. But having used writing to uncover our thinking, having placed our ideas into a medium of permanence, it is necessary then to review our words (often with the help of critical friends) so that we can be sure that we have written something which effectively conveys our thinking to our readers, and we must do this before making the report a public object.

Writing for research

Writing is essential for 'viewing' our thinking, for *discovering* what it is we want to say. And reviewing our words and our thoughts once committed for the first time to paper is crucial in research writing. So, here, we aim to consider ways in which students' research writing can be made more effective and, finally, we suggest a means by which students might review their personal research writing strategies in the light of a series of questions generated throughout this book.

Activity 8.3

You may not agree with our suggestion above on the relationship between writing and thinking. Take a moment to consider what we are saying.

Do *you* write to *record* your thoughts or do you, through the writing process, discover what it is you want to say?

It is worth making some notes about this – you may well want to write something about your process of (and purposes for) writing in your dissertation or thesis.

Hannon (2000) suggests that the research writing process might include five stages: prewriting; drafting; revising; editing; and sharing. Table 8.4 briefly summarises Hannon's explanations of each of these stages.

Students inevitably ask us about the *structure* of a typical thesis or dissertation. We offer the following advice with some ambivalence for three reasons: first,

Table 8.4   Five stages of research writing

Stage	Process
Prewriting	Writing begins well before one sets pen to paper (or fingers to keyboard). At the *prewriting* stage writers take the decision to write something and form the intention of achieving some communicative goal.
Drafting	At this stage writers recognise that what they produce can be very rough – the important thing being to get something down on paper. This stage – like all the others in the writing process – involves the *formation of ideas*. Drafting can mean exploring and playing with ways of expressing ideas.
Revising	Writers can move into the stage of *revision* as soon as they have a draft. There are two key ideas here: *structure* (having the right structure, sticking to it, and making it apparent to the reader through 'signposts' such as headings, subheadings, and key words) and *brevity* (saying what is needed as succinctly as possible).
Editing	*Editing* is the final presentation of a piece of writing in the form expected (or required) by readers. It requires an understanding of genre and of requirements – this is the point where accuracy of presentation matters.
Sharing	*Sharing* can mean giving it to one or more readers: showing your writing to a friend; submitting a report to one's supervisor; presenting a paper at a conference; or publishing a book. It is the final act necessary for all research writing.

Source: adapted from Hannon, 2000: 98–101.

because no dissertation is the same and every dissertation should benefit from original thinking about its structure; second, by the time students have reached the point of writing their thesis or dissertation they have already written, and received feedback on, several pieces of academic writing; and, third, the structure of a piece of writing must depend on the research story it tells.

Nevertheless, we are often asked by our students to give them a 'rough' idea (despite having rehearsed with them our objections above) and so Figure 8.1 represents our 'rough guide' to dissertation writing. All dissertations and theses *should* contain the elements listed here, though your own will have its own unique balance which you will work out in discussion with your supervisor.

There are several texts which support the development of academic writing skills and, specifically, the writing of dissertations and theses (see, for example, O'Hara et al. 2011).

**Dissertation and thesis writing:
'A rough guide' to structure**

ALL INSTITUTIONS WILL ISSUE GUIDANCE ON THE REQUIREMENTS FOR DISSERTATION AND THESIS PRESENTATION – CHECK THE SPECIFIC REQUIREMENTS FOR YOUR OWN PROGRAMME

Title page (succinct and accurate)

Abstract (around 200 words providing a summary of the work)

Contents (lists of chapters, figures and tables)

Chapters

1 **Introduction**
2 **Literature review**
3 **Research context, questions and rationale**
4 **Research methods and methodological issues**
5 **Research action** – data collection and analysis
6 **Research findings** – and their relevance to the wider field of research
7 **Reflection on the study** – contributions, strengths and weaknesses
8 **Conclusions** – including future research questions

References Find out the preferred style and ensure that you follow the appropriate conventions

Appendices Use appendices with reservation – if it is *really* important, ask yourself whether the information you proposed to append should actually appear in the main body of the text.

Caution: The suggested chapters (1–8) will vary from study to study – some will include more than one chapter on, say, 'Research action', others will combine the presentation of analysis, findings and discussion in a series of chapters rather than separate chapters for each element. Studies which report action research investigations might present the report in a series of cycles, thus including more than one 'set' of the chapter headings listed above. Some studies – for example, those which are biographical or autobiographical in nature – may well adopt quite a different style and structure. Given the potential for variety of structures and styles of study, it would be irresponsible to suggest word allocations to the above structure. All students must eventually establish their own particular format in consultation with their academic tutors and drawing on the guidance provided by their own awarding institution.

Figure 8.1   A '*rough guide*' to structure in dissertation and thesis writing

---

Activity 8.4 Critiquing your research writing

When you are drafting and redrafting your dissertation or thesis use this checklist of questions to critique your writing. *Ask:*

- Is this report *persuasive*? How does it persuade? Who does it aim to persuade?
- Is this report *purposive*? Does it make its purposes clear? How does it accomplish this?
- Is this report an expression of the *positional* nature of the research? In which way?

(Continued)

(Continued)

- Is this research *political?* How does the report connect with and articulate political issues?
- Have I justified my enquiry through
  - *radical looking?*
  - *radical listening?*
  - *radical reading?*
  - *radical questioning?*
- Do I need to locate this research within a particular research paradigm?

Ethics: pause for reflection

What are the ethical factors to be considered in preparing and publishing a research report?

We suggest that the writing up element of any research study is filled with as many ethical issues as the fieldwork elements. This is the point where researchers are often 'alone' with their analysed data and there are many decisions to make. It is important that research reports do justice to the enquiry and its participants. Long after decisions about pseudonyms and other issues around anonymity and confidentiality have been made, the research report will remain. It remains an ethical duty of any researcher to write a report which pays attention to the human participants so involved. It is, we suggest, an ethical responsibility of the researcher to write a high-quality report, and this will involve drafting and redrafting the work, taking comment from fellow students and academic supervisors, until the final version submitted is as good as it can possibly be. Following submission of research for academic award, it is worth considering other ways in which the findings can be written for dissemination for a range of audiences, which includes the academy and other research 'users'.

CHAPTER SUMMARY

In this chapter we have:

- *Discussed the essential place of writing and dissemination in research*
- *Invited you to read and critique two examples of research reports, particularly in terms of the extent to which the authors persuade the reader, achieve some purpose, make clear their own research positions, and have some political dimension*
- *Outlined some strategies for writing your research report*
- *Reflected on the ethical issues arising from the chapter contents*

FURTHER READING

Hannon, P. (2000) *Reflecting on Literacy in Education*. London: RoutledgeFalmer.

See particularly Chapter 7, Literacy in Professional Development. This chapter offers useful advice on writing processes, the work involved in getting writing right, and the structure of research writing.

Gilbert, N. (ed.) (2008) *Researching Social Life* (3rd edn). London: Sage.

See particularly Chapter 24, Writing about Social Research. This chapter addresses the end point of research through publication. It discusses truth and persuasion, research literature and reporting research, and includes clear guidance on the shape of a journal article.

9 Research Action: Next Steps

CHAPTER CONTENTS

Introduction 246
Reviewing your research journal 246
Deciding on the key sections of your research reports 247
Getting to it: planning and timetabling your next steps 248
Ethics: pause for reflection 250

LEARNING OBJECTIVES

By studying and doing the activities in this chapter you will:

- have an overview of your own research journal
- have an awareness of the strategies you can use to identify the key sections of your research report
- be able to devise your own writing plan
- have identified your immediate next steps in your research timetable.

Introduction

This is a brief chapter which aims to encourage you to reflect back on the work you have done throughout the book. In this chapter we suggest ways in which you might:

- reflect on your research journal;
- identify what you have learned;
- map out the structure of your research report; and
- create an action plan for the completion of your study.

Our purpose, in this final chapter, is to help you move on, to get on with the completion of your study and to make use of all the thinking you have done as you have worked through this book (much of which you will have recorded in your research journal).

Reviewing your research journal

If you have used your research journal as we have suggested throughout this book, we estimate that by now you will have written around 5,000 words in response to the activities. Some of this writing will – we expect – find its way into your research report, and in this section we offer a suggestion as to how you might review the entries in your journal and 'filter' them for their particular uses.

We said at the start of the book that a research journal is a personal document. Yours may, by now, be crammed with newspaper cuttings, journal references, odd jottings, quotations from articles you have read, reflections on meetings with your supervisor and other items which seemed to be pertinent to your thinking around your enquiry. Equally, you may have a fairly neat document on your personal computer which contains somewhat similar material. Some of the material in your journal may be there because it struck you as interesting and possibly useful, though you did not know why. 'Filtering' the research journal is a process which can help to sort the 'wheat from the chaff' – the notes and reflections which are important to *this* study and *this* time can be highlighted. But the rest need not be discarded – in it may well lie the seeds of future research. Here are two ways of 'filtering' your research journal.

Highlighters and 'post-it' notes

Spend some time reading through the entries in your research journal, use highlighter pens or 'post-it' notes to identify entries which you feel are particularly important. Add additional notes to these entries, such as 'use in literature review' or 'include in discussion of research questions'. You may wish to number or colour-code these selections so that you can easily turn up all the entries which relate to a particular theme. Your research journal – at the point of writing up your research report – remains a 'live' and ever-evolving document.

Activity	Research journal page no.	Focus	Possibly include this in chapter/section... on...
1.3	6	What is the purpose of my research study?	Introduction Rationale for the study
1.7	8	What difference could my study make?	Rationale for the study
1.5	17	My research contexts	Introduction Setting the scene
2.5	23	What assumptions do you make?	Justifying methods and methodological decisions
2.8	33	Refining research questions	Stating and justifying research questions

Figure 9.1   Example of a research journal 'index'

Creating a research journal 'index'

Another way of highlighting the key entries is to draw up a new document which acts as an index to your journal, summarising its contents for easy reference. Revisit the activities recorded in your research journal and note where they might be used in your research report. You may find it helpful to include research journal page numbers to make reference back to the original entry easy. Figure 9.1 gives an example of how such an index might be constructed.

We have made two suggestions in Figure 9.1 as to how you might 'filter' your research journal; neither is mutually exclusive and these are not the only possibilities. However you choose to 'filter' your research journal, do not be tempted to skip this process. You will have done a lot of work which will be useful to your research report; relocating it by reflecting back on your research journal is important and may well uncover ideas which you might not otherwise recollect.

Deciding on the key sections of your research reports

Reflecting back on the entries in your research journal and 'filtering' the entries will help you to decide on the key sections of your research report. In Chapter 8 we presented (with a number of caveats) a 'rough guide' to structuring a dissertation or thesis (see Figure 8.1). At some point you will need to devise your own structure for your research report. Figure 9.2 offers a way of working out this structure, taking the broad chapters identified in Chapter 8 (Figure 8.1) and providing a template for the sketching of individual research reports. As we said in Chapter 8, this process is individual and the involvement of your academic tutor or supervisor is essential.

Remember, this is a flexible template – not a blueprint. It is a tool to help you develop your own structure as best suits your study.

Title	
Abstract	
Chapter 1 Introduction	Title: Summary of contents: Research journal pages:
Chapter 2 Literature review	Title: Summary of contents: Research journal pages:
Chapter 3 Research context, questions and rationale	Title: Summary of contents: Research journal pages:
Chapter 4 Research methods and methodological structures	Title: Summary of contents: Research journal pages:
Chapter 5 Research action data collection and analysis	Title: Summary of contents: Research journal pages:
Chapter 6 Research findings	Title: Summary of contents: Research journal pages:
Chapter 7 Reflections on the study	Title: Summary of contents: Research journal pages:
Chapter 8 Conclusion	Title: Summary of contents: Research journal pages:
Appendices	Titles of appendices: Research journal pages:
References	List of references in preferred style for your institution: Research journal pages

Figure 9.2   Structuring your research report

Getting to it: planning and timetabling your next steps

Whatever point you are at in your own study, it is important to create a timetable to help you plan the remainder of your study to fit the time available before submission, whether this be six weeks, six months or a year or more. This can be simply done and need not take a great deal of time, but it does act as a way of focusing on the remaining work you need to do and how it might be accomplished in the time available. Figure 9.3 is an extract from a student's PhD timetable for her second year of study. It simply maps out the tasks to be done into a time frame which allows the work to be fitted into the timetable of the institution where she was carrying out her fieldwork and her other responsibilities. It does not list the detail of every day, neither does it indicate all times when she will need to meet and discuss progress with her supervisor. It acts as a means for keeping the study on track within the second year of work. The format provides just one example of how a study – its fieldwork, library-based and computer-based tasks – might be accomplished in the time available.

Month: YEAR 2	Tasks
September	Meeting with supervisor following my holiday break Discuss plans for data collection Discuss draft of ethical review application Get advice on how to approach the participants
October	Finalise ethical review application and submit to supervisor for final agreement before formal submission to the Ethics Review Panel Submit Ethical Review Application Begin to approach participants with informal explanations of the study
November	Finalise interview schedules Organise some pilot interviews Get to grips with NVivo using pilot interview data during Christmas break
January	Write up pilot Leave with supervisor for comment Revise research questions for main study Revise interview schedules Go on to Brussels conference, reporting on Literature review completed last year
February–April	Revise interview schedule Obtain informed consent from study participants Begin interviews Aim to complete by April 2013
May	Transcribe interview transcripts Draft methodology chapter – send to supervisor
June–July	Get feedback on Methodology chapter and meet with supervisor to plan revisions Meeting with supervisor to discuss ideas for analytical framework Present at Doctoral student seminar
August	Complete analysis using NVivo Begin to draft analysis chapter

Figure 9.3　Extract from a full-time PhD timetable for the second year of the study

We have provided in this chapter some suggestions for making the best use of your research journal in the development of your research report and of planning your research time to enable you to complete your study in the time frame available. Each chapter has provided you with suggestions for further reading which are selected to help you find the information you need to get you started on the key issues we are discussing, as they relate to your study.

Remember, your study is specific and unique. Your academic tutor or research degree supervisor is a major resource in helping you to 'get it right'.

Ethics: pause for reflection

Your research journal is a personal document which may contain thoughts which are not intended for sharing with a wider audience – formally or informally. What are the ethical implications of keeping of a research journal?

Think about the difference between obtaining ethical approval to carry out your study and the ethical practices in carrying out your research. How do you ensure that you maintain an ethically responsible position throughout your study?

Remember, it is important to find ways of keeping those things which you write that you intend to be private in a safe place. This may sound obvious, but damage can be done if notes you write in your personal research journal accidentally fall into the hands of an unintended audience. Be careful as you make notes and look after your research journal, field notes, photographs and other research documents and data. Think carefully about everything you write.

Ethical approval from your award-bearing institution is the starting point of the ethical processes in your study. As you embark on a piece of research you will encounter a range of issues which may lead to you revisiting your ethical decision-making and reframing your processes and practices. All researchers need to remain ethically alert from the start of the study and throughout, and especially when writing up the study to make it public.

CHAPTER SUMMARY

In this chapter we have:

- *Encouraged you to review your research journal by reflecting back on the work you have done in it and 'filtering' it to identify key themes*
- *Suggested how you might decide on the key sections of your research reports and use an 'index' to your journal to help you to structure your research report*
- *Offered suggestions about taking your next steps in your particular research journey*
- *Reflected on the ethical issues arising from the chapter contents*

References

AERA (2011) 'Inciting the social imagination: educational research for the public good'. Presidential address to the meeting of the American Educational Research Association, Chicago, 11 April.

Agee, J. (2009) 'Developing qualitative research questions: a reflexive process', *International Journal of Qualitative Studies in Education,* 22 (4): 431–47.

Al Kaddah, S. (2001) 'Motivation and learning a second language', in P. Clough and C. Nutbrown (eds), *Voices of Arabia: Essays in Educational Research.* Sheffield: University of Sheffield Papers in Education.

Anderson, J. (1995) 'Listening to parents' voices: cross-cultural perceptions of learning to read and write', *Reading Horizons* 35: 394–413

Arnold, D. and Whitehurst, G. (1994) 'Accelerating language development through picture book reading: a summary of dialogic reading and its effects', in D. Dickinson (ed.), *Bridges to Literacy: Children, Families and Schools.* Oxford: Blackwell.

Barclay, K., Benelli, C. and Curtis, A. (1995) 'Literacy begins at birth: what caregivers can learn from parents of children who read early', *Young Children,* 50 (4): 24–8.

Barone, T.E. (1997) 'Among the chosen: a collaborative educational (auto) biography', *Qualitative Inquiry,* 3 (2): 222–36.

Barrs, M., Ellis, S., Hester, H. and Thomas, A. (1989) *The Primary Language Record.* London: Inner London Education Authority/Centre for Language in Primary Education.

Beck, L.C., Trombetta, W.L. and Share, S. (1986) 'Using focus group sessions before decisions are made', *North Carolina Medical Journal,* 47 (2): 73–4.

Bérubé, M. (2010) *The Left at War.* New York: New York University Press.

Billington, T. (2009) Open Dialogue: 'Working with children: psychologists at the boundaries of knowledge and experience', *The Psychology Review,* 33 (2): 3–11.

Blumenfeld-Jones, D.S. (1995) 'Dance as a mode of research representation', *Qualitative Inquiry,* 1 (4): 391–401.

Booth, T. (2000) 'Reflection', in P. Clough and J. Corbett (eds), *Theories of Inclusive Education: A Students' Guide.* London: Paul Chapman/Sage.

Booth, T. and Booth, W. (1996) 'Sounds of silence: narrative research with inarticulate subjects', *Disability and Society,* 11 (1): 55–70.

Booth, T., Ainscow, M., Black-Hawkins, K., Vaughan, M. and Shaw, L. (2000) *Index for Inclusion: Developing Learning and Participation in Schools.* Bristol: Centre for Studies in Inclusive Education.

Brimer, A. and Raban, B. (1979) *Administrative Manual for the Infant Reading Tests.* London: Education Evaluation Enterprises.

Brown, S. and, Taylor, K. (2008) 'Bullying, education and labour market outcomes: evidence from the National Child Development Study', *Economics of Education Review,* 27 (4): 387–401.

Byers, P.Y. and Wilcox, J.R. (1988) *Focus Groups: An Alternative Method of Gathering Qualitative Data in Communication Research* (Report No. CS-506–291). New Orleans, LA: Speech Communication Association (ERIC Document Reproduction Service No. ED 297 393).

Calvey, B. (2008) 'The art and politics of covert research: doing "situated ethics" in the field', *Sociology*, 42: 905.

Cambourne, B. (1995) 'Toward an educationally relevant theory of literacy learning: twenty years of inquiry', *The Reading Teacher*, 49: 182–90.

Carr, W. *(1995) For Education – Towards Critical Educational Inquiry*. Buckingham: Open University Press.

Capozzola, C. (2002) 'A very American epidemic: memory politics and identity politics in the AIDS memorial...', *Radical History Review*, 82: 91–109.

Clay, M. (1972) *The Early Detection of Reading Difficulties: A Diagnostic Survey*. Auckland, NZ: Heinemann Education Books.

Clough, P. (1995) 'Problems of identity and method in the investigation of special needs', in P. Clough and L. Barton (eds), *Making Difficulties: Research and the Construction of Special Educational Needs*. London: Paul Chapman.

Clough, P. (1996) '"Again Fathers and Sons": the mutual construction of self, story and special educational needs', *Disability and Society*, 112 (1): 71–81.

Clough, P. (ed.) (1998a) *Managing Inclusive Education: From Policy to Experience*. London: Paul Chapman/Sage.

Clough, P. (1998b) 'Bridging "mainstream" and "special" education: a curriculum problem', *Curriculum Studies*, 20 (4): 327–38.

Clough, P. (1998c) 'Differently articulate? Some indices of disturbed/disturbing voices', in P. Clough and L. Barton (eds), *Articulating with Difficulty: Research Voices in Inclusive Education*. London: Paul Chapman.

Clough, P. (2000) 'Routes to inclusion', in P. Clough and J. Corbett, *Theories of Inclusive Education: A Student's Guide*. London: Paul Chapman/Sage.

Clough, P. (2001) 'Bev: an embodied theory of schooling', *Auto/Biography*, 9 (1 and 2): 123–5.

Clough, P. (2002) *Narratives and Fictions in Educational Research*. Buckingham: Open University Press.

Clough, P. (2004) 'Review essay: teaching trivial pursuits: a review of three qualitative research texts', *Qualitative Research*, 4 (3): 447–56.

Clough, P. (2009) 'Finding God in Wellworth High School: legitimations of story-making as research', *Ethnography in Education*, 4 (3): 347–56.

Clough, P. and Barton, L. (eds) (1995*) Making Difficulties: Research and the Construction of Special Educational Needs*. London: Paul Chapman.

Clough, P. and Corbett, J. (2000*) Theories of Inclusive Education: A Student's Guide*. London: Paul Chapman/Sage.

Clough, P. and Nutbrown, C. (eds) (2001*) Voices of Arabia: Essays in Educational Research*. Sheffield: University of Sheffield Papers in Education.

Clough, P. and Nutbrown, C. (2002a) *A Student's Guide to Methodology: Justifying Enquiry*. London: Sage.

Clough, P. and Nutbrown, C. (2002b) 'The index for inclusion: personal perspectives from early years educators', *Early Education*, 36 (Spring): 1–4.

Clough, P. and Nutbrown, C. (2004) 'Special Education Needs and inclusion: multiple perspectives of pre-school educators in the UK', *Journal of Early Childhood Research*, 2 (2): 191–211.

Clough, P. and Nutbrown, C. (2011) 'Mothers and fathers, sons and daughters: dilemmas, difficulties and ethics in the inclusion of family members in research'. Paper presented at the American Educational Research Association Meeting, Chicago, 11 April.

Clymer, T. and Barrett, T.C. (1983) *Clymer-Barrett Readiness Test (CBRT)*. Virginia, USA: Chapman, Brook and Kent.

Cohen, L., Manion, L. and Morrison, K. (2011) *Research Methods in Education* (7th edn). London: Routledge.

Cook, C. (2005) 'It's not what men do: investigating the reasons for the low number of men in the early childhood workforce', in K. Hirst and C. Nutbrown (eds), *Perspectives on Early Childhood Research: Contemporary Research.* Stoke-on-Trent: Trentham Books.

Croll, P. and Moses, D. (1985) *One in Five: The Assessment and Incidence of Special Education Needs.* London: Routledge and Kegan Paul.

Davies, J. (2004) 'Negotiating Femininities Online', *Gender and Education,* 16 (1): 35–49.

Davies, J. (2006) '"Hello newbie! **big welcome hugs** hope u like it here as much as i do!" An exploration of teenagers' informal on-line learning', in D. Buckingham and R. Willett (eds), *Digital Generations: Children, Young People and New Media.* New York: Lawrence Erlbaum, pp. 211–28.

Davies, J. and Merchant, G. (2010) *Web2.0 for Schools.* New York: Peter Lang.

de Vaus, D. (2001) *Research Design in Social Research.* London: Sage.

De Ford, D.E. (1985) 'Validating the constructs of theoretical orientation in reading instruction', *Reading Research Quarterly,* 20: 351–67.

Demn, R. and Brehony, K.J. (1994) 'Why didn't you use a survey to generalise your findings? Methodological issues in a multiple site case study of school governing bodies after the 1988 Education Reform Act', in D. Halpin and B. Troyna (eds), *Researching Education Policy: Ethical and Methodological Issues.* London: Falmer.

Denscombe, M. (1998) *The Good Research Guide for Small-scale Social Research Projects.* Buckingham: Open University Press.

Denzin, N.K. and Lincoln, Y.S. (eds) (2000) *The Handbook of Qualitative Research* (2nd edn). Thousand Oaks, CA: Sage.

Denzin, N. K. and Lincoln, Y.S. (eds) (2005) *The Handbook of Qualitative Research* (3rd edn). London: Sage.

Department for Education and Skills (DfES) (2003) *Birth to Three Matters.* London: HMSO.

Desforges, M. and Lindsay, G. (1995) *The Infant Index.* London: Hodder and Stoughton.

Dickinson, D. (ed.) (1994) *Bridges to Literacy: Children, Families and Schools.* Oxford: Blackwell.

Dirkx, J.M. and Spurgin, M.E. (1992) 'Implicit theories of adult basic education teachers: how their beliefs about students shape classroom practice', *Adult Basic Education,* 2: 20–41.

Downing, J., Ayres, D.M. and Schaeffer, B. (1983) *Linguistic Awareness in Reading Readiness (LARR).* London: National Foundation for Educational Research – Nelson.

Downing, J. and Thackray, D. (1976) *Reading Readiness Inventory.* London: Hodder and Stoughton.

Duffy, G. and Anderson, L. (1984) 'Teachers' theoretical orientations and the real classroom', *Reading Psychology,* 5: 97–104.

Edwards, P.A. (1989) 'Supporting lower SES mothers' attempts to provide scaffolding for book reading', in J. Allen and J.M. Mason (eds), *Risk Makers, Risk Breakers: Reducing the Risks for Young Literacy Learners.* Portsmouth: Heinemann.

Farquhar, C., Blatchford, P., Burke, J., Plewis, I. and Tizard, B. (1985) 'A comparison of the views of parents and reception teachers', *Education 3–13* (13): 17–22.

Farrall, S., Sparks, R., Hough, M. and Maruna, S. (eds) (2011) *Escape Routes: Contemporary Perspectives on Life after Punishment.* London: Routledge.

Faulks, K. (2006) 'Rethinking citizenship education in England: some lessons from contemporary social and political theory', *Education Citizenship and Social Justice,* 1 (2): 123–40.

Fine, M. (1994) 'Dis-stance and other stances: negotiations of power inside feminist research', in A. Gitlin (ed.), *Power and Method: Political Activism and Educational Research.* London: Routledge.

Flewitt, R. (2005) 'Is every child's voice heard? Researching the different ways 3-year-old children communicate and make meaning at home and in a preschool playgroup', *Early Years: International Journal of Research and Development,* 25 (3): 207–22.

Fontana, A. and Frey, J.H. (2000) 'The interview: from structured questions to negotiated text', in N.K. Denzin and Y.S. Lincoln (eds), *The Handbook of Qualitative Research* (2nd edn). Thousand Oaks, CA: Sage.

Geertz, C. (1988) *Works and Lives: The Anthropologist as Author*. Stanford, CA: Stanford University Press.

Gilbert, N. (ed.) (2008) *Researching Social Life* (3rd edn). London: Sage.

Goldsmith, E. and Handel, R. (1990) *Family Reading: An Intergenerational Approach to Literacy*. Syracuse, NY: New Readers Press.

Goodhall, M. (1984) 'Can four year olds "read" words in the environment?', *Reading Teacher*, 37 (6): 478–89.

Goodman, Y. (1980) *The Roots of Literacy*, Claremont Reading Conference Yearbook 44: 1–32.

Goodman, Y. (1986) 'Children coming to know literacy', in W.H. Teale and E. Sulzby (eds), *Emergent Literacy Writing and Reading*. Norwood, NJ: Ablex.

Goodman, Y. and Altwerger, B. (1981) 'Print awareness in preschool children: a working paper', research paper, September, no. 4, University of Arizona, Flagstaff.

Goodwin, W.L. and Goodwin, L.D. (1996) *Understanding Quantitative and Qualitative Research in Early Childhood Education*. New York: Teachers College Press.

Goswami, U. and Bryant, P. (1990) *Phonological Skills and Learning to Read*. Hove: Lawrence Erlbaum Associates.

Green, C. (1987) 'Parental facilitation of young children's writing', *Early Child Development and Care*, 28: 31–7.

Griffiths, A. and Edmonds, M. (1986) *Report on the Calderdale Pre-school Parent Book Project*. Halifax: Schools Psychological Service, Calderdale Education Department.

Guimares, A. and Youngman, M. (1995) 'Portuguese preschool teachers' beliefs about early literacy development', *Journal of Research in Reading*, 19: 1–13.

Hall, N. (1987) *The Emergence of Literacy*. London: Hodder and Stoughton.

Hall, N., Herring, G., Henn., H. and Crawford, L. (1989) *Parental Views on Writing and the Teaching of Writing*. Manchester: Manchester Polytechnic School of Education.

Hannon, P. (1995) *Literacy, Home and School: Research and Practice in Teaching Literacy with Parents*. London: Falmer Press.

Hannon, P. (1998) 'An ecological perspective on educational research', in J. Rudduck and D. McIntyre (eds), *Challenge for Educational Research*. London: Paul Chapman.

Hannon, P. (2000) *Reflecting on Literacy in Education*. London: RoutledgeFalmer.

Hannon, P. and James, S. (1990) 'Parents' and teachers' perspectives on preschool literacy development', *British Educational Research Journal*, 16 (3): 259–72.

Hannon, P. and Nutbrown, C. (1997) 'Teachers' use of a conceptual framework for early literacy education involving parents', Teacher Development, 3: 405–20.

Hannon, P. and Nutbrown, C. (2001) 'Emerging findings from an experimental study of early literacy education involving parents', paper presented at the United Kingdom Reading Association Annual Conference, Canterbury, Christ Church University College.

Hannon, P., Morgan, A. and Nutbrown, C. (2006) 'Parents' experiences of a family literacy programme', *Journal of Early Childhood Research*, 3 (3): 19–44.

Harper, D. (2005) 'What's new visually', in N. K. Denzin, and Y. S. Lincoln (eds), *The Sage Handbook of Qualitative Research* (3rd edn). London: Sage.

Hart, C. (1998) *Doing a Literature Review: Releasing the Social Science Research Imagination*. London: Sage/The Open University.

Hart, C. (2001) *Doing a Literature Search: A Comprehensive Guide for the Social Sciences*. London: Sage/The Open University.

Heath, S.B. (1983) *Ways with Words: Language, Life and Work in Communities and Classrooms*. Cambridge: Cambridge University Press.

Hedenus, A. (2011) 'Finding Prosperity as a Lottery Winner: Presentations of Self after Acquisitions of Sudden Wealth, *Sociology*, 45 (1): 22–37.

Heibert, E.H. (1983) 'Knowing about reading before reading: preschool children's concepts of reading', *Reading Psychology*, 4 (3): 253–60.

Hess, J.M. (1968) 'Group interviewing', in R.L. King (ed.), *New Science of Planning*. Chicago: American Marketing Association.

Hine, C. (2009) 'How can qualitative internet researchers define the boundaries of their projects?', in A.N. Markham and N.K. Baym (eds), *Internet Inquiry: Conversations about Method*. London: Sage.

Hooks, B. (1991) *Breaking Bread: Insurgent Black Intellectual Life*. Boston, MA: South End Press.

Hurdley, R. (2006) 'Dismanthing Mantelpieces: Narrating Identites and Materializing Culture in the Home', *Sociology*, 40 (8): 717–33.

Hurdley, R. (2010) 'The power of corridors: connecting doors, mobilising materials, plotting openness', *The Sociological Review* 58 (1): 45–64.

Hutton-Jarvis, C. (1999) 'Text or testament? A comparison of educational and literary critical approaches to research', *International Journal of Qualitative Studies in Education*, 12 (6): 645–58.

Israel, M. and Hay, I. (2006) *Research Ethics for Social Scientists: Between Ethical Conduct and Regulatory Compliance*. London: Sage.

Jarrett-Macauley, D. (1996) *Reconstructing Womanhood, Reconstructing Feminism: Writings on Black Women*. London: Routledge.

Jones, M. and Hendrickson, N. (1970) 'Recognition by preschool children of advertised products and book covers', *Journal of Home Economics*, 62 (4): 263–7.

Kaomea, J. (2003) 'Reading erasures, making the familiar strange', *Educational Researcher*, 32 (2): 14–25.

Kaplan, A. (1973) *The Conduct of Inquiry*. Aylesbury: Intertext Books.

Kawulich, B.B. (2011) 'Gatekeeping: an ongoing adventure in research', *Field Methods*, 23 (1): 57–76.

Kent LEA (1992) *Reading Assessment Profile*. Kent: Kent County Council.

Khan, R. (2002) 'No need to smack', in C. Nutbrown (ed.), *Research Studies in Early Childhood Education*. Stoke-on-Trent: Trentham Books.

Kiesinger, C.E. (1998) 'From interviewing to story: writing Abbie's life', *Qualitative Inquiry*, 4 (1): 71–95.

Koch, C. (2001) 'Choosing post-secondary education: what influences women students?', in P. Clough and C. Nutbrown (eds), *Voices of Arabia: Essays in Educational Research*. Sheffield: University of Sheffield Papers in Education.

Levande, D.I. (1989) 'Theoretical orientation to reading and classroom practice', *Reading Improvement*, 26: 274–80.

Lewis, A. (2002) 'The development of children's ideas about others' difficulties in learning', *British Journal of Special Education*, 29 (2): 59–65.

Lewin, K. (1951) *Field Theory in Social Science: Selected Theoretical Papers*. New York: Harper and Bros.

Lujan, M.E., Stolworthy, D.L. and Wooden, S.L. (1986) *A Parent Training Early Intervention Program in Preschool Literacy*, ERIC Descriptive Report, ED 270 988.

Maclean, M., Bryant, P. and Bradley, L. (1987) 'Rhymes, nursery rhymes and reading in early childhood', *Merrill-Palmer Quarterly*, 33 (3): 255–81.

Madriz, E.I. (1998) 'Using focus groups with lower socioeconomic status Latina women', *Qualitative Inquiry*, 24 (1): 114–28.

Manchester LEA (1988) *Early Literacy Project: A Framework for Assessment*. Manchester: Manchester City Council Education Department.

Markham, A. (2005) 'The methods, politics, and ethics of representation in online ethnography', in N.K. Denzin and Y.S. Lincoln (eds), *The Sage Handbook of Qualitative Inquiry*. London: Sage.

Markham, A.N. and Baym, N.K. (eds) (2009) *Internet Inquiry: Conversations about Method.* London: Sage.

McCormick, C.E. and Mason, J.M. (1986) 'Intervention procedures for increasing preschool children's interest in and knowledge about reading', in W. Teale and E. Sulzby (eds), *Emergent Literacy: Writing and Reading.* Norwood, NJ: Ablex Publishing Corporation.

McCracken, G. (1988) *The Long Interview.* Qualitative Research Methods 13. London: Sage.

McCulloch, G. and Richardson, W. (2001) *Historical Research in Educational Settings.* Buckingham: Open University Press.

Meek, M. (1982) *Learning to Read.* London: Bodley Head.

Merleau-Ponty, M. (1962) *The Phenomenology of Perception.* New York: Humanities Press.

Mertens, D.M. and Ginsberg, P.E. (2009) *The Handbook of Social Research Ethics.* London: Sage.

Merton, R.K. and Kendall, P.L. (1986) 'The focused interview', *American Journal of Sociology*, 51: 541–57.

Miles, M.B. and Huberman, A.M. (1994) *Qualitative Data Analysis: An Expanded Sourcebook.* London: Sage.

Mitchell, R.G. (1993) *Secrecy and Fieldwork.* Qualitative Research Methods 29. London: Sage.

Morgan, D.L. (1998) *Planning Focus Groups.* London: Sage.

Nutbrown, C. (ed.) (1996) *Respectful Educators: Capable Learners – Children's Rights and Early Education.* London: Paul Chapman/Sage.

Nutbrown, C. (1997) *Recognising Early Literacy Development: Assessing Children's Achievements.* London: Paul Chapman.

Nutbrown, C. (1999) *Focused Conversations in Research.* MA Study Unit Sheffield, University of Sheffield School of Education.

Nutbrown, C. (2001) 'Creating a palette of opportunities: situations of learning in the early years', in L. Abbott and C. Nutbrown, *Experiencing Reggio Emilia: Implications for Preschool.* Buckingham: Open University Press.

Nutbrown, C. (forthcoming) Children's Views of their Early Years Settings, research summary available at: http://www.shef.ac.uk/content/1/06/02/76/73/childview.pdf.

Nutbrown, C. (2005) *Key Concepts in Early Childhood Education and Care.* London: Sage.

Nutbrown, C. (2010) *Key Concepts in Early Childhood Education and Care* (2nd edn). London: Sage.

Nutbrown, C. (2010) *Threads of Thinking: Young Children Learning and the Role of Early Education.* London: Sage.

Nutbrown, C. (2011a) 'Naked by the pool? Blurring the image? Ethical and moral issues in the portrayal of young children in arts-based educational research', *Qualitative Inquiry*, 17 (1): 234–67.

Nutbrown, C. (2011b) *Conceptualising Arts-based learning in the early years.* Research Papers in education onlinefirst06 July 2011.

Nutbrown, C. and Clough, P. (2002) 'The Index for Inclusion: Personal Perspectives from Early Years Educators', *Early Education*, 17 (1): 1–4.

Nutbrown, C. and Clough, P. (2004) 'Inclusion in the early years: conversations with European educators', *European Journal of Special Needs Education*, 19 (3): 311–39.

Nutbrown, C. and Clough, P. (2006) *Inclusion in the Early Years: Critical Analyses and Enabling Narratives.* London: Sage.

Nutbrown, C. and Clough, P. (2009) 'Citizenship and inclusion in the early years: understanding and responding to children's perspectives on "belonging"', *International Journal of Early Years Education*, 17 (3): 191–206.

Nutbrown, C. and Hannon, P. (eds) (1996) *Preparing for Early Literacy Development with Parents: A Professional Development Manual.* Nottingham/Sheffield: NES Arnold/The REAL Project.

Nutbrown, C. and Hannon, P. (1997) 'Teachers' use of a conceptual framework for early literacy education involving parents', *Teacher Development*, 1 (3).

Nutbrown, C. and Hannon, P. (2003) 'Children's perspectives on family literacy: methodological issues, findings and implications for practice', *Journal of Early Childhood Literacy*, 3 (2): 115–45.

Nutbrown, C. and Jones, H. (2006) *Daring Discoveries: Arts-based Learning in the Early Years*. Doncaster: Darts, Community Partnerships and University of Sheffield.

Nutbrown, C., Hannon, P. and Weinberger, J. (1991) 'Training teachers to work with parents to promote early literacy development', *International Journal of Early Childhood*, 23(2): 1–10.

Nutbrown, C., Clough, P. and Selbie, P. (2008) *Early Childhood Education: History, Philosophy and Experience* London: Sage.

Nutbrown, C., Hannon, P. and Morgan, A. (2005) *Early Literacy Work with Families: Research, Theory and Practice*. London: Sage.

Oakeshott, M. (1933) *Experience and Its Modes*. Cambridge: Cambridge University Press.

Oakley, A. (1993) 'Interviewing women: a contradiction in terms', in H. Roberts (ed.), *Doing Feminist Research* (2nd edn). London: Routledge.

O'Hara, M. (2011) 'Young children's ICT experiences in the home: some parental perspectives', *Journal of Early Childhood Research*, 9 (3): 220–31.

O'Hara, M. Carter, C., Denis, P., Kay, J. and Wainwright, J. (2011) *Successful Dissertations: The Complete Guide for Education and Childhood Studies Students*. London: Continuum.

Oliver, M. (2000) 'Profile', in P. Clough and J. Corbett, *Theories of Inclusive Education: A Students' Guide*. London: Paul Chapman/Sage.

Oppenheim, A.N. (1992) *Questionnaire Design: Interviewing and Attitude Measurement*. London: Pinter.

Pink, S. (2009) *Doing Sensory Ethnography*. London: Sage.

Pahl, K. And Rowsell, J. (2010) *Artifactual Literacies: Every Object Tells a Story*. New York: Teachers College Press.

Parackal, M. (2001) 'Special educators in Beirut: a case study', in P. Clough and C. Nutbrown (eds), *Voices of Arabia: Essays in Educational Research*. Sheffield: University of Sheffield Papers in Education.

Perera, S. (2001) 'Living with "Special Educational Needs": mothers' perspectives', in P. Clough and C. Nutbrown (eds), *Voices of Arabia: Essays in Educational Research*. Sheffield: University of Sheffield Papers in Education.

Pink, S. (2006) *Doing Visual Ethnography: Images, Media and Representation in Research* (2nd edn). London: Sage.

Raymond, S. (2001) 'Excellent teaching: perceptions of Arab, Chinese and Canadian students', in P. Clough and C. Nutbrown (eds), *Voices of Arabia: Essays in Educational Research*. Sheffield: University of Sheffield Papers in Education.

Ritchie, J. and Lewis, J. (2003) *Qualitative Research Practice: A Guide for Social Science Students and Researchers*. London: Sage.

Rorty, R. (1989) *Contingency, Irony and Solidarity*. Cambridge: Cambridge University Press.

Rossman, G.B. and Rallis, S.F. (2011) *Learning in the Field: An Introduction to Qualitative Research* (2nd edn). London: Sage.

Rudd, T., Suth, D. and Facer, K. (2006) *'Towards new learning networks'* Futurelab Available at: http://www.futurelab.org.uk/resources/publications-report-articles/opening-education-reports/Opening.Education.Report.121/

School Curriculum and Assessment Authority (SCAA) (1996) *Baseline Assessment – Draft Proposals*. London: SCAA.

Schmidt, R. B., Boraie, D. and Kassabgy, O. (1996) 'Foreign Language Motivation; internal structure and external connections', in R. Oxford (ed.), *Language Learning Motivation: Pathways to the New Century*. Honolulu: University of Hawaii.

Segel, F. and Friedberg, J.B. (1991) 'Is today Liberry Day? Community support for family literacy', *Language Arts*, 68: 654–7.

Seidman, I.E. (1991) *Interviewing as Qualitative Research: A Guide for Researchers in Education and the Social Sciences.* New York: Teachers College Press.

Shklovsky, V.B (1965) 'Art as Technique essay', available at http://ecmd.nju.edu.cn/Uploadfile/17/8082/technique.doc

Silverman, D. (2001) *Interpreting Qualitative Data: Methods for Analysing Talk, Text and Interaction* (2nd edn). London: Sage.

Silverman, D. (2006) *Interpreting Qualitative Data: Methods for Analysing Talk, Text and Interaction* (3rd edn). London: Sage.

Snape, D. and Spencer, L. (2003) 'The foundations of qualitative research', in D. Snape and L. Spencer, *Qualitative Research Practice: A Guide for Social Science Students and Researchers.* London: Sage.

Snow, C. (1991) 'The theoretical basis for relationships between language and literacy in development', *Journal of Research in Childhood Education,* 6: 5–10.

Somerset Maugham, W. (1938) The *Summing Up* [See p. 406]

Sparkes, A. (1994) 'Life histories and the issue of voice: reflections on an emerging relationship, *International Journal of Qualitative Studies in Education,* 7 (2): 165–83.

Sparkes, A. (2005) 'Narrative Analysis: exploring the whats and hows of personal stories', in M. Holloway (ed.), *Qualitative Research in Health Care,* Milton Keynes: Open University Press.

Srinivas, L. (2010) 'Cinema Halls, Locality and Urban Life', *Ethnography* 11 (1): 189–205.

Stanley, L. and Wise, S. (1993) *Breaking Out Again.* London: Routledge.

Stenhouse, L. (1975) *An Introduction to Curriculum Research and Development.* London: Heinemann.

Stewart, D.W. and Shamdasani, P.N. (1990) *Focus Groups: Theory and Practice.* Applied Social Research Methods Series 20. London: Sage.

Sulzby, E. (1990) 'Assessment of emergent writing and children's language while writing', in L.M. Morrow and J.K. Smith (eds), *Assessment for Instruction in Early Literacy.* Englewood Cliffs, NJ: Prentice Hall.

Sveningsson, E. (2009) 'How do various notions of privacy influence decisions in qualitative internet research?', in A.N. Markham, and N.K. Baym (eds), *Internet Inquiry: Conversations about Method.* London: Sage.

Swinson, J. (1985) 'A parental involvement project in a nursery school', *Educational Psychology in Practice,* 1: 19–22.

Tacey, C. (2005) 'Why do boys like to build and girls like to draw? Gender issues surrounding four and five year old girls in a small British military community', in K. Hirst and C. Nutbrown (eds), *Perspectives on Early Childhood Research: Contemporary Research.* Stoke-on-Trent: Trentham Books.

Taylor, D. (1983) *Family Literacy: Young Children Learning to Read and Write.* Exeter, NH: Heinemann.

Taylor, D. and Dorsey-Gaines, C. (1988) *Growing Up Literate: Learning from Inner-City Families.* Portsmouth, NH: Heinemann.

Teale, W.H. and Sulzby, E. (eds) (1986) *Emergent Literacy: Writing and Reading.* Norwood, NJ: Ablex.

Thackray, D.V. and Thackray, L.E. (1974) *Thackray Reading Readiness Profiles.* London: Hodder and Stoughton.

Tierney, W.G. (1998) 'Life history's history: subjects foretold', *Qualitative Inquiry,* 4 (1): 49–70.

Tizard, B., Blatchford, P., Burke, J., Farquhar, C. and Plewis, I. (1988) *Young Children at School in the Inner City.* London: Lawrence Erlbaum Associates.

Toomey, D. and Sloane, J. (1994) 'Fostering children's early literacy development through parent involvement: a five-year program', in D.K. Dickinson (ed.), *Bridges to Literacy: Children, Families and Schools.* Oxford: Blackwell .

Vaughn, K., Schumm, J.S. and Sunagub, J. (1996) *Focus Group Interviews in Education and Psychology.* London: Sage.

Vincent, D., Green, L., Francis, J. and Powney, J. (1983) *A Review of Reading Tests*. London: National Foundation for Educational Research.

Vulliamy, G. and Webb, R. (eds) (1992) *Teacher Research and Special Educational Needs*. London: David Fulton.

Wacquant, L. (2002) 'The curious eclipse of prison ethnography in the age of mass incarceration', *Ethnography*, 3 (4): 371–97.

Wade, B. (1984) *Story at Home and School*. Educational Review Publication, 10. Birmingham: University of Birmingham, Faculty of Education.

Wade, B. and Moore, M. (1993) *Bookstart in Birmingham*. Book Trust Report No. 2. London: Book Trust.

Walford, G. (ed.) (1991) *Doing Educational Research*. London: Routledge.

Walker, R. (1985) *Doing Research: A Handbook for Teachers*. London: Methuen.

Wandsworth Borough Council Education Department (1994) *Baseline Assessment Handbook*. London: Wandsworth LEA.

Waterland, L. (1989) *Apprenticeship in Action*. Stroud: Thimble Press.

Weinberger, J. (1996) *Literacy Goes to School*. London: Paul Chapman Publishing.

Weir, B. (1989) 'A research base for prekindergarten literacy programs', *The Reading Teacher*, 42: 456–60.

Wells, G. (1987) *The Meaning Makers: Children Learning Language and Using Language to Learn*. London: Hodder and Stoughton.

Wham, M.A. (1993) 'The relationship between undergraduate course work and beliefs about reading instruction', *Journal of Research and Development in Education*, 27: 9–17.

Williams, R. (1965) *The Long Revolution*. Harmondsworth: Penguin.

Wilson, C., Bates, A. and Völlm, B. (2010) 'Circles of support and accountability: an innovative approach to manage high-risk sex offenders in the community', *The Open Criminology Journal*, 3: 48–57.

Wilson, J. and Cowell, B. (1984) 'How shall we define handicap?', *British Journal of Special Education*, 1 (2): 33–5.

Winter, M. and Rouse, J. (1990) 'Fostering intergenerational literacy: the Missouri parents as teachers programme', *The Reading Teacher*, 24: 382–6.

Wolfendale, S. and Topping, K. (eds) (1996) *Family Involvement in Literacy: Effective Partnerships in Education*. London: Cassell.

Woolley, H., Armitage, M., Bishop, J., Curtis, B. and Ginsborg, J. (2005) *Inclusion of Disabled Children in Primary School Playgrounds*. London: National Children's Bureau and Joseph Rowntree Foundation.

Yakira, E. (2010) 'Whose Left, Which War? A Comment from Jerusalem', *Politics and Culture*, December, Issues 3 and 4.

Ylisto, I. (1977) 'Early reading responses of young Finnish children', *Reading Teacher*, November: 167–72.

Appendix 1: Research Planning Audit

Name ....

Date ....

What is the topic of my research?	
Why have I chosen this topic?	Previous research (the literature) Professional relevance (my current work) Other reasons (such as ...)
Are my reasons good enough?	Yes, because ... No, because ...

What are my research questions?	1. 2. 3. Are there more?
Where do these come from?	(Literature, practice, other? ...)
Can I justify the research questions? How can I do this?	
Where will I do the research?	
Have I negotiated access to the research setting? How? What?	

When will I do the research? Is my time-table realistic?	
What methods will I use to investigate the research questions?	
How can I justify these methods?	
What are the ethical considerations? How will I address these? Does the study need ethical approval?	
Is there anything I need to rethink?	The topic? The methods? The timetable? The location?
Do I need to revise the research questions? Are they clear? Are they researchable?	1. 2. 3. (others?)
Where have I got to in my research?	

What is my first/next step?	
What help do I need?	

Author Index

Agee 48
Al Kaddah 160, 169

Baym 98, 171
Beck 92
Bérubé 11, 12
Billington 32
Blumfeld-Jones 86
Booth 69, 145, 152, 155
Brehony 196
Brown 17, 63
Byers 93

Calvey 60, 61
Capozzola 86
Clough 54, 58, 65, 66, 69, 70, 71, 86,
    100, 101, 104, 120, 147, 148, 149,
    151, 155, 191, 192, 230, 236,
    237, 238
Cohen 19, 21, 23, 37, 55, 56,
    149, 159
Cook 121, 122, 136
Corbett 65, 155

Davies 97, 145
Demn 196
Denscombe 19
Denzin 21
deVaus 20, 48

Farall 63
Faulks 15
Fine 100
Fine 94, 95
Fontana 141
Frey 141

Geertz 70
Gilbert 244
Ginsberg 190, 196
Goodwin 6

Hannon 10, 32, 113, 114, 116, 117,
    199, 236, 237, 238, 241, 244
Harper 86
Hart 138
Hedenus 12
Herbert 150
Hess 93
Hine 99, 103
Huberman 37
Hurdley 43, 119

Jones 58

Kaomea 54
Kaplan 36
Kawulich 30, 31, 48
Kendall 19
Khan 11
Kiesinger 100
Koch 11

Lewin 113
Lewis 23, 91
Lincoln 21

MacNaughton 13
Madriz 94, 95
Manion 19, 23, 37, 55, 149
Markham 98, 99, 103, 171
McCracken 91
McCulloch 53

Merchant 97
Mertens 190, 196
Merton 19
Miles 37
Mitchell 63, 101
Morgan 94
Morrison 19, 23, 37, 55, 149

Nutbrown 32, 52, 53, 57, 58, 71, 86, 96, 113, 114, 116, 117, 147, 148, 149, 154, 199, 236, 237

O'Hara 241
Oakshott 25
Oalkey 64
Oliver 65

Pahl 86
Parackal 11
Perera 66
Pink 138
Plummer 15

Rallis 196
Raymond 160, 161, 169
Richardson 53
Ritchie 23
Rorty 70
Rossman 196
Rowsell 86
Rudd 97

Sachdev 151
Schumm 93

Sebba 151
Seidman 90, 91
Shamdasani 94
Share 92
Shklovsky 54
Silverman 61, 112
Snape 23
Somerset Maugham 238
Sparkes 69
Spencer 23
Srinivas 53
Stenhouse 10, 14
Stewart 94
Sunagub 93
Sveningsson 143

Tacey 13, 14
Taylor 17, 63
Teirney 100
Trombetta 92

Vaughn 93
Vulliamy 100

Wacquant 53, 61
Walford 100
Walker, 31, 64, 90
Webb 100
Wilcox 93
Wilson 17, 18
Wolfendale 153
Woolley 63

Yakira 12

Subject Index

Analysis of research reports 226, 237

Analysis 12, 20, 21, 28, 29, 39, 59, 61, 82, 83, 91, 93, 94, 108, 117, 130, 136, 138, 146, 148, 159, 161, 187, 189, 191, 193, 208, 226, 237, 238, 239, 242, 248, 249, 256, 258

Arrest of Experience 24, 26, 46, 198

Assumptions 8, 15, 25, 37, 52, 89, 120, 193, 225, 247

Audio Recording 142, 148

Breadth viii, 20, 77, 176, 177, 188, 190

Case studies 20, 69, 84, 192, 196, 202

Clarification 7, 40, 41, 48, 88, 89, 165, 204

Confidentiality 39, 83, 92, 101, 102, 103, 142, 143, 162, 185, 243

Critical literature review 28, 39, 71, 105, 106, 108, 111, 112, 116, 136, 137, 138, 176, 237

Critical readers ix, 18, 31, 37, 240

Culture 26, 30, 31, 33, 34, 52, 69, 72, 74, 92, 110, 115, 119, 120, 149, 154, 155, 156, 161, 170, 171, 212, 219, 224, 255, 259

Critical reflection 46, 63, 106, 107, 116, 121, 136, 139, 175, 179, 195, 235

Computer Assisted Analysis 149

Critical relationships in research 175, 176, 188, 189, 195, 196

Critical theory 18, 19, 37

Change xiv, 3, 4, 5, 6, 8, 9, 10, 14, 15, 17, 18, 19, 23, 35, 38, 44, 45, 58, 59, 65, 71, 72, 73, 74, 77, 78, 79, 80, 82, 83, 89, 95, 98, 108, 114, 134, 145, 147, 149, 155, 161, 165, 169, 178

Contexts of research 11, 13, 14, 52, 53, 54, 170, 178, 191, 194

Decisions viii, ix, xi, 4, 10, 15, 19, 20, 21, 25, 27, 29, 32, 35, 37, 46, 64, 67, 68, 101, 102, 108, 111, 117, 120, 136, 141, 143, 145, 150, 161, 162, 168, 170, 177, 187, 191, 193, 196, 243, 247

Depth viii, 5, 6, 7, 9, 91, 93, 94, 141, 157, 176, 177, 183, 186, 187, 190, 191

Design of research studies x, xi, xii, xiii, xv, 4, 8, 10, 13, 19, 20, 21, 22, 28, 29, 32, 37, 39, 41, 43, 46, 48, 74, 78, 99, 101, 102, 135, 137, 138, 146, 151, 154, 158, 161, 162, 163, 168, 170, 175, 166, 177, 178, 179, 187–196, 200–203, 236, 253

Dissemination xii, 79, 190, 198, 235, 243

Dissertation xi, 13, 22, 27, 45, 66, 157, 183, 186, 240, 241, 242, 247, 257

Drafting 100, 240, 241, 242, 243

Empirical studies 29, 37, 40, 41, 135, 170, 188, 198

Ethics x, 3, 4, 19, 22, 24, 41, 46, 52, 55, 60, 61, 63, 83, 99, 102, 103, 105, 136, 137, 140, 170, 175, 185, 187, 188, 189, 195, 196, 197, 226, 243, 245, 247, 250, 252, 255, 256

Ethnography 38, 60, 61, 103, 104, 138, 238, 252, 255, 257, 258, 259
Evidence 17, 18, 27, 34, 54, 59, 60, 61, 82, 107, 108, 109, 116, 123, 131, 132, 236, 239

Feel/feeling of research 12, 29, 30, 31, 33, 41, 65, 90, 91, 96, 123, 125, 148, 246
Field questions x, 25, 29, 36, 39, 40, 45, 48, 65, 101, 103, 112, 113, 117, 140, 159, 161, 162, 169, 176, 180, 181, 182, 188, 189, 190, 193, 196, 249
Fieldwork 39, 84, 101, 228, 243, 249, 256
Findings ix, 7, 8, 17, 21, 22, 61, 69, 85, 94, 102, 107, 109, 114, 125, 128, 131, 137, 170, 171, 184, 186, 189, 196, 236, 242, 243, 248, 253, 254, 257
Focused Conversations 91–96, 103, 256
Framework 19, 21, 27, 39, 44, 45, 116, 117, 137, 155, 163, 165, 176, 187, 236, 237, 254, 255, 256
Framework for analysis of research report 39, 237

Gender 9, 13, 16, 29, 74, 79, 80, 82, 84, 85, 121, 136, 141, 145, 155
General/specific 19, 35, 36, 176, 177, 190
Goldilocks Test 41–45, 111, 180, 184, 186

Identity/identities 9, 67, 103, 120, 229, 252
Informed consent 60, 79, 142, 143, 171, 187, 190, 196, 203, 249
Internet 62, 96, 97, 98, 99, 102, 103, 110, 141, 142, 143, 144, 145, 170, 171, 255, 256, 258
Interpretations 21, 69, 100, 105, 117, 150
Interpretive 18–21, 23, 95
Interview 9, 12, 25, 27, 32, 34, 35, 38, 39, 67, 68, 69, 89–95, 98, 100, 102, 117, 124, 134, 135, 139–149, 153, 157, 158, 160, 161, 168–172, 185–187, 190, 191, 193, 194, 195, 199, 202–207, 226, 229, 249, 254, 255–258

Journal xi, xii, xiii, xiv, xv, 5, 6, 15, 22, 30, 37, 46, 56, 59, 69, 106, 110, 146, 149, 162, 169, 170, 179, 181, 182, 198, 245, 246, 247, 250
Justification ix, x, 24, 25, 28, 37, 46, 47, 55, 62, 63, 67, 106, 109, 140, 143, 175, 178, 181, 196

Lenses 26, 53, 60
Life historical research 177, 187, 195
Literature review 21, 28, 39, 47, 71, 105, 106, 108, 111, 112, 116, 123, 136, 137, 138, 176, 180, 186, 236, 237, 242, 246, 248, 249, 254

Making a difference ix, 3, 5, 7, 9, 14, 16, 22, 105, 126, 155, 156, 157, 180, 226
Making the familiar strange 26, 46, 47, 51, 52, 53, 54, 59, 61, 178, 255
Meanings 59, 60, 61, 107, 119, 191
Methodology – what is? 24–48
Methods viii, ix, x, xi, 5, 6, 10, 18, 19, 20, 21, 23, 24, 25, 26, 27, 31, 33, 34, 36, 38, 42, 44, 46, 48, 55, 56, 61, 63, 64, 76, 86, 90, 91, 92, 93, 94, 99, 103, 124, 134, 135, 138, 140, 141, 149, 159, 161, 169, 172, 179, 181, 182, 185, 186, 187, 189, 190, 194, 195, 202, 242, 247, 248, 252, 255, 256, 258, 262
Moral 4, 10, 11, 13, 22, 28, 29, 60, 64, 67, 73, 74, 78, 79, 84, 97, 98, 99, 137, 140, 170, 178, 187, 201, 238, 256
Motivation 11, 19, 54, 65, 86, 97, 140, 160, 169, 170, 192, 252, 257

Observation xiii, 13, 20, 26, 51, 52, 54, 5, 56, 59, 61, 69, 108, 112, 169, 184, 185, 186, 192, 195

Paradigms 18, 19, 20, 21, 22, 23, 28, 93, 94, 235, 243

Participants ix, 25, 27, 28, 29, 39, 40, 44, 46, 47, 48, 54, 60, 63, 64, 67, 68, 78, 83, 86, 88, 89, 90, 91, 92, 93, 95, 97, 99, 100, 101, 102, 103, 108, 124, 126, 127, 130, 136, 140, 141, 142, 144, 146, 148, 149, 157, 159, 162, 170, 177, 181, 185, 187, 190, 196, 243, 249

Personal xiii, 9, 13, 16, 28, 29, 34, 52, 64, 65, 66, 67, 72, 89, 92, 100, 106, 133, 144, 146, 149, 152, 155, 157, 159, 171, 180, 181, 187, 190, 194, 208, 236, 237, 239, 240, 246, 250, 252, 256, 258

Persuasive xi, xii, 3, 5, 21, 22, 23, 28, 39, 70, 86, 106, 107, 159, 178, 181, 198, 240, 242

Policy x, 8, 11, 14, 15, 16, 17, 19, 26, 53, 54, 72, 73, 74, 75, 78, 83, 108, 117, 120, 135, 150, 158, 176, 177, 178, 180, 191, 192, 194, 196, 201, 233, 237, 252, 253

Political xii, 3, 4, 11, 12, 13, 14, 15, 16, 18, 22, 23, 27, 28, 34, 54, 63, 65, 69, 70, 73, 75, 78, 84, 86, 106, 107, 108, 110, 140, 151, 152, 153, 170, 178, 181, 190, 194, 197, 198, 201, 227, 235, 236, 237, 238, 239, 243, 253

Positional 3, 10, 11, 12, 13, 22, 23, 27, 28, 63, 68, 86, 105, 178, 181, 235, 236, 237, 238, 239, 242

Positivist 18, 19, 23

Power 13, 14, 27, 34, 69, 70, 83, 87, 95, 96, 97, 100, 101, 114, 115, 141, 227, 28, 238, 239, 253, 255

Practice 7, 8, 9, 10, 11, 13, 15, 16, 19, 20, 23, 28, 35, 39, 41, 42, 44, 46, 47, 52, 59, 60, 61, 99, 103, 105, 106, 111, 136, 137, 142, 144, 146, 150, 151, 159, 170, 171, 178, 181, 187, 191, 250, 258

Presentation 48, 96, 162, 241, 242

Professional development 9, 15, 16, 72, 76, 81, 82, 83, 114, 115, 154, 244

Protection (of research participants) 9, 15, 16, 72, 76, 81, 82, 83, 114, 115, 154, 244

Publication xii, 187, 237

Purposive xii, 3, 6, 22, 23, 28, 86, 106, 178, 181, 193, 198, 235, 236, 242

Qualitative research x, 12, 14, 18, 20, 21, 23, 37, 48, 61, 93, 99, 102, 103, 124, 134, 143, 159, 160, 161, 168, 190, 196, 228, 238, 251, 252, 253, 255, 256, 257, 258

Quantitative research 18, 20, 21, 99, 124, 134, 148, 159, 161, 190, 254

Questionnaires 3, 9, 20, 91, 124, 125, 136, 139, 140, 156, 158, 159, 160, 161, 162, 163, 168, 169, 171, 172, 190, 193

Radical enqiry xi, xii, 26, 107, 108, 119, 176, 178, 181, 196, 198

Radical listening xii, 26, 27, 28, 29, 46, 63, 99, 101, 102, 107, 175, 176, 178, 181, 185, 196, 198, 243

Radical looking xii, 26, 27, 29, 46, 47, 51, 52, 53, 54, 59, 60, 61, 101, 107, 109, 175, 176, 178, 181, 185, 196, 198, 243

Radical questioning xii, 26, 28, 29, 47, 107, 140, 159, 170, 171, 175, 176, 178, 181, 185, 193, 196, 198, 243

Radical reading xii, 28, 46, 47, 105, 106, 107, 108, 109, 116, 117, 119, 121, 136, 137, 175, 176, 178, 181, 185, 196, 198, 243

Report xi, xii, xiv, xv, 10, 11, 13, 15, 17, 18, 20, 22, 27, 31, 33, 37, 39, 46, 47, 52, 55, 59, 61, 62, 64, 63, 67, 69, 96, 98, 99, 101, 102, 103, 107, 108, 109, 113, 116, 119, 121, 136, 137, 139, 140, 141, 143, 146, 149, 162, 182, 197–244, 246–250

Research – what is? 3–24

Research action 16, 37, 63, 70, 184, 242, 245–250

Research design x, xi, xii, xv, 4, 10, 13, 19, 20, 21, 22, 28, 29, 34, 37, 39, 41, 43, 46, 48, 99, 101, 102, 137, 159, 163, 170, 175–196
Research Journal viii–xv, 5, 6, 15, 22, 30, 37, 42, 46, 50, 59, 69, 106, 110, 146, 149, 162, 169, 170, 179, 181, 182, 245, 246, 247, 248, 250
Research planning audit 176, 179, 180–186, 260–265
Research planning 19, 111, 112, 138, 143, 169, 175, 176, 178, 179, 180–186, 188, 190, 195, 196, 198, 203, 248, 250, 260–263
Research questions ix, x, xi, xv, 11, 13, 19, 24, 25, 29, 36, 38, 39, 40, 41, 42, 43, 44, 45, 46, 47, 48, 54, 108, 111, 112, 113, 139, 140, 146, 148, 155, 159, 161, 162, 163, 170, 171, 175, 176, 177, 179, 180, 181, 182, 184, 187, 188, 190, 194, 195, 242, 246, 248, 249
Russian Doll Principle 41–45, 180, 184, 186

Self 9, 34, 39, 54, 64, 100, 102, 198
Self critical research 14, 198

Six steps of social science enquiry 106, 107
Significance 4, 18, 25, 31, 107, 159, 178, 192

Theoretical basis 14, 19, 20, 112, 116, 137, 163, 191, 236
Theory 5, 6, 18, 19, 37, 112, 113, 136, 137
Thesis 67, 68, 121, 135, 178, 240, 241, 242, 247
Timetable 120, 179, 181, 182, 185, 186, 231, 245, 248, 249, 262

Unique/niqueness x, 60, 67, 107, 112, 113, 116, 117, 181, 241, 250

Values 4, 13, 16, 21, 25, 28, 35, 52, 63, 64, 67, 106, 189, 192
Voice vii, ix, 26, 27, 28, 46, 47, 54, 58, 62–105, 146, 148, 153, 154, 157, 178, 182, 201, 202, 227, 229, 236

Writing xii, xiii, 18, 20, 40, 86, 87, 88, 89, 90, 91, 92, 94, 100, 108, 110, 111, 121, 136, 137, 145, 162, 170, 197, 198–243, 250